ENVIRONMENTAL DECISION-MAKING IN CONTEXT

A Toolbox

*Advancing excellence
in public service . . .*

American Society for Public Administration
Book Series on Public Administration & Public Policy

David H. Rosenbloom, Ph.D.
Editor-in-Chief

Mission: Throughout its history, ASPA has sought to be true to its founding principles of promoting scholarship and professionalism within the public service. The ASPA Book Series on Public Administration and Public Policy publishes books that increase national and international interest for public administration and which discuss practical or cutting edge topics in engaging ways of interest to practitioners, policy-makers, and those concerned with bringing scholarship to the practice of public administration.

RECENT PUBLICATIONS

Environmental Decision-Making in Context: A Toolbox
by Chad J. McGuire

**Government Performance and Results: An Evaluation of
GPRA's First Decade**
by Jerry Ellig, Maurice McTigue, and Henry Wray

**Practical Human Resources for Public Managers:
A Case Study Approach**
by Nicolas A. Valcik and Teodoro J. Benavides

The Practice of Government Public Relations
edited by Mordecai Lee, Grant Neeley, and Kendra Stewart

Promoting Sustainable Local and Community Economic Development
by Roland V. Anglin

Government Contracting: Promises and Perils
by William Sims Curry

**Strategic Collaboration in Public and Nonprofit Administration:
A Practice-Based Approach to Solving Shared Problems**
edited by Dorothy Norris-Tirrell and Joy A. Clay

American Society for Public Administration
Series in Public Administration and Public Policy

Advancing excellence in public service . . .

ENVIRONMENTAL DECISION-MAKING IN CONTEXT

A Toolbox

CHAD J. MCGUIRE

CRC Press
Taylor & Francis Group
Boca Raton   London   New York

CRC Press is an imprint of the
Taylor & Francis Group, an **Informa** business

CRC Press
Taylor & Francis Group
6000 Broken Sound Parkway NW, Suite 300
Boca Raton, FL 33487-2742

© 2012 by Taylor & Francis Group, LLC
CRC Press is an imprint of Taylor & Francis Group, an Informa business

No claim to original U.S. Government works

Printed in the United States of America on acid-free paper
Version Date: 20120308

International Standard Book Number: 978-1-4398-8575-8 (Hardback)

Library of Congress Cataloging-in-Publication Data

McGuire, Chad J.
    Environmental decision-making in context : a toolbox / Chad J. McGuire.
        pages cm. -- (Public administration and public policy)
    Includes bibliographical references and index.
    ISBN 978-1-4398-8575-8 (hardcover : alk. paper)
    1. Environmental policy--Decision making. I. Title.

GE170.M44 2012
333.7--dc23   2012005955

Visit the Taylor & Francis Web site at
http://www.taylorandfrancis.com

and the CRC Press Web site at
http://www.crcpress.com

Contents

Acknowledgments ix

About the Author xi

1   Introduction 1

2   Science of Environmental Decision-Making 7
    Introduction 7
    Natural Systems 9
      Ecosystem Principles..17
        Components: Biotic and Abiotic...18
        Services Provided: Provisioning, Regulating, Cultural............20
      Biodiversity...23
        Definitions 24
        Interactions..25
        Importance 27
      Ecosystem-Based Management...29
        Definition and Purpose 30
        Role in Environmental Management......................................31
        Examples in Environmental Policy Management Techniques... 34
    Systems Thinking 39
      Box Modeling: Wrapping Our Heads around the Problem............. 40
      Underlying Scientific Principles 43
        $E = mc^2$, or the Relationship between Energy and Matter
        (Mass–Energy Equivalence)...43
        Equilibrium Theory, or $dC/dT = 0$ 45
      Parts of the Box in Context: Inflows, Outflows, and Feedback
      Mechanisms...49
    Conclusion...59
    References..60

3 Economics of Environmental Decision-Making **63**
Introduction 63
Categories of Economics Relevant to Environmental Decision-Making 65
Natural Resource Economics..68
Ecological Economics...72
The Role of Discounting, Substitution, and Trade-Offs...................76
Defining Value: Linking Environment and Human Interactions..............81
Measurements of Well-Being and Progress 81
Gross Domestic Product..82
Alternatives.. 84
Total Valuation Technique (Tv = Dv + Iv + Nuv) 91
Direct Values (Dvs) 92
Indirect Values (Ivs) 95
Nonuse Values (Nuvs) 98
Benefit–Cost Analysis... 101
Conclusion..106
References...108

4 Values of Environmental Decision-Making **113**
Introduction 113
Objective Values 115
Risk Assessment and the Role of Science 115
Quantification Methods 120
Subjective Values..129
Emotion and Public Outrage.. 131
NIMBY and Other Perceived Values 138
Scaling Value Decisions 146
Values and Individual Decision-Making...............................148
Self-Interest 149
Learning Dynamics... 157
Values and Multiparty Decision-Making...............................166
Consensus Building and Majority Voting..........................167
Other Collective Value System Considerations.....................170
Conclusion.. 174
References... 176

Case Problems **179**
Introduction to Case Problems 179
Case Problem 1. Watershed Management: Linking Terrestrial and
Aquatic Environmental Problems 179
Relevant Information..180
Hints for Analysis.. 181

Case Problem 2. Fisheries Management: Managing Public Resources
through a Mix of Private Incentives 181
    Current Government Fishery Policy 182
    Alternative Policy 1 182
    Alternative Policy 2 183
    Alternative Policy 3 184
    Hints for Analysis 184
Case Problem 3. Sustainability: Setting Priorities between Today and
Tomorrow, a Total Valuation Application 185
    Current Policy 185
    Alternative 1 186
    Alternative 2 186
    Alternative 3 187
    Hints for Analysis 187
Case Problem 4. Climate Change: Making Environmental Decisions
in the Face of Uncertainty 187
    Hints for Analysis 189

Index **191**

Acknowledgments

I acknowledge everyone who has helped me make this book a reality. This includes, but is not limited to, the following people: family and friends who have supported me in my endeavors, your love and support are always appreciated; students who have helped to stimulate the idea for this book based on a lack of alternative resources, your frustrations and good suggestions have helped pave the way; the University of Massachusetts, Dartmouth and specifically my colleagues in the Department of Public Policy, your support has been unwavering and your collegiality unmatched. Thank you all!

About the Author

Chad J. McGuire is a professor of environmental policy within the Department of Public Policy at the University of Massachusetts, Dartmouth. His background is in environmental law and environmental science. Chad writes extensively in the fields of environmental law, policy, sustainability, and dispute resolution. He has worked on policy issues related to fisheries management, climate change, globalization, and land use patterns. His expertise has been sought in private and public forums, and he has served on committees for both nonprofit and government entities. He has over 15 years in the environmental management field. This book is based on his experiences teaching and practicing environmental policy.

Chapter 1

Introduction

Making decisions about the environment is not easy. Probably the most honest reason for this is the environment is a very complex and dynamic place, and as such it requires knowing a lot of things about these complex interactions, at least if we want our decisions to be as informed and accurate as possible. Because of the complexity involved in understanding the environment, the choices we make about environmental issues are often incomplete. A focus on objective data associated with risk assessment may prevent consideration of important community values. Focusing on the direct economic benefits to the community in developing a tract of land may fail to consider the costs to the natural services provided by the land in an undeveloped state. In a perfect world, those who make environmental decisions would be armed with a foundation for making decisions that attempt to identify a broad range of issues that are at stake when making such decisions. The purpose of this book is to help provide that foundation.

This book should be seen as a handbook or reference manual. Its intended purpose is to introduce the reader to a set of common tools used in environmental decision-making, and provide a framework for analyzing environmental problems. No expertise or background knowledge in any discipline is required, just a desire to become better versed in how environmental decisions are made. While no specialized knowledge is required, this book does draw upon a set of intellectual tools from several academic disciplines, including both the natural and social sciences. All of the information required to understand the principles discussed in this text is clearly identified in each section of the text. Within each section, recommendations identifying more in-depth study opportunities are made for those seeking a greater level of understanding in any subject matter described throughout this book.

In order to understand the purpose of this book, you need to understand a major assumption it relies upon about how environmental decisions are made. That assumption is the following: *there exists a general lack of understanding as to the basic tools required to properly engage in environmental decision-making; this is particularly true when we think about making fully informed decisions regarding environmental choices.* For example, scientists may offer an opinion regarding an environmental issue based on their specific expertise, and their expertise is often limited to their area of specialization. If scientists are offering an opinion on essential habitat for a particular species of animal, they usually do not include in their assessment any discussion of what other uses—specifically human uses—might apply to that habitat (this is outside their area of expertise). An economist might be able to more particularly describe the other uses for the habitat in terms of economic values and substitutions, balancing a set of defined costs versus benefits. However, that economist may know little about local value judgments that might apply to the property, for example, what cultural value the local citizens find in the area that includes the essential animal habitat defined by the scientists. Finally, those citizens and the general public of the area may offer competing judgments on the exact value of the habitat based on their personal assumptions, all of which may have little or nothing to do with the value of the land to the animal as essential habitat.

In the above example, each discipline (science, economics, values) is acting independently of the other, and the collective information described is often not aggregated in such a way that incorporates the underlying principles from each discipline. This can lead to decisions that do not properly consider the information being provided. This is particularly true in local government settings, where the task of making environmental decisions often falls upon individuals or groups without access to specialized expertise in one or more of the aforementioned areas. Even when expertise is available, local decision-makers often lack a comprehensive understanding of how to aggregate this to make informed environmental decisions. What is needed, then, is a general practice guide that highlights some of the major tools of environmental decision-making, allowing for a more comprehensive evaluation of environmental issues. Providing a simple yet effective means of learning these basic skills is one of the major goals of this book.

To meet the goals described above, this book is broken down into three main sections followed by a case problem section where readers can apply the skills developed in the three main parts to hypothetical cases. Each major part of the book is devoted to one of three basic areas of consideration, all of which are based on the assumption that environmental decision-making occurs at the intersection of science, economics, and value judgments. A representation of this connection is shown in Figure 1.1.

Chapter 1 of this book deals with how *science* interacts with environmental decision-making. In many ways, science provides the objective information that informs the decisions we make about the environment. We often think of science as having a more applied approach in environmental questions, solving environmental problems through, for example, technological advancements. Science has helped us to harness the wind and sun to create energy in a manner that limits the carbon

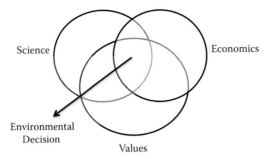

Figure 1.1 Relationship between science, economics, and values in environmental decisions.

intensity of energy production. Since the burning or carbon is linked to a warming climate, we can see science having a role in providing us with important technological solutions. However, if we dig a bit deeper, we can also see that science helped us to understand the relationship between carbon and a warming planet in the first place. Science helped us to understand how our actions of releasing stored carbon into the atmosphere have led to a greenhouse effect on earth. This is the kind of science we will be focusing on in this book; the scientific principles that help us understand the connections between our actions and the environment.

The science section of this book is divided into two parts, one focusing on natural systems and the other focusing on systems thinking. The systems focus provides the necessary framework for making environmental decisions. Specifically, environmental decisions require a basic understanding of cause and effect; those making decisions need to understand how past, current, and future actions might impact the environment. Understanding natural system processes provides a big picture, identifying the relationships that exist between the earth system and the components of that system. Moving from a discussion of natural systems, the section goes on to provide a detailed understanding of systems thinking, a way of understanding causes and effects of human actions within the earth system. With a foundation of systems thinking in hand, the reader is then able to connect small-scale environmental issues with larger-scale impacts, an essential part of understanding the context of environmental decisions.

Chapter 2 of this book is focused on *economic* principles involved in environmental decisions. Economics is the language in which we evaluate the benefits and costs of our actions. This evaluation can be done retrospectively (in the past), concurrently (today), and prospectively (toward the future). Economics applied to environmental decisions is really about understanding what goes into our methodology in valuing natural resources, and how we compare those valuations to our past, current, and future actions. Understanding fundamental aspects of economic analysis within the context of environmental decision-making is a critical part of becoming versed in how decisions in this field are made.

The economics section is divided into four separate parts. The first part discusses several economic categories that apply to environmental decision-making. These categories identify the methods by which we determine the value of natural resources. The second part discusses economic valuation, focusing on the assumptions traditional economic analysis uses in defining the concepts of human well-being, and explaining some alternative ways well-being may be defined. The third part focuses on a specific economic method—*total valuation*—used to identify a variety of values associated with natural resources. The purpose here is to show that natural resource value can extend beyond traditional economic valuation techniques. Finally, the fourth part discusses benefit–cost analysis, a fundamental economic technique used in analyzing environmental decisions.

Chapter 3 focuses on how *values* impact environmental decision-making. Most environmental decisions are ultimately decided through a framework where the individual or group makes a decision based on a set of assumptions. These assumptions, based in fundamental value systems, provide the relative weights that ultimately drive decisions. It is in this process that, for example, objective information can be put aside and decisions can be made to counter the hard evidence presented. In this way, we can see that values are an important driver of environmental decisions, and understanding what goes into value judgments is an essential part of understanding how environmental decisions are made.

The value section is broken down into three main parts. The first part discusses objective forms of valuation, focusing on traditional methods of risk assessment, specifically how risk is quantified through a variety of techniques. The second part focuses on subjective forms of valuation, identifying the role that different factors like individual emotions and community outrage can have on how we form our value judgments. Specific environmental issues steeped in subjective criteria are also highlighted here, including such phenomenon as NIMBY (not in my back yard). Finally, the scaling of value decisions is discussed. Scaling refers to the manner in which value judgments can change between individual choices and that of the group. In some cases individual value judgments can be shown to flip in a group setting where a person can think one way about an issue, but then think completely opposite about that same issue when placed in a group setting. The implications of this phenomenon are discussed as it relates to values as a driver of environmental decisions.

A set of four case problems follows the three main parts of this book. The case problems allow the reader to apply the knowledge learned throughout the text to a set of hypothetical situations. The goal is to show how the environmental toolbox described in the book informs decision-makers, allowing readers to apply the skills to several hypothetical examples. Each example focuses on different issues presented in environmental management. Some are focused on property rights characteristics, while others ask you to consider intergenerational issues, comparing what is good for people today against what is good for future generations. Collectively, the case problems allow for greater exploration of the issues presented in the main body of the text.

Another goal of this book is to move beyond the traditional pillars of academic discipline in order to provide readers with the most fundamental aspects of what is actually involved in making environmental decisions. It is not meant to be a tightly bound academic text. Nor is it meant to be a loosely defined set of principles. Rather, it is meant to provide a reference to a set of skills that are fundamental in making environmental decisions. In order to be comprehensive on the subject without making it too dense, some shortcuts had to be taken with the amount of depth applied to any one subject. This is made explicit at relevant points in the text itself. However, readers are directed to areas of further study and inquiry as appropriate, allowing for greater depth of study as the reader sees fit.

Chapter 2

Science of Environmental Decision-Making

Introduction

The goal of this opening chapter is to introduce the reader to some basic scientific concepts that are applicable to environmental decision-making. This chapter is separated into two major categories: *natural systems* and *systems thinking*. The natural systems section is devoted to explaining scientific principles that are often used when making environmental decisions. The scientific principles focused on here include ecosystem science as a way of understanding natural system interactions, the concept of biodiversity as an indicator of natural system health, and ecosystem-based management as a science-based tool for implementing human-based policies related to the environment.

The systems thinking section adds to the information provided in the natural systems section, moving toward an operation understanding of the system itself, including the development of analytical tools that allow us to understand interactions of the natural environment and how these interactions are influenced by human activities. These analytical tools provide a foundation for understanding causal connections within a systems context, for example, understanding the impacts of carbon forcing from one component of the system to another. Once we understand these basic principles of systems thinking, we are then prepared to begin making judgments about our environment, including judgments about our interactions with the environment.*

Before we begin a more in-depth exploration of science as it relates to environmental decision-making, let us take a moment to consider the term *science*, and what we really mean by the term in the context of environmental decisions. The reason we should fully consider the role of science contextually is because we rely on science as a society to provide us with objective, factually based information. Its role as the basis of objectivity is critical to understanding how it influences environmental decisions, and this statement should become more clear to you as we move through the materials in this text.

Science is a term that is used to describe a great deal of disciplines and interactions humans have with the world, and as such its meaning can vary depending on the context in which it is being used. Broadly speaking, science can be distinguished from other disciplines through the *scientific method*, a process defined mostly by the ability to replicate the steps used to achieve a particular result, for example, a simple experiment that shows whenever liquid A is mixed with liquid B, the resulting combination liquid is blue in color. The hallmark of the legitimacy of this claim is that the same results—resulting liquid being blue—will occur every time, no matter who attempts the procedure.† The ability to replicate results is one way we distinguish science as something more objective or fact based than other subjective aspects of our lives. In this way science helps us to know *what is*, rather than *what should be*.

Because it focuses on objective statements about our world that can be tested, the term *science* tends to take on an air of legitimacy; if some fact derives from a direct scientific-type observation, then that fact it is general held to be true. In this way, science serves an important function in environmental decisions; it helps us understand cause and effect in the natural environment, including how human actions might be a cause of a particular effect on the environment. The objective nature of science helps us identify environmental problems by pointing out important facts, and it also helps us identify and develop solutions to environmental problems by showing us ways in which our actions can be more harmonious with background environmental conditions.

---

* Formal judgments about how we choose to interact with the environment will be discussed in more detail in Chapter 3.

† There may be other limiting factors to this experiment that must be closely observed by those conducting the experiment. For example, temperature might be an important factor; the resulting color of blue might only occur if the two liquids are kept within a specific temperature range. Also, other factors might be important to ensure that the result can be replicated. The key is to pay close attention to all things that can be measured (temperature, timeframe, mixing conditions, etc.) when presenting the results. We will be returning to the importance of conditions (generally termed *variables*) in our discussion of environmental decision-making throughout this text.

From the standpoint of the environment, science can be an important foundation from which decisions are made. Science aids in establishing what is known, what is potentially knowable, and what is not capable of being known about the environment.* Having this foundation helps decision-makers set priorities; it helps them understand what is important in relation to the level of scientific understanding. For example, science has helped us refine our understanding about climate change, especially the existence of climate change as an observable trend over time and the impact human activities are having on this observed trend. As science certainly increases the causal relationships associated with climate change, institutional leaders are aided by this increasing certainty in making decisions that respond to climate change. Without science helping to uncover the causal connections, it is less likely decisions will be made that directly deal with the issue of climate change. Even if decisions were being made to deal with climate change without the help of science, they would likely be "shots in the dark" without the help of scientific causal connections.

Even though science is important in environmental decisions, it is not the only consideration that matters. As will be shown in Chapter 4, objective information is but one factor—and sometimes a seriously discounted factor—in how humans make decisions. Moreover, translating scientific information into values that then form the basis of decisions is equally difficult because, depending on the value systems being influenced, the impact of the scientific information can vary. For example, those who value intergenerational environmental health tend to look at the scientific information about climate change as indicative of immediate and substantial changes to current policy directions. Others who value more immediate needs of humans and account for difficult economic conditions tend to devalue or otherwise discount the scientific information supporting climate change, especially where such information calls for policy directions they see as a threat to current prosperity. We will revisit these issues in later chapters and sections of this text. For now, it is enough to see that science helps us in establishing important objective information when making decisions, but its importance is not absolute in environmental decision-making. Rather, its importance is subject to conflicting views, perceptions, and preferences of individuals and groups. We now begin our exploration of science by looking at natural systems.

Natural Systems

In this section, the immediate goal is on providing a descriptive understanding of natural systems, emphasizing three recurring themes that often arise in the

---

* At least what is not capable of being known under current conditions. Science is constantly changing our understanding of what is known and not known. Environmental decisions have to account for this variability of scientific understanding over time.

environmental context: ecosystem principles, biodiversity, and ecosystem-based management. We will explore systems-related thinking in more detail in the second part of this chapter. For now our goal is to understand the meaning of a natural system within the context of the three recurring themes identified above. Before we get into the three themes, let us take some time to consider the meaning of a natural system.

Let us begin by dissecting the term *natural system* into its two components, *natural* and *system*. Let us start by focusing on the latter term, *system*. A system may be said to be a set of components that contain energy flows between the components and where these energy flows are regulated between components in some manner (Bertaianffy 1968). A system can technically be either open or closed, an open system allowing energy to flow into it from some outside source and a closed system not allowing outside energy transfer. The structure of a basic system, including components, is shown in Figure 2.1.

To better understand the concepts behind a system, let us look at an example, a residential home baseboard heating system. Such a system operates by having a set of interlinked pipes that flow to and from a heat source. The heat source is controlled by a thermostat, which can be programmed to establish a set temperature in the area being heated. The components of the system are the pipes, the water, the heater, and the thermostat. Once the water has filled the system, the system is closed because all of the interactions occur without influence from outside energy sources.* The thermostat provides the regulation of energy flow in the system; depending on the setting of the thermostat, heating of the water is either generated or not. In this way, the thermostat acts as the feedback mechanism of the system.

Feedback mechanisms, in our example the thermostat controlling the temperature of the house, create a kind of *equilibrium* within the system over time. For example, if the thermostat is set to 72° but the ambient temperature of the room is 60°, then we can expect the heating system to turn on and heat the room until the ambient air temperature reaches 72°. Once this occurs, the thermostat will shut off the heating system. When the temperature of the room goes below the threshold of 72°, the heating system will turn back on and heat the room until it returns to 72°. It will then turn off again, repeating the cycle as the ambient air temperature dictates. If we draw out this repetition on a graph, we will likely find room temperatures representing something like what is shown in Figure 2.2.

Notice from the figure that air temperature is kept within a range of a few degrees—say from 70 to 74°—representing a 2° buffer in the thermostat. Within

---

* A human changing the setting of the thermostat may be argued to be an outside influence. One might argue the system is not technically closed in the absolute sense because of this interaction. Also, if the heater is based on natural gas or oil, for instance, then there is an energy source emanating from outside the system making it more open than closed. These are points of contention in a true sense and have applicability about assumptions made regarding our Earth system that will be pointed out later in this section. However, these points can be put aside for now so we can simplify for purposes of understanding the concepts being discussed.

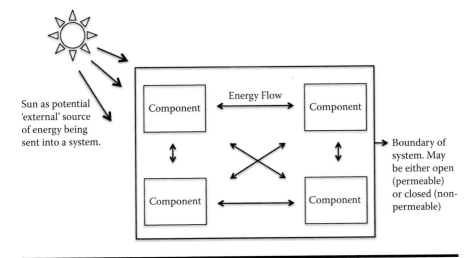

Figure 2.1   Representation of a basic system with interactions.

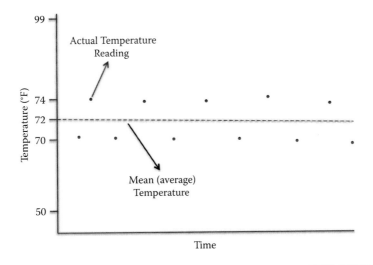

Figure 2.2   Representation of system interaction based on temperature control.

this range one can determine the mean temperature—the straight line on the figure—between these two numbers, in this case 72°. The state of the system—72° in our example—can be said to be an equilibrium state that is created through the feedback mechanism of the thermostat setting.* Unless someone changes the settings of the thermostat, or the system breaks or malfunctions, we can expect the heating

---

* We will be discussing the concept of *equilibrium* in more detail in the systems thinking portion of this section.

system described to maintain a set mean temperature of about 72°, understanding that we will find variability within the system between 70 and 74° at any given time.

Natural systems operate on similar principles as just described above, with one distinction being the system is not made by human hands, but rather described using the Earth as the largest component of the system.* What this means is that ecological science assumes that planet earth operates much in the same way as the heating system described above. To test this theory, we can see whether our definition of *system* applies to the earth. Is the earth a (1) set of components, (2) linked together by energy flows, (3) where these energy flows are regulated in some way?

Many scientists see the earth as a set of components that interact with one another. The four major components of the earth system are the lithosphere or land of the earth, including the rocks and crust; the atmosphere where a lot of exchanges occur between system components, the hydrosphere or water bodies of the earth; and the biosphere or all living things that inhabit the earth. These are the four major components that make up the earth system. Using the term *category* is a bit of a misnomer because it may lead us to believe these components are truly distinct from one another. In fact, the components of the earth system are very much interrelated through processes that create interactions within and between these components. Some of the interactions are necessary for maintaining life as we know it within certain components; for example, the interaction between the ocean and air is an important pathway for carbon to be absorbed from the atmosphere into the ocean.

One way to understand how the components of the earth system are connected is looking at energy flows between components, and a good example of energy flows between system components is heat transitions. Heat energy comes from sources both within the earth (endogenous) and outside the earth (exogenous) (Schlesinger 1997, 48–53). Endogenous sources of energy come from within the earth itself, with the largest source of such energy being the heat contained in the earth's inner layers.† We see examples of this energy every time a volcano erupts or the earth's tectonic plates shift. Exogenous sources come from outside the earth, with the most obvious source of external energy coming from our sun. The sun provides heat through radiation energy, and this heat helps to create ocean currents and air mass flows across the earth. The sun is also the way in which photosynthetic organisms derive energy, leading to the existence of life.‡

---

* For our purposes, the word *natural* in the term *natural systems* is meant to refer to system-like processes similar to the radiant heating system described above that occur without being solely created by human beings.

† Recall that the earth is actually a small crust of hard surface that is cooled in recent geologic history, under which lies molten rock (magma) that is concentrated at different densities with the largest density being at the core, or center, of the earth.

‡ Another exogenous source of energy is gravity, for example, the force exhibited by the moon during different phases. This results in the pulling and pushing of tides, which provides a source of energy between components of our earth system.

The last element in our definition of a system—the active regulation of the energy flows—is a bit controversial. In order to meet this part of the definition, we need to know whether the earth has mechanisms like that of the thermostat, where the purpose of the component is to actively regulate the system within a particular range; in the case of the earth, the range we are looking at is the conditions that actively support life as we know it today. To answer this question, we need to observe the current conditions of the earth system to see how those concentrations came to be, and whether there is some mechanism (like the thermostat) keeping conditions on earth within a range that supports life. We can explore this question by reviewing an interesting experiment developed by James Lovelock in support of his Gaia hypothesis (Lovelock 2000).

The Gaia hypothesis is a theory advanced by James Lovelock, a naturalist who has expertise in chemistry, earth science, and medicine. The Gaia hypothesis suggests the earth is a living thing, much like a human being is a living thing.* The idea is that a key element of living is the ability to self-regulate, and like any self-regulating system, the earth also self-regulates to keep itself within a defined range of conditions that are suitable for life.

The Gaia hypothesis posits components of the earth system are regulated by other components; for example, the atmosphere is regulated to a great extent by the biosphere. The claim suggests the biosphere has developed over time to act like the thermostat from our example above. Essentially, if something happens to cause environmental conditions in the atmosphere to shift—a perturbation—then the biosphere reacts, bringing the system back into balance. Lovelock used the model of the "daisy world" to illustrate this point (Lovelock 2000). A quick summary of the model will help explain the point.

The daisy world model envisions an imaginary earth that is inhabited by only two varieties of flowers, white- and black-colored daisies. Each of these flowers responds differently to the amount of sunlight that enters the earth. Black daisies are stimulated by low levels of sunlight entering the earth, while white daisies are stimulated by high amounts of sunlight. In this way, the proportion of white to black daisies will depend on the amount of sunlight-derived heat entering the earth; when sunlight is abundant there will be more white daisies than black daisies, and when sunlight is low there will be more black daisies than white daisies.

Let us now assume the sun begins to deliver more sunlight energy into the earth system than normal. Under the rules outlined by Lovelock above, this would mean that more sunlight would increase the number of white daisies and decrease the number of black daisies. The question we want answered now is what *effect*, or feedback, this change in ratio of white to black daisies might have on the earth. In order to answer this question, we need to know something about the reflective and absorption capacities of colors, specifically white and black.

---

* Lovelock used the term *Gaia* to refer to the earth, giving it a name and thus an identity as a living thing.

White colors tend to reflect sunlight and therefore heat. This is a phenomenon known as the albedo effect.* Black colors tend to absorb heat energy, the opposite of the color white. Thus, a black-colored object will tend to retain heat, making the surrounding environment hotter, while a white-colored object will tend to repel heat, making the surrounding environment cooler. So, the fact that white daisies increase when there is more sunlight while black daisies increase in number when there is less sunlight tells us something about how the biosphere (the two varieties of daisies in this case) reacts to changes in the ambient air temperature of the earth. If we assume greater amounts of sunlight are entering the atmosphere of the earth, the dark-colored daisies would absorb more of this sunlight, ultimately causing the dark daisies to die off because of too much absorbed heat; say they get too hot. White daisies, however, would not get too hot because they repel sunlight; this allows the white daisies to flourish in the space that is left once occupied by the black daisies. In addition, the expansion of white daisies repels more of the additional sunlight entering the earth, keeping the earth's temperatures within a constant range even though more sunlight is entering the earth.

Decreases in sunlight would result in cooler temperatures, but also a greater abundance of dark daisies. The white daisies would die off because the ambient temperature of the area would immediately cool due to the decrease in sunlight coming into the earth.† The dark daisies would absorb more heat, allowing them to not only survive the lower amount of sunlight entering the earth, but also allowing them to thrive by taking over the space left by the dying white daisies. The heat absorbed by the expanding black daisy population would also moderate the cooling effect on the earth by retaining heat, thereby offsetting the decrease in sunlight entering the earth.

Now that we understand the relationship between color and heat, we need to see the impact this relationship would have on the earth as a system. First, we need to acknowledge the fact that the black and white daisies represent the *biosphere* of our earth system. So, what we are asking in the context of Lovelock's Gaia hypothesis in this example is what impact, if any, do these changes in the makeup of the biosphere have on the earth system?

We know the earth, like our heating system example, operates within a narrow range of average temperatures over time. What Lovelock is trying to reveal in the daisy world example is that a component of the earth system—in this case the biosphere—can help to regulate something like temperature. In other words, the

---

* The *albedo effect* is a main reason snowpack and glacial ice takes a long time to melt, even under warm conditions; the snow and glaciers repel most of the heat energy from the sunlight because of the light color.

† This is similar to our heating system example. The thermostat in our example allowed for a range of temperatures, something between 70° and 74°, with the ideal temperature being 72°. Reduced sunlight entering the atmosphere would allow for the temperature to drop below a threshold, like the thermostat allowing the room to drop to 70° even though the ideal temperature is 72°.

temperature of the earth is not dependent on how much sunlight reaches the earth; it can also be manipulated by other components of the earth. In this way, we see the *relationship* between components of the earth system, and this relationship helps us understand the interrelated importance of all parts of the earth. Taken even further, thinking of the various parts of the earth as a self-regulating system creates some undeniable moral questions, questions we will consider more fully in Chapter 4. For now, it is enough that we recognize the earth does indeed exhibit the characteristics of a system. Moreover, because it is not man-made, we may say it is a natural system.

Now that we have some understanding of what constitutes a natural system, including the application of this term to the earth itself, we can begin to think about the importance of natural systems in context. For example, why should we care about natural systems at all? If the system is self-regulating, as Lovelock's theory might suggest, then why should we worry about it? If we do something to perturb the system, we can simply rely on the thermostat-like regulator within the earth system to create a feedback mechanism to bring us back within normal limits of what is a healthy environment for our survival—correct? In actuality, equilibrium is no guarantee, meaning what is considered normal within a given natural system can change over time. Now that we have some understanding of system dynamics, we need to add on to this understanding the concept of system change. The key goal of understanding here is to know that while systems tend to remain within observed limits, a system can be pushed to a point where it changes forever, creating a new normal range of limits.

Almost all known systems have some level of vulnerability where sufficient amounts of stress placed on the system can cause long-term change. The question of change depends on the overall vulnerability of a system, usually referred to as the *threshold* of the system. Thresholds are the limits of the system; place sufficient pressure to move a system beyond a threshold and the system may change forever. If that same stress does not go beyond a system's threshold, then the system can usually rebalance to the usual equilibrium state. However, if a stress goes beyond the system's threshold, then a new equilibrium state will occur, meaning the system has changed from its previous condition. A representation of how this occurs is shown in Figure 2.3.

If we accept the premise that natural systems have thresholds that can be exceeded, then we can begin to see the importance of systems thinking in environmental decision-making. The premise tells us a story that the earth is not entirely resilient, as it can be pushed to a new state that is different from the current state seen today. So what if human actions have a role in pushing our earth system toward, and possibly beyond, a certain threshold? How might we know when this is occurring even on the smallest of scales? And if it may indeed be occurring, what actions might we take in order to lessen or prevent a change that has negative consequences for us?

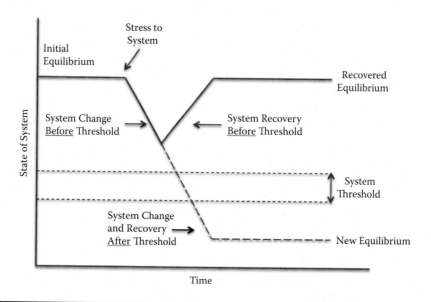

Figure 2.3 Representation of equilibrium response to differing stress levels placed on system.

We worry about our impacts on the environment because we worry about the potential for changes in equilibrium states that go beyond our capacity to deal with those changes; a shift from one equilibrium state to another is a prime reason for this concern. Climate change has to be the best example of whether or not we are pushing our earth system toward thresholds that could result in a dynamic shift to a new equilibrium state. Most important, we do not know if such a new state would be as conducive to human survival and prosperity as the current state has been. This is but one reason why we are concerned with the natural systems. However, let us now move on to an overview of the parts of this section. As you view these parts, consider how they are important in equipping one in making environmental decisions, especially in light of the need to understand how human actions impact our natural system and the degree to which our actions might push our system up against natural limits.

This section is broken down into three distinct parts. The first part deals with *ecosystem principles*. In this part, we will discuss the relevant considerations of ecosystem science, or the interactions among individuals, species, communities, biomes, etc. The purpose here is to begin thinking about scales of interactions and how actions locally can have a regional or global impact. The second part discusses concepts surrounding *biodiversity*. What is biodiversity, why is it important, and how are we impacting it? We may begin to see an understanding of human impacts on biodiversity aids in our understanding of sustainability (again, depending on our perspective). The final part in this section deals with the relatively new concept of *ecosystem-based management*. In many ways, we are attempting to manage our resources from an ecosystem standpoint. Is this possible? If so, what information is necessary to know in order to manage ecosystems? How should we act if we do not have perfect information identifying the true effects of our actions? Finally, we may begin to consider the *trade-offs* apparent in ecosystem-based management, including the cost of protecting natural resources.

Ecosystem Principles

With our understanding of natural systems in hand, we now begin a further exploration of system thinking by looking at *ecosystems*. Ecosystems can be said to be units of the larger earth system described above. Recall the components of the earth system: atmosphere, hydrosphere, lithosphere, and biosphere. These are large-scale components, meaning they represent the largest units of the earth system we can imagine. Also recall that systems are characterized in part by the fact that energy flows between components of the system. Another way of saying this is the components of the system interact with each other. For example, the hydrosphere interacts with the atmosphere; water and air have all kinds of interactions, including the exchange of heat and chemicals through both systems. These same kinds of interactions occur in all components of the earth system.

We can refine the scale of our analysis down further by focusing on subunits of the larger system components. For example, consider the Amazon Rainforest as a system. The Amazon contains all the components of the earth system: air, water, land, and living things. If we look on a map, we can see there are boundaries of the Amazon. However, we can think about how these boundaries are established; what creates the beginning and end of the Amazon in such a way that we can describe it as a distinct subunit of the earth system?* While we may not know the precise answer to this question, we can presume there are unique characteristics and interactions within the Amazon system that allow it to be viewed as a discrete unit of study. We can focus our attention on what makes the interactions between the components of the Amazon unique, and by doing so allow for a more particularized study of interactions within this subunit. This is the essence of ecosystem principles—a scientific focus of natural systems that limits our analysis to a specific area that contains all of the components of a system regardless of the scale. The key is that the unit is capable of standing alone, meaning it can support the life that thrives within the system without additional inputs from outside the system.†

---

* We have much less trouble identifying the boundaries of the earth system because the earth is a distinct unit as a planet; its beginning and end are shaped by the boundaries of the planet itself. It is interesting, however, to conceptualize other kinds of boundaries, including non-visible boundaries, which might end up extending our concept of the earth system. Certainly, if we include exogenous heat sources like the sun, then we may begin to draw the lines of the system a bit differently than simply ending at the boundaries of planet earth.

† With the exception of external sources of energy like the sun.

An ecosystem can be said to be the whole system of an environment, whether that environment is large or small.* It includes both the *biotic* (living) and *abiotic* (nonliving) parts of an environment (Molles 2008). Ecosystems should include all of the necessary *parts* or *components* of the system being analyzed, which, standing alone, can support all of the living things within the ecosystem. The largest ecosystem, arguably, is the earth itself. As mentioned earlier, James Lovelock proposed the earth is a *self-regulating* system when he formulated his Gaia hypothesis. The purpose of his argument was to suggest the earth, in many respects, acts much like a living thing. It maintains (regulates) life within a range of temperatures, pressures, and concentrations. For example, oxygen abundance in the atmosphere has been relatively stable since life obtained a foothold. It now stands at approximately 21% of atmospheric concentrations. This is completely necessary for life. Lowering oxygen levels a few percentage points would result in death of most living heterotrophs (consumers) (Bryant 1997). Increasing oxygen concentrations would result in a super-saturation of the substance, resulting in fires being maintained on wet surfaces. It is truly a fascinating theory and brings us closer to understanding the level of interconnectedness that supports existence on earth.

From an environmental standpoint, ecosystems represent an important part of determining the overall health of a natural system. Whether it is looking at something large like the Amazon Rainforest, or something quite small, like a pond, ecosystem analysis allows us to get a sense of the overall health of the natural system under observation. From a human standpoint we can divide health of an ecosystem into three primary services (benefits) that natural systems provide. These three services are provisioning, regulating, and cultural services (Millennium Ecosystem Assessment 2003). By focusing on the components of the ecosystem, as well as the services provided, we gain stronger insights into what impacts these systems the most. Understanding what impacts ecosystems is important because if we agree that these ecosystem services are important for human survival and well-being, then as humans, we certainly want to maintain the conditions on earth that support our species' current and continued survival. We now turn to a more in-depth review of the living and nonliving components of the ecosystem to develop the background knowledge necessary for understanding what impacts ecosystems.

Components: Biotic and Abiotic

We have previously identified ecosystems as a kind of natural system. Like the earth system, ecosystems are made up of a variety of natural system components: the

---

* Some ecosystems are incredibly small. One example is the ecosphere, which is an enclosed glass case that contains all components of a natural system. Tiny shrimp live in the enclosed sphere for years, meaning the system is entirely closed (with the exception of light), and capable of fully supporting life.

biosphere, lithosphere, hydrosphere, and atmosphere. Three of these components (lithosphere, hydrosphere, and atmosphere) are abiotic (nonliving), while one component (biosphere) is biotic (living). Our goal in this section is to summarize the major interactions between the biotic and abiotic parts of a natural system. The reason is to identify aspects of these interactions in context, allowing us to see the importance of the entire ecosystem from an environmental decision-making perspective.

The environment contains both living and nonliving things, both of which are critical to the survival and propagation of life. Much of environmental decision-making tends to focus on the living parts of life. This might not really be surprising, simply because most environmental issues tend to focus on the impact actions have toward living things. However, the nonliving parts of the environment are just as important, and understanding this point is the purpose of this section.

Nonliving components of an ecosystem include the chemical and physical processes in the environment. All biology at its core is chemistry, and this means the elements forming compounds are the basis of life (Bolsover et al. 2011). Moreover, forces such as light, temperature, and pressure all play a role in life. For example, some organisms can only survive at extreme temperatures and pressures, the kinds that would be fatal to human beings. However, these same organisms cannot survive at the pressures and temperatures that we are accustomed to; the factors that help to make life possible vary depending on the reference point of the organism under consideration. Abiotic factors can also be limiting for life to exist. Light only travels to a certain depth in the ocean, after which photosynthesis is made impossible because of a lack of available photons from the sun. Elements such as nitrogen, silicon, and phosphorous might also be limiting factors for the growth and development of certain aquatic organisms. The point here is that nonliving factors are just as important for life, and failing to consider these factors in environmental decisions means we fail to account for everything that may have an impact on living things.

Nonliving factors impact the living factors in a variety of ways. Consider our example of the Amazon Rainforest above. What kinds of plants and animals do you find there? What is the level of diversity of species—the number of different species—present? Now, consider contrasting what you see in the Amazon with the Sahara Desert. What types of plants and animals do you find in this desert? Are they the same as what you find in the Amazon? Is the diversity of species the same? The obvious answers here suggest the two areas are quite different, but what is really different about them? For one thing, the Amazon gets a lot more rain than the Sahara. Rain—or water—is a nonliving thing, but absolutely necessary for life. When you have a lot of rain (and a lot of sunlight and constantly warm temperatures), you get something that looks like the Amazon. When you have very little rain, you get something that looks more like the Sahara. So, we might suggest that a lot of rain, or water, is an important attribute of the Amazon; meanwhile, lots of rain is a not so critical component of the Sahara.* Understanding this relationship helps us connect the abiotic and biotic parts of life together. It also helps us understand how feedback within the system depends on the particular attributes of the system that is being observed.

From a very general perspective, one would worry less about an environmental decision that would divert water resources from a desert than they would about a decision to divert that same water from a rainforest. The reason brings us back to the point about system thresholds; the desert likely has a threshold that is less impacted by water than the rainforest.† So, diversion of water will less likely lead to an equilibrium shift in a desert, while it might more likely cause a shift in a rainforest. Therefore, what we are really taking about is an understanding of the energy flow within the specific ecosystem under consideration.

Knowing what parts of the particular system are most at risk helps us identify important values related to that system. In the parlance of ecosystem principles, we can think of those values as services provided by each ecosystem. If we know the services provided by the ecosystem, we have a better chance of prioritizing what is most critical in support of that ecosystem, both for its own sake and in relation to human well-being. We now turn to a discussion of the different kinds of services that can be provided by an ecosystem; these services also form the basis of our accounting system for establishing value in order to begin making environmental decisions.

Services Provided: Provisioning, Regulating, Cultural

If ecosystems are about understanding connections between components of the system, then we must find a way to identify the value of those connections, whether that is in direct relation to human benefits or something more indirect.‡ The reason we need to link the components of the natural system to identified values is so that we may begin to judge the merits of our actions in relation to the environment. For example, we can determine the trade-offs between values gained in a land development setting versus the values lost from the undeveloped land that has been altered from the environment. At the heart of this trade-off analysis is the identification and accounting of natural values.

In this section, we focus our attention on three categories of services provided by natural systems: provisioning, regulating, and cultural services. Provisioning

---

* There is little doubt water is an important factor for all life, including life that exists in desert settings. However, the organisms of the desert are more adapted to living with little water availability than the organisms that live in the rainforest. Move them from one location to the other, and their ill adaptability to the new climate will likely become apparent.

† It is important to reiterate that this is a generalization to make a point. All water that is made available to a desert ecosystem is undoubtedly important and necessary for the life that has evolved within that system.

‡ The term *value* that is being used here is a relative term that is based in large part on the criteria by which we determine value in context. This is discussed at greater length in Chapter 4.

and regulating services are connected to human well-being, but are focused more on the natural conditions provided from the resource itself. Cultural services more directly relate the natural value of the resource to a human-centered value, the resource providing the value that is almost entirely human based. Each service will be explained in greater detail below, followed by a discussion of how these services help us begin to account for values in environmental decisions.

Provisioning services are the types of things we get from the environment that help to sustain us as a species (Chapin 2009, 41). For example, an ecosystem can contain many different types of animals, deer being one example. The deer are part of the ecosystem, but they are also a potential food source for predators, including humans. In this way, the ecosystem helps to provision the deer as a source of food.* Freshwater is another example of a provisioning service provided by an ecosystem; it is necessary for the survival of most living things.† The key with a provisioning service is that the resource provides direct consumptive value to the recipient (beneficiary) in question; the provisioning service is something tangible that can be touched, smelled, and generally consumed for personal survival. As humans, we derive direct consumptive value from a variety of ecosystem sources. These sources include categorically: food (crops, livestock, wild foods, fisheries, aquaculture), fiber (timber, cotton, hemp, silk, wood fuel), freshwater, and others (Chapin 2009, 42). The relative value of provisioning services is obvious; they provide us with the basic necessities of supporting and maintaining life. It is generally easy to defend the importance of provisioning services when making environmental decisions because of the direct and obvious connection between the resource and human survival.

Regulating services are values provided by ecosystems that are not directly linked to sustaining humans. Rather than providing immediate forms of sustenance, regulating services are connected to feedback that helps maintain the integrity of provisioning services. For example, photosynthetic plants help to clean the atmosphere through the natural process of respiration (taking in carbon dioxide and releasing oxygen); this process helps to regulate the amount of oxygen in the air, keeping it within a range that is healthy for human survival and prosperity. Said another way, we may care about the wood in a tree as a provisioning service that provides us with building materials or as a source of fuel. However, we also care about the regulating capacity of the tree to clean the air, making our lives possible. We may be most directly aware of the provisioning services of the tree, but it is the regulating services that help to provide the foundation for our very existence, whether we are aware of this fact or not.

---

* Most deer are herbivores or plant eaters, so plants are an important provisioning resource for the deer (as well as other animals, including humans).

† For simplicity sake, we are looking at these different kinds of services from the human lens, meaning we are interested in how these different parts of a natural system provide the associated services to humans.

There are many different examples of provisioning services. For example, wetlands help to filter water, making it available for human consumption (Chapin 2009, 203). Mangroves provide important nursery habitat for a variety of fish species, some of which are of commercial importance (Chapin 2009, 223). Forests help to prevent erosion of nutrient-rich topsoil aiding in agricultural production (Chapin 2009, 32, 189–94). Other categories of regulating services provided by different ecosystem components include the following: air quality regulation, climate regulation, water regulation, erosion regulation, water purification and waste treatment, disease regulation, pest regulation, pollination, and natural hazard regulation (Chapin 2009).

Cultural services identify the human connections to ecosystem services. They include values associated with recreation and tourism, aesthetics, and spiritual/religious considerations. John Muir often referred to natural areas as "God's cathedral" (Worster 2008). His revelation being that natural places imbue the human spirit with a sense of awe and inspiration. Places like the Grand Canyon and Yosemite National Park are examples of nature's aesthetic and inspirational power; we are both inspired and humbled by the scenes we see in nature.

What we draw from this discussion is the inherent value ecosystems provide that go beyond providing us with literal sustenance. Said another way, where provisioning services provide us with the basic necessities for literal survival—food, shelter, clothing—cultural services provide us with a different kind of "food" or "shelter" that goes beyond literal sustenance; in cultural services we find our connection to natural things in a more intimate yet informal way. All of these values are important considerations when engaging in environmental decisions.

Consider that when making environmental decisions, one needs to have a solid understanding of the background environmental factors at play. Natural systems give us the largest-scale picture of what those background environmental factors are in a particular instance. Included in ecosystem principles are two main points: the components of an ecosystem include both living and nonliving things, and the services provided by an ecosystem can be categorized into provisioning, regulating, and cultural services. Any environmental decision must include consideration of the living and nonliving factors of a natural system. Also, all services provided by that natural system must be assessed and accounted for. Otherwise, it is likely whatever environmental decision is being made will be discounting the true value of the environment under consideration (simply because not all services are being considered).

Assume a government official is trying to decide whether to allow for development to occur in a natural area. Failure to consider the regulating and cultural services provided by the ecosystem could allow for the decision-maker to come to the incorrect conclusion about the total value of the environment at stake. It is not unlike a potential employer considering only two of your credentials when you actually have three; you know all three credentials are important to the job, and the consideration of just two of them might prevent you from getting the position. Meanwhile consideration of all three credentials would show that you are perfectly qualified for the position. Accounting for all services provided by an ecosystem is the same thing; failure to properly identify and account for all value can lead to a decision about the resource that is incomplete.

The point attempting to be made here is that a full understanding of ecosystem principles—even without being a trained ecologist—increases the likelihood that environmental decisions will be made with full information, and full information should be the goal of any environmental decision-maker. However, ecosystem principles are not the entire focus of understanding natural systems. From an environmental decision-making standpoint, certain aspects of natural systems are considered of crucial importance, one being the issue of *biodiversity*. The next section highlights some of the more critical concepts of biodiversity for consideration.

Biodiversity

Have you ever heard the saying "everything is connected"? In some respect, biodiversity seems to be at the heart of that saying. Remember James Lovelock and the Gaia hypothesis? Dr. Lovelock hypothesized the earth was a self-regulating system, that is was equipped with the means to maintain itself within a certain boundary of limits. This is similar to how our bodies self-regulate internal temperatures. We have inputs: nutrients from food, oxygen, and liquids. These inputs interact with various chemicals inside our body that are catalyzed through various reactions (including the use of bacteria in our stomachs to aid in digestion). These reactions then fuel the functions of our bodies (including growth, repair, and otherwise maintaining the system). Lovelock believes the earth works in much the same way; but what is helping to regulate the earth system? Many believe biodiversity is a large part of the answer.

The term *biodiversity* refers to a richness and diversity of life. It is meant to express the idea that a healthy natural system is one that contains a lot of variety: variety of plants, animals, fungus, bacteria, and variety of the different landscapes in which living things thrive.* A major tenet behind biodiversity theory is, all things being equal, the more species of things that are present, the healthier the natural system (Hubbell 2001). So, for example, it is presumed that areas where we find lots of species density (a high number of species per unit of area observed) are

---

* The term *landscape* is being used here to refer to the different types of environments created in which various forms of life are found. Recall the example of the different types of things we find in the Amazon Rainforest ecosystem versus the Sahara Desert ecosystem. The different landscapes or environments set the stage for the development of different kinds of plants and animals, each suited to surviving in the environment in which they are found. Further, within each landscape exist different micro-landscapes. For example, the oceans are a type of ecosystem. However, within the ocean there are many different types of landscapes; the open ocean is like a vast desert of water. Meanwhile, a near shore coral reef contains a structure quite different from the open ocean, allowing a variety of marine species to live and thrive among the niches created by the coral mosaic. The coral reef and open ocean represent two types of landscapes within the larger ecosystem of the ocean itself.

hotspots of biodiversity and are therefore important for life (Hubbell 2001, 30–47). The Amazon Rainforest is one area where we find a lot of living things per area. The Amazon actually contains some of the highest densities of biodiversity on earth (Gardner 2010). Thus, beyond the importance of the Amazon as a sink for carbon (often mentioned in climate change discussions), it also represents an important repository of biodiversity.

The importance of biodiversity may also be connected to some of the ecosystem services described in the previous section. One example is that of pharmaceutical applications of different types of plants, animals, and bacteria still waiting to be found in biodiversity hotspots. Many current medical treatments have come from chemical compounds found in living things found in places like the Amazon. This is but one example of why biodiversity may have importance for human well-being. There are many other examples, but let us identify these examples within a context of looking at biodiversity through an exploration of its definitions, interactions, and some of the more common arguments of its overall importance.

Definitions

Formal definitions of biodiversity differ depending on what scientific discipline is defining the term, and in what context the term is being used. From a genetic standpoint, biodiversity means the diversity of genetic materials being shared between populations of the same species (Krishnamurthy 2003). In this definition, biodiversity is directly linked to the health of a species because it identifies the importance of genetic diversity as a factor in healthy populations of a species. A lack of such diversity can lead to species inbreeding, or a "bottlenecking" of genetic diversity, which can limit reproductive rates of species (Krishnamurthy 2003, 81–83). One example in recent years has been the low genetic diversity among Cheetah populations in Africa, which has led to inbreeding and resulted in very low reproductive success, endangering the survival of certain populations of Cheetah (Krishnamurthy 2003, 81–94).

Other disciplines take a broader approach to defining the term *biodiversity*. Ecologists tend to look at larger scales of biodiversity than the cellular genetic level. They tend to focus on populations of species, interactions between populations of species, and even larger components (Molles 2008). A broader focus allows one to see the more obvious implications of human activities and how they impact biological diversity. Development of roads and other structures that interfere with the natural habitat of a species can limit interaction between populations of species over time because of geographic isolation (Lindenmayer and Fischer 2006, 125–32). Researchers in evolutionary theory find corollaries to this effect in places like Australia, which represent an island effect because of plate tectonics; where Australia was once connected to other large land masses and the animals interacted, its isolation since separating from these land masses has allowed for species to exist in Australia that do not exist anywhere else on earth (Rice 2007, 51–54).

Human activities can create the same kind of island effect on species. In more extreme cases, human activity can lead directly to the extinction of a species by altering essential habitat for the species (Suter 1993, 371). Larger-scale definitions of biodiversity help us understand the potential impacts of our actions on the earth system by allowing us to see the physical impacts of human activities on members of the earth's biosphere.

A more generalized definition of biodiversity tends to account for both the micro- and macro-scales of diversity. At the famous 1992 United Nations Earth Summit, a general consensus for the definition of *biological diversity* included the importance of understanding and valuing diversity within species, between species, and of ecosystems (Convention on Biological Diversity 2011). This definition is broad but also comprehensive, suggesting an appreciation of biological diversity at all levels is an important precondition to making informed environmental decisions. Connecting this broad definitional understanding of biodiversity as a component of making sound environmental decisions is a key element in understanding the importance of biodiversity as an indicator of ecosystem health. Let us now look at some of the interactions between biodiversity and general ecosystem health.

Interactions

It is generally presumed that biologically diverse systems have a greater potential for beneficial outcomes like a high system resiliency to stress (Holling 2010). Recalling that systems under stress can sometimes cross a threshold that results in a fundamental change to the system, we can see the value biodiversity can play in preventing this from occurring by increasing the resiliency of the system. Consider recent changes in the production of agricultural products and how such changes have modified background levels of biodiversity. Let us begin this consideration by summarizing recent changes in modern agriculture.

In modern agricultural production there is a lot of direct human interaction in the development, growing, and harvesting of the food that is produced. Technological innovations and scientific advancements in genetics have allowed us to manipulate genes to create strains of crops that are highly resistant to stresses (drought, heat, predation, etc.), while also being capable of producing a high yield product (larger corn kernels, etc.) (Murray 2003). The ability to create artificial fertilizer through the fixing of nitrogen has also added to our capacity to manipulate the natural system of growing food. Our ability to manipulate the natural system has also changed the system, providing new feedback into the system through the introduction of genetically modified species, and also through the changing of ground cover from natural conditions to agricultural land for growing these crops. Let us place these changes into context with an example.

Say a field is cultivated to grow a variety of wheat for human consumption. Let us assume there are approximately ten varieties of wheat species represented in the field. It may be that some of the wheat varieties have attributes favorable for human consumption: they grow faster, have a larger yield of edible portions, and overall tend to have a more pleasant taste. We might want to select only these species of wheat because they will provider larger yields of better-tasting food in a shorter amount of time.

Now let us consider a potential outcome of our conscious rational choice to grow a select few varieties of wheat. If we agree biodiversity is positively correlated with resiliency, meaning the more diversity the more diverse the system, what do you think the resilience of the field is if it only has one or two varieties of wheat as opposed to ten? It is likely our choice to grow only a few varieties has reduced the overall resiliency of the field. For example, what if a fungus or some disease finds its way onto the field and attacks the high-yielding variety of wheat because of characteristics unique to that wheat? In a field with ten varieties of the wheat, there is a greater chance of still yielding a good harvest overall because some of the other wheat species will be resilient to the fungus/disease. However, with a field of only a few varieties, it is possible the fungus/disease completely destroys the entire crop. This is the lesson of the importance of biodiversity; the lower numbers of biological variety provide less resistance to stresses against the system.

The use of single crop species because they contain preferred characteristics is generally referred to as a monoculture planting (Murray 2003). Monoculture planting is considered dangerous by many who advocate for the diversity of agricultural species. They argue that it places all of your proverbial eggs into one basket; if a disease or pest comes along that cannot be controlled, the entire crop is destroyed. Biological diversity between the species of wheat (some using different genes than others) can provide a buffer against such possibilities.

There are a number of examples throughout human history that support the problems of relying on a single crop or species for agricultural production, the Irish potato blight of 1846 being a well-known example (Freeman 2007, 101). This is one reason farmers today often employ a strategy of planting various species in the same field. Some of the planting is done to protect a target crop from insects or other pests. In certain cases, a crop of plant A closely planted to the target crop of plant B can help to prevent predation, meaning crop A's purpose is to prevent the predation of another crop (Center, van Driesche, and Hoddle 2008, 266–78). Crop A is not being grown for human consumption, but rather to increase the resiliency of crop B, another example of how biological diversity can aid in protecting target species.

Beyond the example of agricultural crops, we can also point to non-human-induced interactions among biologically diverse systems that are relevant for background understanding in environmental decision-making. If we recall our summary of the Gaia hypothesis championed by James Lovelock, we remember that feedback between parts of a natural system helps us see how important interactions are for the system to function properly. In the daisy world example, recall how increasing heat input from the sun is moderated by the biological response of more white daisies beginning to grow, reflecting more of the sun back into space. When the earth cools, more heat is absorbed by the black daisies, which increase in number because of the niche left open by dying light daisies. Now, imagine if one of the varieties of daisies no longer existed? Say white daisies go extinct, and we are only left with black daisies. If the earth begins to take on additional heat into the system, we do not have white daisies to repel the heat; this means the regulation offered by the biosphere is reduced (at least in Lovelock's example), resulting in either heat being trapped on earth, or the death of all biological life.* We can say in this example that a lack of diversity among the daisy plants has resulted in a hotter planet, likely leading to threshold limits that could create a new equilibrium state on earth.

The daisy world example is helpful because it allows us to conceptualize the importance of biodiversity at some of the largest scales, in this case the entire earth system. Through these examples, we hopefully begin to gain a basic sense of how the interactions between the biosphere and other natural system components are impacted through the lens of biological diversity. We cannot spend too much time delving into the details of this topic, as it represents an entire discipline of study in itself. Rather, our job here is to gain a sense of understanding of the issues that arise from biodiversity interactions as they relate to environmental questions. Ultimately, the relevance of biodiversity is its importance to our understanding of natural systems, the subject we review next.

Importance

Biodiversity provides the earth with necessary *nutrients* and *processes*. Plants and other autotrophs help to synthesize sunlight and water into organic matter through the process of photosynthesis (Schlesinger 1997, 34–35). This in turn provides a supply of oxygen as a by-product of this reaction. Animals and certain bacteria (heterotrophs) consume oxygen as part of their metabolic processes, ensuring the oxygen levels remain at a relative constant (Gagosian and Lee 1981, 96–97). If there were too many plants stimulating too much oxygen in the atmosphere, the response would be an increase in consumers of plants, limiting their growth. At the same time, too many consumers without corresponding plant growth would overeat the plants, causing a die-off of the consumer population, further ensuring the ratio of oxygen in the atmosphere remains within a given range. In this way, regulation of the amount of oxygen in the atmosphere is achieved, keeping the relative concentration of oxygen consistent (Schlesinger 1997, 37).

Another example of the importance of biodiversity in maintaining overall function of the natural system is the role of honeybees as pollinators of plant species. Without the existence of bees to aid in pollination, we might have a significant reduction in the variety of fruits and vegetables (Kremen 2008). This would certainly

---

* In a world where only white and black daisies comprise the entire diversity of the biosphere, the increasing heat would kill off the black daisies (recall they absorb too much heat and die off), leaving no biological species left to inhabit the earth.

impact human well-being. Honeybees are one of the few species that serve as a major pollination pathway for most of the fruits and vegetables humans consume. Since these fruits and vegetables require a conduit like the bee to procreate, the honeybee becomes an indispensible partner in the process of procreation for these plants.

The importance of biodiversity is directly related to human well-being. Without a biologically diverse environment to support life, there is no life capable of being supported for humans; the relevance of biodiversity in this context could not be clearer. But can we do more than simply identify a correlation between general biological activity and human well-being? It seems one might argue a number of species are important for human survival, say a percentage of the photosynthetic autotrophs, but that does not suggest every single species alive today is absolutely necessary, correct? There certainly is strong evidence that some background level of extinction is a part of our natural systems, being observed in the fossil record over time. So, while one might argue that diversity to some degree is important, what is the relevance of thinking we must maintain all diversity currently observed?* Let us explore this question in a bit more detail now.

Research suggests the services provided by a biologically diverse set of organisms within a natural system are both important and valuable (Costanza et al. 1997, 253). So, all things being equal, there is an argument to be made that suggests greater levels of biodiversity yield greater amounts of value. The value we are describing here is precisely the kind of value found in the ecosystem services identified earlier in this chapter. This includes air quality, climate control, water purification, pollination, and erosion prevention. These are representative of the regulating services that we discussed earlier.

Ecosystem stability is another consideration; there is evidence in the fossil record that high rates of biodiversity correlate strongly with stable climate and populations (Freeman 2007, 88–91). Conversely, high rates of extinction—lowering of biodiversity—tend to correlate with strong shifts in ecosystem stability (Freeman 2007, 88–91). Of course, it is possible that not all species are created equal; some species may have more importance than others in maintaining a stable and healthy environment. We already mentioned that species go extinct under natural (nonhuman) pressures all the time. Obviously those that have gone extinct could not have been essential in maintaining the overall health of ecosystems; if they were, we should see a dramatic shift in those systems, say to another equilibrium

---

* It is important to know that our current rates of extinction in species lost per year are substantial and reflect the kinds of extinction rates observed in the fossil record where the relative abundance and distribution of species altered substantially and irreversibly. So, while we entertain this argument for illustrative purposes of learning, the overall *rate* of extinction is the primary factor that should be considered when determining the overall health of the natural system. (Rate of extinction can be determined by averaging the number of species going extinct in 1 year over the number of new species coming into existence in the same year, and looking at this number in relationship to the total number of species within a system.)

state.* Other species might be more like the black and white daisies from Lovelock's example; they might be critical to maintaining important ecosystem functions. How are we to know the difference? What if we make a mistake and label one species unimportant when it actually is important? This is precisely the problem with trying to pick and choose species; we simply do not know enough to make intelligent decisions. So, what might be the more logical approach?

When our knowledge is insufficient to determine the relative importance of a particular species, we likely have to default back to a position that presumes all known species existing today are important. We default to this position because we can be assured that species currently existing, in aggregate, have aided in establishing the current conditions of the earth system that support our own survival. Until we know more, this position should dominate our means of evaluating the importance of any particular species.

If we think about this position, it really says biodiversity is critical, and this applies to each individual species present on the earth today. So, unless we have absolute information to the contrary, each species must be presumed to be a critical component for the health of our earth system. If we correlate this presumption to a decision-orientated perspective, then this means biodiversity has to be a consideration in environmental decisions. So to summarize, if we are making decisions about the environment that discount the diversity of life, then we are placing ourselves in a precarious position simply because we cannot say with absolute assurance that the species placed in peril are unimportant for our survival. This is one of the main reasons biodiversity is an important consideration when making environmental decisions.

From these examples we may begin to see biodiversity as an important indicator in assessing the overall health of the earth. Thus, in order for us to have healthy ecosystems, we really need to have strong biodiversity—they are interchangeable, and the one cannot function without the other. So now we have some evidence to support a foundational belief that biodiversity is an important means by which ecosystem health is determined. But how do we take ecosystem principles and apply them to actual environmental management decisions? We now turn to attempts to actively manage our interactions with natural systems, focusing on what is referred to as *ecosystem-based management*.

Ecosystem-Based Management

Our attention now turns to the interactions between humans and natural systems through a discussion of ecosystem-based management. Ecosystem principles helped us understand the importance of natural systems, how systems are connected, and the impact these connections have on the overall health and well-being

---

* Another way of saying this is: just because one species goes extinct does not mean a threshold has been reached in the system, forcing the system to a new equilibrium state.

of all species on planet earth. Biodiversity helps us understand the importance of species richness and diversity. We now take this knowledge and attempt to apply it to a form of human-based management toward natural systems. The focus here is on combining our thinking of natural systems with our human-created institutions. The goal is to begin to think about ways in which our institutions can handle the type of natural system interactions discussed in meaningful ways to handle environmental questions.

Definition and Purpose

Ecosystem-based management is a management framework for making environmental decisions. Heavy emphasis should be placed on the term *framework* here because it really is about how we perceive our interactions with the natural system. It includes assumptions we make about the natural system and human interactions within that system. A generalized definition of ecosystem-based management is an approach to environmental decision-making that emphasizes and incorporates all of the potential interactions within an ecosystem, including human interactions, rather than considering single components of the ecosystem in isolation (Millennium Ecosystem Assessment 2003). One of the key components of ecosystem-based management is the interactions occurring between components of the ecosystem. Ecosystem-based management has multiple objectives, focusing on the diverse benefits provided by the natural system, rather than focusing on any single ecosystem service. In ecosystem-based management all ecosystem services identified earlier (provisioning, regulating, and cultural) become important. Finally, ecosystem-based management principles adopt an adaptive management strategy, meaning the assumption of complexity in both the natural and social components of the system requires the need to constantly evaluate and reassess management decisions. Adaptive management is best suited to this task because it embraces an iterative process of management: a constant implementation, evaluation, learning, and adaption to what is learned about a new implementation strategy occurring in a repetitive cycle. Collectively this process helps to formulate a definition of precisely what is ecosystem-based management. What an ecosystem-based management process looks like visually is represented in Figure 2.4.

Ecosystem-based management is a type of management scheme that seeks a more holistic approach to understanding the causative factors involved in environmental impacts. As such, it is not meant to be singular in scope or perspective. For example, consider a proposal to build a large dock next to a pristine estuary lake that feeds into an ocean bay. Let us consider the potential impacts of this proposed development on both the natural and man-made components of the relevant ecosystem. Certainly, the building of the dock would have some impact on the water quality of the immediate area; testing might be required as a condition of development to ensure that water quality levels do not drop below a threshold. However, the dock will likely also disrupt the bottom sediment and local habitat of

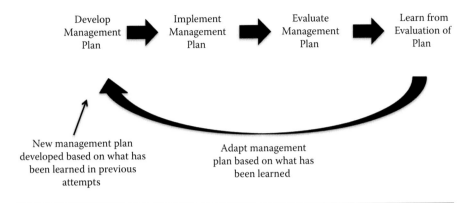

Figure 2.4   Representation of an ecosystem-based management process.

the marine life in the immediate vicinity of the dock. Depending on what is at the seafloor, this can include important grasses and structures that are used by commercially important fish species as a nursery for young. Disturbing this area can have an impact on these species. Moreover, the proposed use of the dock will likely bring boats to the area, meaning there will be additional impacts to the water and local marine and wildlife from the boats themselves (loud motors, discarding waste into the water, etc.). The dock, depending on how it is built, might also disrupt water flow around the area, causing sediment buildup around the dock. This can impact the local marine life. There are also human-based ecosystem component considerations. For example, the dock can impede navigation of other boats in the area, and also impact the view and other aesthetic considerations.

Imagine if we stopped our analysis of the example in the preceding paragraph at water quality measurements? What would we be missing in terms of understanding the overall impacts of the proposed dock development? We would miss the impacts between components of the ecosystem, for example, the impacts to the things living in the water, as well as impacts to the surrounding habitat of those living things. Ecosystem-based management offers the potential for a more comprehensive analysis because it requires us to think about all of the connections and impacts related to a proposed activity. Considering all of the connections and impacts of a proposed activity can allow us to better assess the relative merits of that activity, or at least compare the values between the activity and the impacted parts of the natural system. The very idea of comparison gets us into the role of ecosystem-based management in environmental decisions, a topic discussed in greater detail below.

Role in Environmental Management

The example of the immediately preceding dock-building proposal helps us place the role of ecosystem-based management in the larger context of environmental management. We can also refer this question back to the concepts discussed earlier in this chapter under ecosystem principles, specifically the three categories of services provided by ecosystems: provisioning, regulating, and cultural. If we take the example and consider the various services provided by ecosystems, we get a sense of the role of this kind of management system in making environmental decisions.

First, we see that ecosystem-based management provides a fuller accounting of how environmental values are being impacted. By identifying all environmental values present under an ecosystem management analysis, we have a better accounting of what environmental values are at stake. Second, we see human values being considered along with environmental values, as human institutions are considered components of the system that is being analyzed. This helps us identify trade-offs where appropriate, including instances where harm to natural system values might be offset by significant gains in human-based values. Third, we see that the iterative process, or adaptive management component, of ecosystem-based management ensures a continual review of impacts; it is not as if one evaluation of environmental impact will be conclusive, but rather multiple and constant review of impacts over time will tell a fuller story. Thus, we see the role of environmental management as one of a continuing process when seen through the lens of ecosystem-based management.

Let us now compare what we know about ecosystem-based management to traditional forms of environmental management and see where there are differences. (We will look at examples of ecosystem-based management being implemented in current environmental policy initiatives in the next section.)

Traditional forms of environmental management include the statutes passed mainly in the 1970s known as the media-specific environmental laws.* These laws are known as media specific because they were just that, specific to a particular medium like the air or the water. So, the laws focused mainly on what we were doing that had an immediate impact on the medium at issue. Let us look at the Clean Water Act as an example in depth.

The Clean Water Act contained two main parts, both aimed at remediating and maintaining the chemical, physical, and biological integrity of the nation's waters (Gross and Dodge 2005). These two main parts were point sources and non-point sources of pollution. The early focus was on point sources of pollution, things like major factories and manufacturing plants (and also sewage discharge facilities)—all man-made facilities that had a discrete instrument that was discharging waste into waterways.

The obvious example is a factory that generates a by-product in the manufacturing process of waste chemicals that it simply discharged directly into an immediately adjacent stream, river, lake, or other water body. The Clean Water Act requires any such point source polluter to immediately cease polluting, and apply for and get a

---

* This includes, but is not limited to, such laws as the Clean Air Act, the Clean Water Act, the Resource Conservation and Recovery Act, the National Environmental Policy Act, and the Toxic Substances Control Act.

permit from a federal agency before commencing any further polluting (Gross and Dodge 2005). The permit limits the amount of chemicals (defined as pollutants) the facility can dump into the waterway within a set period (say a total amount per day, week, month, or year). The purpose of the permit is to ensure the water quality of the water body by limiting total amounts of pollutants into the system.

So, how well does the Clean Water Act do in preventing pollution of the waterway? Our first query should be to ask what is being defined as pollution? Does it include everything that can impact the integrity of the relevant ecosystem, or something less? If it is less, then we are not really considering ecosystem principles in the protection of the water system, are we? If the pollution is only certain chemicals known to cause adverse impacts to humans, then impacts to the natural system might be missed. For example, say the factory is discharging four different kinds of chemicals, only one of which is known to be hazardous to humans. Regulating only this one chemical may miss impacts of the other chemicals on other components of the ecosystem. What if one of the other chemicals interacts with the water to cause problems to the marine wildlife in the area? Should this not be considered important when controlling what comes out of the factory simply because there is no direct impact on humans? The answer is a likely no from an ecosystem perspective.

Let us also consider that the Clean Water Act separates pollution into two categories: *point* and *non-point* sources of pollution. We have identified examples of point sources (factories and public water treatment facilities as two examples), but we have not really discussed non-point sources. Non-point sources include things that do not have an obvious form of pollution delivery, like a pipe or ditch (Gross and Dodge 2005). They include things like runoff, which includes accumulated chemicals and debris that builds up on roads and other surfaces; when it rains, this debris is collected in the rainwater and tends to move toward water bodies. The water bodies can be ponds, streams, rivers, lakes, and certainly the ocean. They can also be underground water sources such as aquifers that represent important sources of drinking water for human consumption (Pierzyniski, Sims, and Vance 2005, 116–18).

Other sources of non-point pollution include animal feedlots where food animals (steer, cows, pigs, chicken, turkey, etc.) are raised for human consumption or the production of things like milk (Millennium Ecosystem Assessment 2005, 301–3). Fertilizer runoff from agricultural and residential lawn maintenance represents a particularly difficult example of non-point source pollution; a prime example is the runoff from the Mississippi River that aggregates in the Gulf of Mexico, causing a dead zone in the Gulf waters where large areas exhibit low-oxygen conditions (known as *hypoxia*) during parts of the year (Hill 2010, 276–78).

The non-point sources of pollution are particularly difficult to control because they contain no single source like the factory-type point sources identified above. However, these sources of pollution represent some of the more dangerous forms from an ecosystem management standpoint. Consider the Gulf of Mexico example above; the cumulative impacts of using fertilizer from farming operations and residential lawns developed along the Mississippi result in a condition in the Gulf of

Mexico ecosystem that fundamentally changes the ecosystem of the Gulf waters. This dead zone that is created impacts all the ecosystem services identified: provisioning, regulating, and cultural. So why hasn't the Clean Water Act been more successful at dealing with non-point sources of pollution? We will attempt to answer this question in the following section.

Examples in Environmental Policy Management Techniques

The purpose of this section is to review examples of ecosystem-based management in existing environmental policy management techniques. The goal is to see how ecosystem principles can be implemented in environmental decisions. We will do this by reviewing examples where ecosystem principles have been implemented to varying degrees of success. In one example, we find failure to implement ecosystem-based management techniques. In the other example, we find a more successful implementation strategy. Try and understand what shared differences might exist between the two examples to indicate just how ecosystem principles can consistently be implemented into environmental decisions in a way that maximizes benefits to all components of the system, both natural and human.

We begin here carrying forward the question raised in the previous section: Why has the Clean Water Act failed at comprehensively dealing with non-point source pollution? Let us carry forward the example of the dead zone in the Gulf of Mexico, which is mainly caused by fertilizer runoff entering the Gulf from the Mississippi River (Hill 2010, 276). If we look at the history of the Clean Water Act,* we find that the law has been successful at controlling point sources of pollution, sources where the pollution emanates from a specific source, like a pipe. However, the Clean Water Act has been less successful at controlling non-point sources. What are the main differences?

One difference between point and non-point sources of pollution is that point sources are mainly stationary, allowing the source of the pollution to be clearly identified. The term often used to describe such sources is *discrete*. Non-point sources are more *diffuse*, meaning they are spread out, making them hard to identify. Even when non-point sources can be identified, the particular mechanisms of pollution are not obvious; fertilizer, for instance, is not easily observed as entering a nearby waterway during a rain event, and even if it is, one must be around during the event to detect it occurring.

---

* Our ability here to review the entire history of the Clean Water Act is severely limited. Major aspects of its history, implementation, and subsequent amendments are purposefully left out here because the resulting material would take up too much room within this text. I acknowledge I have taken liberties with the history in order to make the example useful for identifying ecosystem-based management principles (mainly expressing the difference between point source and non-point source controls). Those seeking a more in-depth treatment of the history of the Clean Water Act have a multitude of available resources at their disposal.

The diffuse nature of non-point sources creates a dynamic management setting. Consider the permit system identified above that exists for point sources of pollution; one can monitor the creation and quantity of a pollutant from a facility, and then also monitor the amount of pollution that is sent into the environment. Enforcement of this kind of pollution creation and dispersal is, conceptually at least, linear. Try and image how such a permit system would be implemented for non-point sources of pollution. One may create a limit for the amount of fertilizer that can be emitted into the water from a particular source, but how do you actually enforce this amount? How does one even tell how much of the pollution is actually getting into the waterway? There is no pipe or other direct means that aggregates all of the pollution prior to it making its way to the water. It seems conceptually impossible to use the same kind of permit system for non-point sources of pollution that is employed for point sources of pollution.

Let us now conceptualize some of the ways in which non-point source pollution might actually be managed. (We will get into some of the economic ways of internalizing costs and creating incentives in Chapter 3; this will help us to really begin answering this question. However, I believe it is worthwhile to begin thinking about solutions as we come across the opportunity.) If direct enforcement is hard to impossible, then what might be a way to limit and even prevent certain pollution from diffuse sources? Let us consider taxation as a way to manage non-point source pollution.

Maybe a pollution tax can be levied on the things making the pollution. In our example of the dead zone, fertilizer was determined to be a main ingredient in the nutrient enrichment of the Gulf that ultimately leads to the creation of a dead zone. Taxing the fertilizer that is used in areas adjacent to the Mississippi River Basin may be one way to attack the pollution problem. If this were done, the tax would have to be calculated sufficiently to encourage a more conservative use of fertilizer. The revenue created from the tax could be used to help prevent runoff in these areas, say with the creation of buffer zones, near water areas that soak up the pollutants before they have a chance to get to the water body. There are actually many examples of how the tax could be used to both change behaviors and subsidize solutions. Again, more will be discussed on this concept in Chapter 3. Let us now turn to an example where we can envision ecosystem-based management principles being successfully implemented in an environmental policy decision-making process.

Let us first consider what would be an idealized situation for ecosystem-based management; we can use the Clean Water Act discussion above, especially the part about non-point source pollution, to help direct us by reminding ourselves of what is difficult in this kind of management. The first thing that comes to my mind is the importance of information, not just any kind of information, but as complete a set of information helping me determine causal relationships between ecosystem components as is available. I say complete information here because understanding of the system is really based on integrating information about all components of the system. So, information is a key ingredient in making ecosystem-based decisions.

How would I go about getting complete information? If I am a government, I might try to "hire" the resources directly through employment at an agency, or indirectly through grant funding of expert research. Of course, the expense of doing so would be substantial and borne mostly by the taxpayer in such a situation, which can have political consequences. If I am a stakeholder, I might try to obtain the information firsthand, but I would run into the same cost problem as the government, except I would likely have less resources at my disposal.* As such, I might try and share information with other private stakeholders. By combining knowledge about the resource, I might develop a more complete understanding of how the natural system works.

Focusing for a moment on the idea of sharing information between private stakeholders a number of issues arise, at least when we place the idea within the context of the following example. Consider a small near-shore fishery, say one that focuses on three interacting species: sea urchin, albacore, and lobster. Assume there are approximately 50 individuals who fish for these three species collectively within a defined area.† Together they have knowledge of the entire spatial area under consideration, but individually they have expertise based on a subset of the defined area. Another way of saying this is each individual is an expert on the area he or she fishes, but has little expertise on the areas he or she does not fish, and no individual fishes every area that encompasses the boundaries under consideration. The only way to gain a more complete understanding of this system is for the stakeholders to share their individual expertise. If they do, then there is an increased chance of gaining sufficient knowledge to manage the area holistically, in line with ecosystem-based principles. If they do not share information, then it is less likely that complete ecosystem-based management is possible. We now need to consider what would impact each individual's willingness to share their expertise with the group. To answer this question, we have to consider incentives.

What incentives might exist for an individual fisher to share his or her personal information with the group? For one, the collective sharing of information can lead to a better understanding of the dynamics operating in this system: knowing where the urchins, abalone, and lobster breed; understanding where the adults of the species congregate; what areas provide important nursery habitat to ensure new generations grow, thrive, and produce offspring of their own. If this information is shared collectively, then the group can better manage how they collectively fish to ensure the long-term viability of the species (at least based on the impact their collective fishing effort makes on the long-term viability of the species).

---

* The availability of resources to private versus public entities depends on a variety of factors.
† The area we would define would be the spatial boundary of interest. We need to be reminded that the physical boundary created by these individuals might be based on a number of factors, including human-derived boundaries like political borders. It is important to note, however these boundaries are defined, that they may overlap natural ecosystems, be wholly within one natural ecosystem, perfectly define a natural ecosystem (unlikely), or any combination of these options.

Of course, the information can also be used for illicit purposes. For example, a fisher can decide to use group information to determine the best spots to fish; the individual efforts of other fishers to find their best spots through trial and error over time has become available to the group collectively.* This information could also help to form the basis of government management decisions that determine certain fishing grounds should be protected because they contain sensitive habitat for the target species; if one of the proposed areas for protection includes your fishing grounds, you will lose your prime fishing spots that likely took years (even generations) to develop. Unless you are assured of gaining access to equally viable fishing grounds, you may feel less inclined to share your information. Now our analysis begins to move away from the information itself to a different discussion about the *impact* of sharing information on individual fishers.

The purpose of our current example is not to go too far into a discussion of human decision-making dynamics; this is discussed in greater detail in Chapter 4, and you should carry forward the questions raised above when you get to that section. The purpose now is to touch upon the issue of environmental management questions in ecosystem-based management to understand the importance of how complete information can lead us into a difficult discussion about the process of gaining that information, at least when the process includes actors that are directly impacted by the aggregation of that information. In the current example information is power, both in terms of understanding the natural system (a benefit) and in terms of understanding the impact on the human system (a potential detriment to stakeholders, depending on a variety of factors). So, while complete information is an important goal in engaging in ecosystem-based management, we can see the actual sharing of that information is more difficult to envision.† This leads us back into our discussion of aspects of human-based interactions that pose difficulty when making ecosystem-based decisions.

---

* In this way, the individual efforts put into understanding the ecological dynamics of a particular fishing area is no longer proprietary to the individual, meaning the sharing of the information reduces the value of the information to the individual (because the value was based, in large part, on its proprietary nature. This value has now been transitioned to a larger group value, but we must acknowledge the loss in value to the individual fisher who shares this information.

† We can use the same problem of sharing information with our Clean Water Act example of non-point source pollution along the Mississippi River. Consider that in order to properly manage the runoff of fertilizer, each individual (resident, farmer, etc.) that lives along the Mississippi would likely have to monitor and provide, voluntarily, what they know about their individual fertilizer use and practices. The aggregation of this information could yield important insights about nutrient enrichment, including the capacity of the Mississippi River system to deal with nutrient inputs. Of course, since the nutrients are leading to toxic conditions in the Gulf of Mexico, the result of this new knowledge would likely require restrictions on current uses and practices by some or all of those who provided the information. Knowing this up front, do you think it is more or less likely that some individuals within the group might "defect" from sharing their information? Again, these questions of how humans and groups make decisions will be discussed in greater detail in Chapter 4.

In addition to the problem of aggregating information to create a holistic understanding of the natural system when structures encourage the nonsharing of that information, another difficulty surrounds consideration of the framework in which that information might be used. Said another way, consideration of the impact of the information on human systems is equally important. The term *framework* here refers to the regulatory conditions in which management decisions are made. How is the information that is generated being shared and used to make regulatory decisions? For example, if the information is being used solely to describe and ascertain the health of a natural system, then the information may be failing to account for all components of the system. Remember, humans are of equal importance in overall ecosystem understanding, and this includes an understanding of social and economic aspects of human interactions. How information about the natural system is used to make decisions about human interactions with the system is important. Using our example of the near-shore fishery, we can consider how a more complete understanding of the natural environment should impact those who regularly fish the resource. Let us focus our attention here on what kind of system of governance would lead to sustainable outcomes as humans interact with the environment.

Remember our working premise: in order to gain complete information about the resource from an ecosystem standpoint, information concerning the resource should be readily shared. When information is held by private actors who have no incentive to share that information, policy choices must be made that motivate the sharing of information. To encourage sharing of information, there must be a system of governance that ensures such sharing. Sharing can be either compelled or volunteered, and a system of governance can look to either method for ways of creating compliance.

Compulsion in our current fishery example would be difficult to imagine, especially if we consider the methods that might be employed and the likely rate of compliance (likely very low). Under most federal fishery management regimes, private citizens are given a right to fish in the ocean, which is deemed a public resource (Saunders 1973). Traditionally, this license to fish the resource does not include specific information about areas fished, including what areas are generally considered the most viable and productive grounds. The current use of monitors—people hired by the federal government to assess what is being caught on a fishing trip—might be used to take note of locations with high catch rates. Considering how the government would use this information and the expense of having monitors on every fishing vessel and trip, it is somewhat difficult imagining the costs involved in such a process.

Voluntary coercion may be a better means, where each member who shares information believes himself or herself to be in a better position for sharing the information than if he or she kept the information to himself or herself. To create such a system, rewards that exceeded the costs in helping to create the body of knowledge about the natural system would have to be created. Moreover, these rewards would have to accrue directly to the fishers giving the information. Direct guarantees to the fishers providing this information giving priority access to the resource, both today and in the future, is one obvious way to make the reward exceed the cost. This is particularly true where guarantees are given to both access and quantity of the resources. The point here is one has to conceive of ways to develop the human component of the system that reinforces the understanding and ultimate strategy of management related to the natural component of the system. Disregarding either component will likely lead to inefficient outcomes from an ecosystem-based management model.

We are discussing the human side of thinking holistically, or within a systems framework; if we are to consider ecosystem-based management as a way of managing environmental issues, we must also consider the human element of such a management strategy. What we have yet to cover in this section under ecosystem-based management is the fundamental scientific components of systems thinking.

Based on what we have discussed thus far, we understand the concept of a natural system in relation to ecosystem principles, biodiversity, and ecosystem-based management. However, the foundations of systems thinking—why natural things operate in systems context—have yet to be discussed. In order to be grounded in the basic principles of systems science, we will now explore the second main section of this text, *systems thinking*. The goal is to provide fundamental theoretical concepts that lay the foundation of systems analysis. This way the complex environmental problems can be reduced to their basic components so the problem observed can move toward consideration of environmental solutions. Important in this section will be the understanding of basic scientific principles that can provide a rough objective estimate of system interactions.

Systems Thinking

In this section, we delve into the topic of *systems thinking*. This section is intended to provide a greater understanding of how we consider systems in environmental decisions through analyzing the processes of the system between components. The concepts we discuss here are an important part of working with the problem sets at the end of this text, so pay close attention to the principles identified in this section.

We begin with a discussion of *box modeling*, a process often used by earth scientists to better understand the basic components of an environmental problem. The section then discusses the underlying scientific principles that describe the processes of energy flows between components of the system; this includes Einstein's famous equation $E = mc^2$, which describes the relationship between energy and matter (the mass–energy equivalence). Finally this section concludes with an overview of *equilibrium theory*, or the notion that all natural flows of energy return to a base equilibrium. This is generally represented by the equation $dC/dT = 0$, which means the change in concentrations within a component system (dC) over the change in time (dT) is 0; there is no change in the concentration of energy within a system component over time.

Before fully exploring this section, let us take a moment to review what we have already learned in this chapter and try to place it within the context of systems thinking generally. Recall that all systems are comprised of components that interact with one another, forming the complex processes of the system itself. Natural system components include the hydrosphere, biosphere, lithosphere, and atmosphere. Human system components include social institutions and economic considerations.

Our emphasis on systems thinking relies heavily on the second characteristic of systems—energy flows between components of the system—and focuses our attention on this process of energy flow between components. Consider that all life as we know it exists within the natural components of the system described above. If we consider the actual physical space of the earth where life exists, it is something along the lines of physical space between the upper layers of crust near the earth's surface (to include the oceans floors), to somewhere in the upper atmosphere—around 22 km above the earth's surface (Margulis and Sagan 1995). It is this zone that we are really focused on when considering environmental impacts.

Box modeling helps us see the big picture of these interactions. The underlying scientific principles help us define our expectations so we can justify our assumptions and expectations about the natural world, and then see how well our assumptions match what we observe. Understanding the parts of the box model helps us see how these energy flows might be impacted by our decisions; we get a sense of what the natural flows are and how a potential action might impact those flows in one direction or another. This is particularly important when we think about managing environmental decisions from an ecosystem perspective, where we might be identifying aspects of the environment that are not readily assumed to be at stake in the context of the environmental action being reviewed. Now that we have a general sense of the purpose of this section as applied to our understanding of environmental decision-making, we can begin our exploration of this section in earnest by looking at box modeling in detail.

Box Modeling: Wrapping Our Heads around the Problem

Box modeling serves a variety of purposes for the environmental decision-maker. Fundamentally, box modeling is a way of creating a holistic perspective of an environmental issue, simplifying the issue into a concrete set of interactions so potential cause-and-effect relationships can be observed and analyzed. Separating the two words, we can say that box modeling is a form of modeling the energy flows within components of a system. The components (and system) are represented as boxes. A representation of a box model is presented in Figure 2.5.

The component boxes contain inflows, outflows, and feedback loops, signifying the direction that energy is flowing within the components of the system. (Each of these flows will be discussed in more detail later in this section.) Proposed human

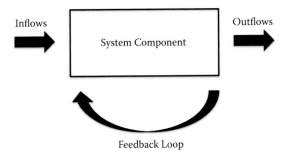

Figure 2.5 **Representation of a simple box model.**

actions that may impact energy flows can be modeled and the potential impacts observed. I say potential impacts here because there is doubt whether these potential impacts will be the actual impacts. Remember we are simply modeling the natural world; models are not absolute representations of what will occur.

An important piece of information derived from developing the box model is the determination of feedback loops. A feedback helps us determine current energy flow directions of a natural system, and also how potential actions might alter those current flows giving some indication of the overall impact that might occur within the system. For example, there is a large sink of carbon that rests within the lithosphere of the earth; some of this carbon is in the form of coal, while the other major form is oil. The normal time it takes for the carbon to naturally be removed from this sink to other parts of the earth system (say the atmosphere) is on the order of hundreds of thousands of years to millions of years (Schlesinger 1997). We say the carbon is buried within a sink (meaning it is there for the indefinite future) because of the long period of time it stays there relative to human timeframes; while it rests in the deep earth it does not interact with the other components of the natural system.

If we look at the human action of actively drilling for coal and oil within the earth's crust, we can see how this activity changes some of the directions observed in our box model. If an arrow points to the lithosphere as a sink of carbon, we can now see how human actions create a small arrow pointing from the lithosphere into the atmosphere (especially after the coal/oil is burned). This is a change in the normal dynamic of the energy between system components, in this case making the lithosphere a new source of carbon for other components (specifically the atmosphere) through human activity.

Beyond the crust of the earth becoming a source of carbon through human drilling (creating a new input of carbon from this normal sink), we can also observe the feedback this human activity causes to the earth system. For example, we can see how this stored carbon in the ground now becomes available carbon, adding to the carbon that already exists in the atmosphere. The feedback mechanism creates additional carbon in the atmosphere unless there is yet another feedback from another component of the system to absorb this additional carbon from the atmosphere.

We have observed an increase in the amount of carbon in the atmosphere since industrialization, in the form of carbon dioxide (CO_2). In fact, this observed increase in the amount of atmospheric carbon is one of the leading indicators of climate change (Intergovernmental Panel on Climate Change 2007). Box modeling allows us to imagine this result without actually having to see it occur.* Using the model, we see that the activity—removing carbon from the lithosphere and burning it—will result in some additional carbon being sent to other components of the system. The amount calculated to enter the atmosphere might not be as much as actually observed, or it might not occur as fast as imagined, but the simple expectation that the carbon has to wind up somewhere else in the system is an important way of mentally observing the environmental issue. The capacity to do this leads to understanding of the issue, which then forms the foundation for making informed environmental decisions.

Going back to the question of feedback observations for a moment, let us think about some other potential feedback that can occur when carbon is removed from the lithosphere. We know that burning the carbon (like burning coal to create electricity or burning oil as a distillate form like gasoline) will send most of the carbon into the atmosphere—this has been readily observed (Tennesen 2008). However, we can look to the other components of the natural system in the box model to try and see if there are feedback from those systems that might moderate the amount of carbon going into the atmosphere.

It is possible that the two other components of the system—the biosphere and hydrosphere—offer some carbon sequestration capacity that would deal with additional carbon flows from the lithosphere. In looking solely at the biosphere, consider that carbon dioxide is a form of food for vegetation (Schlesinger 1997, 34–35). We know carbon dioxide in the atmosphere provides a major food source for plant life on land; is it possible that more CO_2 in the atmosphere will simply provide more food for those plants? If so, is there a capacity for those plants to absorb some of the additional CO_2 that is being removed from the ground? The box model allows us to see this potential feedback—greater uptake of additional carbon by plants—as another pathway for the carbon within the larger system.

What about the hydrosphere? Photosynthetic organisms—known as phytoplankton—in the ocean also absorb CO^2 as a form of food (Schlesinger 1997, 301). Also, there is a chemical reaction that occurs in the ocean whereby CO^2 from the atmosphere is absorbed by the ocean, combining to make some additional compounds (Schlesinger 1997, 310–20). Without going into too much detail, the point is there is likely some capacity between the components of the natural system to share in the distribution of this additional carbon being removed from the

---

* Of course, the actual phenomenon must be observed and recorded in reality to confirm the presumption we see in the box model analysis. Relying solely on the model itself to initiate environmental policy would be similar to preventing science (objective information) as an important contribution to our understanding when making environmental decisions.

lithosphere. Indeed, if the carbon makes it to the bottom of the ocean, it stays there for a long period of time in human terms, which means the hydrosphere can act as a sink of carbon, just to a lesser extent than the lithosphere (Schlesinger 1997, 320).

Finally, we should also consider some of the human components of the system. Beyond humans creating an input from the lithosphere through mining and drilling activities, they can also use technology to sequester some of that additional carbon. New technological advances are allowing humans to find ways to manipulate the natural system's capacity to move carbon between natural components of the system (Hemming and Hagler 2007, 283–84), as well as human-created ways of actively removing carbon from one component to another (Katzer 2011).

The points being made here highlight the importance of box modeling; it allows us to see the interactions between components of the system, which then allows for an understanding of potential cause-effect relationships between components. This is a powerful way of shaping environmental problems. We will get into additional details of how the components of the box work in context later in this section.

We now move into a discussion of the underlying scientific principles that help us make decisions about the box. For example, when we discuss potential interactions between components of the natural system, why do we believe some interactions have to occur? Why do we have to account for all of the carbon removed from the lithosphere by humans even if we cannot find an equal amount in the atmosphere? Does that absolutely mean the carbon must exist in another component of the system? If so, why? These are the kinds of questions that are answered in the following section on underlying scientific principles.

Underlying Scientific Principles

Most of this chapter has been focused on understanding natural systems, with human actions as part of natural systems. Underlying systems thinking as a concept comprises many different scientific principles. In this section, we focus on two principles that are key to understanding systems thinking. These basic principles help us to understand some of the assumptions in our modeling of environmental problems from a systems standpoint. The two principles discussed here are *mass–energy equivalence* and *equilibrium theory*. These scientific principles help us create a foundational understanding of what kinds of results (feedback) we might expect from certain interactions with the environment. We begin with an exploration of the mass–energy equivalence.

$E = mc^2$, or the Relationship between Energy and Matter (Mass–Energy Equivalence)

Mass–energy equivalence (derived from the equation $E = mc^2$ made famous by Albert Einstein) helps us understand the *relationship* between energy and matter

(Moring 2004, 171). It suggests that energy (E) is equal to the mass of an object (m) multiplied by the square root of the speed of light (c). Removing the speed of light variable from the equation, we see there is a direct relationship expressed here between mass and energy. Focusing only on this relationship, we can then suggest that things we see in our natural environment can change form between a physical and a nonphysical state while still existing is relative equivalent terms.

There are simple examples of the mass–energy relationship. Carbon that exists in hard coal—a physical thing—can be burned. The carbon molecule can then change its state into a gaseous form once it is burned, combined with oxygen, and form carbon dioxide (Katzer 2011). So the element at issue, carbon, has the capacity to change forms through a reaction like burning the carbon, but it still exists in its elemental state as carbon; the burning of the coal did not destroy the carbon, and a new molecule of carbon was not created when the carbon dioxide formed. Rather, the same carbon moved from one state, a complete physical form, into another state, a complete gaseous form (Tennesen 2008).

The carbon molecule in the example maintains its elemental form as carbon. What is happening when we detect additional carbon in the atmosphere is that there is a movement of carbon from one source to another; we are not actually creating new carbon. In fact, carbon that exists in the atmosphere as carbon dioxide can be further altered into different forms, carbon monoxide, for instance (Schlesinger 1997, 64). As discussed in the box modeling section, this same carbon can also change forms again, finding its way into the oceans, combining with calcium and oxygen to form calcium carbonate (Schlesinger 1997, 312–13), creating a hard shell for things like clams or coral structures, and ultimately finding its way to the bottom of the ocean where it is buried in sediment and slowly absorbed into the lithosphere, where it stays for eons until forces like plate tectonics or other earth-shifting activities cause it to be sent into another component of the earth system.*

The carbon molecule might be absorbed into the biosphere component of the system, being taken up by a large sequoia tree as nutrients (Lorenz and Lal 2010), helping to form additional girth of the tree itself and thereby being stored as part of the tree for hundreds to thousands of years, depending on the fate of the sequoia itself.† If the tree is cut down by humans and burned as a source of heat, the carbon trapped in the tree will then be released back into the atmosphere as a gas (Lorenz and Lal 2010, 124–26). Rather than being cut down by humans, the carbon might exist in a seed of the tree itself and be eaten by an herbivore, a squirrel, for instance. The carbon may then become part of the squirrel itself, incorporated as muscle tissue, for instance (Gautier 2008, 72), or it may become part of the waste stream of the squirrel (Gautier 2008, 75). If it becomes part of the squirrel, we can then follow the fate of the squirrel to determine the future course of the carbon,

---

* Human activities we have already discussed can also cause the carbon to be removed from the lithospheric "grave" prior to other natural forces.
† Sequoias can live for thousands of years under natural conditions.

moving on when the squirrel is either eaten or dies. If it is part of the waste stream, then the carbon may become a gas, being removed back into the atmosphere (say as methane, CH4) (Gautier 2008, 70–75). Or, the carbon can become part of the fertilizer base for new life, being absorbed by a seedling that rests under the space in which the squirrel discarded its waste.

It is interesting to follow the fate of the carbon molecule as it makes its way across different components of our system. A few points during our observation here are worth considering in more detail. First, we can see that the carbon molecule is always the same molecule; it simply changes its relationship as it flows between different components of the system. This observation helps us see the box system as a dynamic structure, with different base elements transitioning from one component of the system to another. Why is this important? It helps us understand the dynamics that occur within a system, and thus we are better prepared to begin to think systematically about human interactions with the environment.

A second point focuses on what is driving the change in carbon between components of the system. As the carbon moves between components of the system, there are interactions that are occurring, all driven by work or energy. Whether the action is physical (humans digging up coal from the lithosphere) or chemical (the burning of coal transitioning the carbon from a physical state to a chemical state), energy is required to make these transitions occur. Recall that there are two main energy sources for life; an exogenous source like the sun and endogenous sources like the geothermal heat derived from the center of the earth. These are the base forms of energy inputs into the system (like the gas that makes the motor run in an automobile). Without these inputs, it would be hard to imagine life as we know it on earth.

There are also flows of energy between component parts of the earth system. Understanding the ways in which energy flows between these components helps us understand environmental decisions. Because at the core of environmental decisions is a base understanding of these interactions, understanding the interactions between system components helps us understand how the environment is operating in context.

A final question to ask is: What expectations can we have of these energy flows over time? Are they always in flux, meaning we can never know what to expect in terms of how much carbon exists in one component of the system over time? This is the subject of our next section, which focuses on equilibrium theory. We now turn to this subject for additional insights on understanding our box system.

Equilibrium Theory, or dC/dT = 0

If the mass–energy equivalence theory is about helping us understand the relationship between mass and energy, then equilibrium theory is about helping us understand what concentrations of constituents between system components we should expect in our system over time. Using the example above of the carbon molecule, equilibrium theory helps us determine what we should expect to see in the system regarding concentrations of carbon over time.

Establishing a baseline of what we should expect to see through our assumption of equilibrium of the system, we can then compare this baseline against what we actually observe and focus our attention appropriately. In fact, this is precisely what drew scientists like Keeling* to take note of changes in the average concentration of carbon in the atmosphere over time; the additional concentration of carbon over time went against the expectations of what should be observed over time (Tennesen 2008). So, what precisely should we be observing? This question is answered through understanding equilibrium theory.

Equilibrium theory suggests the earth is a well-mixed natural system, meaning the relative concentrations of things we find in the system should be about the same; they should not change significantly from current concentrations (Schlesinger 1997, 12–14). Precisely, the equation for equilibrium theory, dC/dT = 0, is broken down as follows: the change in the concentration of some component of the earth system (dC) over a period of time (dT) is zero; there is no change in concentrations over time.

As stated above, a base presumption in equilibrium theory is that the earth is a well-mixed system. This assumption is founded in the fact that the earth has been around for billions of years, and if we look at the planet's recent history, the earth has shown a pretty stable cycle. Think of the beginning of a new job or the beginning of a new semester at a university. At the very beginning, things are in flux—there is a general sense of chaos. There is little consistency or pattern because everything is new. However, over time we tend to create patterns; we begin to understand the general requirements of a job or university semester. After a while, we settle into a pretty predictable pattern, at least much more predictable than at the beginning of the job or university semester.

Equilibrium theory is similar in that it suggests the earth was really dynamic, constantly changing when it was first formed. However, after so many billions of years, the earth system has become pretty stable and predictable. When talking about the concentrations of things that make up the earth, we see they are also pretty well mixed, or at a state of equilibrium. The concentration of oxygen we see today in the atmosphere, for example, is what we should expect to see over time; the concentrations should not change. This applies to most things that make up the earth.

To summarize, due to the long period of the earth's existence, things that cycle throughout the components of the earth do so in a relatively steady state. In this

---

* Charles David Keeling is the scientist who began to measure the average concentration of atmospheric carbon dioxide over time. He began his measurements in the late 1950s, and his measurements are a significant contribution to our awareness of climate change today. He is known for the Keeling curve, which represents the seasonal variation seen in carbon dioxide today.

way the earth is said to have achieved a form of equilibrium between these different compounds. This applies not only to the concentrations of things we find around the earth (the amount of oxygen molecules found in the atmosphere), but it also applies to the state of the energy flows between system components; the processes that move compounds between system components is also relatively stable and existing at equilibrium (Schlesinger 1997, 12–14).

Does the assumption of equilibrium work all the time? Does it apply to snapshots of time of the earth, meaning if we look at concentrations of things right now on the earth, will they show precise equilibrium? Of course not! There are variations in the normal range of the system on a regular basis. We usually tend to refer to these periodic disturbances as natural disasters; volcano eruptions, earthquakes, tsunamis, hurricanes, and similar events are all examples of an abnormal jolt to the natural system. Sometimes these abnormalities exhibit consistent patterns; for example, we know the normal heating of the northern hemisphere summer can lead to hurricane seasons along the eastern portion of the Atlantic Ocean (Del Moral and Walker 2007, 159–66). Other phenomena, like earthquakes and volcano eruptions, are harder to predict with a strong degree of accuracy; many of these natural phenomena show little to no pattern of consistency.

Even though some phenomena show little to no direct patterns, the vast majority of processes between earth system components do show regular patterns and cycles. In fact, it is the consistency of natural patterns that has created the environment for humans to develop from hunter-gatherers to a more place-based agricultural existence, ultimately leading to the development of civilization as we know it today (Fagan 2004). In short, consistent patterns within nature have allowed us to thrive as a species; if they did not exist, our existence would likely be near impossible in its current form. So, while we can expect some variation from equilibrium at any given point in time (a hurricane here, an earthquake there), the overall trend of the earth's recent history has been that of representing a well-mixed system that operates under equilibrium assumptions.

Applying equilibrium assumptions to our box model, we can identify the following observations. First, whatever concentrations we find in one system component should be relatively consistent over time. For example, if we observe 100 units of carbon buried in the earth, then equilibrium theory suggests this amount should stay consistent over time. If substantially less carbon is observed in the earth at some point in the future, we should assume, all things being equal, current earth conditions will seek to be at 100 units of carbon in the lithosphere. As mentioned earlier in this section, the atmosphere is made up of approximately 21% oxygen. Under current conditions, we would expect the atmosphere to be comprised of approximately 21% oxygen; if it changes dramatically we should look for a cause for that change, and assume the shift is out of the norm. The reason we should look for a cause out of the norm is because we assume the earth is a well-mixed system at equilibrium.

One other assumption attached to equilibrium theory as it relates to the earth is that the planet is a *closed system*, meaning the concentration observed in the system remains constant over time (Schlesinger 1997, 4). For example, if the entire earth were to contain 100 units of carbon, then we would expect there always to be 100 units of carbon found within the earth system, no more and no less. The ratio of the 100 units of carbon found in any given component of the system can change over time (say some additional carbon being moved from the lithosphere to the atmosphere due to human interactions), but the overall amount of carbon will never exceed or be less than 100 units.* Combine this assumption of a closed system with a well-mixed system, and we have our equilibrium theory.

So why is equilibrium theory an important concept in environmental decision-making? To answer this question, we need to look back at our box modeling discussion. Recall that box modeling aids us in simplifying the world around us; it allows us to focus on trends by making simple assumptions about energy flows between components of our system. Equilibrium theory helps us legitimize the assumptions we make in box modeling. Because of the major assumptions contained in equilibrium theory (a well-mixed, closed system where the concentrations of things that make up the system are invariant over time), our box model analysis is more likely to be true under normal circumstances. Since our model is more likely to be true, it becomes a powerful tool in environmental planning.

Consider the example of carbon management between system components. If we assume concentrations of carbon are relatively stable in different components of the system, then we need to account for our nonnatural movement of carbon (often referred to as anthropogenic forcing) (Philander 2008, 64); this is especially true where we are taking long-term stored carbon from a sink (like the lithosphere) and forcing it into a different component like the atmosphere. Although we can assume certain feedback between the system components as mentioned above (the biosphere or hydrosphere capturing some of that carbon from the atmosphere), we need to consider all potential impacts of these actions. What will be the response of the other components of the system? If some of the forced carbon remains in the atmosphere, how long will it remain there and what impact might it have on the earth system?

It is generally better to proactively consider these questions before actions are taken because of the potential irreversibility of the impact from the actions

---

* In reality, the earth is not really a closed system. For example, we know meteors and "space dust" often fall onto the earth bringing new sources of matter. However, this amount is inconsequential to the amount of matter already present on the earth. Because of this, the assumption of a closed system is safe concerning matter. However, we also have discussed a major source of heat energy coming from the sun, something we referred to as an exogenous source of energy. Since much of our heat budget on earth comes from the sun, it may be inappropriate to think of the earth as entirely closed concerning heat, especially since our heat budget is being potentially impacted by increased concentrations of carbon in the atmosphere, leading to a greenhouse effect.

after the fact.* Box modeling, when done well, can provide environmental decision-makers a degree of forecasting, determining potential issues with proposed initiatives that may have an impact on the environment. Box modeling may also serve to highlight proposals that are likely to have a positive impact on the environment. For example, forest regrowth projects, open space planning, and other such initiatives can identify carbon sequestration opportunities, as well as other positive net impacts (Lorenz and Lal 2010). These potential impacts can be reviewed on a biogeochemical scale through a box model. Now that we are describing the importance of box modeling in some additional detail, it is time to return to the model. In this following section we will describe the box in more detail, particularly focusing on the energy flows between components of the system: inflows, outflows, and feedback mechanisms.

Parts of the Box in Context: Inflows, Outflows, and Feedback Mechanisms

To begin, refer to the simple diagram showing a basic box model, above in Figure 2.5. As you can see, we have the box (component of the system) represented in the center of the diagram. Inputs are identified by the arrow to the left of the box leading into the box (indicating something is being moved into the component), while outflows are shown as an arrow leaving the box from the other end (things moving out of the system component). The looping arrow that moves from the outflow to the input represents a feedback mechanism; in this representation, the inputs are impacted by what is flowing out of the component. If this were the only component of a system, then we would be viewing a simplified version of an entire system cycle in this diagram.

A few points can be made about how the inputs, outflows, and feedback mechanisms interact. First, we can apply basic underlying scientific principles, specifically equilibrium theory, to begin placing some numbers on these lines. For example, say the input has 10 units of carbon entering the component, and the output only has 7 units of carbon leaving the component. A representation of the system component diagram with these numbers added is shown in Figure 2.6.

Would this component be at equilibrium? Obviously not, and we would need to think about what is happening to the other 3 units of carbon. It is probably safe to assume the additional 3 units of carbon are remaining in the specific component of the system. Since this violates the assumption of equilibrium, we should be concerned about this observation (less carbon leaving the system than is entering

---

* *Irreversibility* is a term that is relative in its application here. While the earth system would return to some state of equilibrium at some point (whether that be the known equilibrium state or a new equilibrium state), the time it takes for the earth to establish this equilibrium can be anywhere from centuries, millennia, and even much longer. Considering these long timeframes, the actions are considered irreversible in human timeframes.

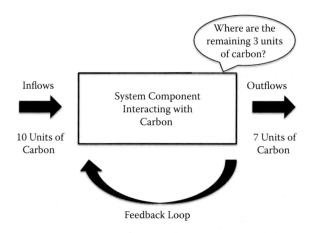

Figure 2.6   Box model representing a system component of carbon interactions.

the system). What this tells us is that our box here likely contains a "sink" for carbon. So, if these were real-life numbers that were observed, our ability to box model the results would help us zero in on the issue.

Focusing our attention on this system component, we can try to determine an answer to our lost carbon problem. We would do this by identifying the potential sinks that exist in the box and try to determine the resting place of the additional carbon. We might also pay close attention to any feedback being observed within this system because of the increased carbon remaining within the component. We should pay close attention to changes from the expected norm (nonequilibrium changes) and see whether those changes are one-time events or more representative of a trend over time. If the phenomenon keeps recurring over time, this fact will reinforce a new trend within the system, maybe leading toward a threshold shift within the current system paradigm. Remember, a consistently observed trend of increasing carbon concentrations in our atmosphere is evidence that the atmosphere is absorbing additional carbon outside the normal range of equilibrium dynamics usually observed in our earth system.

Let us now expand this idea further with a more complex set of boxes and arrows. Figure 2.7 shows a set of boxes and interacting arrows representing a more realistic representation of a system, with each box representing a component of the system (rather than one box alone); while the overall picture looks complex, we see it is made up of the basic parts of the box model: boxes with inflows, outflows, and feedback mechanisms. There are just more boxes and more arrows. However, the information can be interpreted in the exact same way as our simplified previous example. Moreover, the insights that can be gained are in many ways more elaborate and detailed, like the box model itself. You will still find inputs and outflows into each component box of the system represented here. However, you will also find that some of these inputs are the result of outflows from other components,

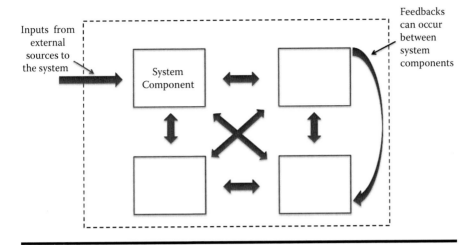

Figure 2.7 Representation of a complex box model showing various system component interactions.

while some of the outflows become the inputs for yet other components. You should also see that this process creates a cyclical interaction in several cases, resulting in a sort of recycling phenomenon where some of the outputs of one component become the inputs for that same component. Let us look at this cycling phenomenon in a bit more detail.

Consider as an example the interaction between the biosphere and atmosphere in relation to carbon cycling. We can review this interaction beginning in either component of the system, as the flow we are describing is cyclic in nature, meaning the carbon will be found cycling between both components of the system. For simplicity let us begin in the atmosphere.

Carbon exists in a variety of forms in the atmosphere (Schlesinger 1997, 47–87). The gas carbon dioxide is taken up by plants on the surface of the earth and used as a primary nutrient in the development of simple sugars commonly referred to as carbohydrates (Schlesinger 1997, 128–32). The chemical reaction looks something like this:

$$CO_2 + H_2O \rightarrow CH_2O \text{ (carbohydrate)} + O_2{}^*$$

Much of the carbon is then used to make additional plant material, let us say something relatively long lasting, like the hardwood trunk of a tree. So, in this case, the carbon from the atmosphere has been pulled into the biosphere by the work of plants; we can model this as an outflow of carbon from the atmosphere, and also as an input of carbon into the biosphere. At some point in time, the tree will die,

---

* We can see how oxygen (O_2) is a by-product of the plants combining carbon dioxide (CO_2) with water (H_2O).

burn, or come to some other fate. When this occurs, the carbon stored in the tree will be released.* That carbon will then become an input into the atmosphere or an outflow from the biosphere; both are correct. That carbon will then be in the atmosphere available to be taken up again by another plant in the biosphere. This cycle can theoretically continue indefinitely.

The type of carbon being described in the previous example is known as available carbon, or carbon that is capable of being taken up between different components of the system. We should distinguish this type of carbon from the more nonavailable carbon, which is carbon that is no longer readily available for use because of where and how it is currently being stored (Schlesinger 1997, 127–28). Probably the most unavailable form of carbon is that which is buried deep in the lithosphere. Crude oil is one example of this form of carbon; it is unavailable mainly because of its location, buried deep below the surface of the earth (Princiotta 2011). Coal is more available than most current deposits of oil in terms of location (closer to the surface), but it is relatively unavailable itself, also because the carbon is stored in a relatively hard structure (Schlesinger 1997, 359–66). Depending on the relative amounts of available to nonavailable coal in the system, one can get a sense of how disturbances to one component can impact other components. For example, the vast amount of carbon is stored in the deep lithosphere of the earth. Second in terms of storage of carbon are the oceans (hydrosphere) of the earth. Knowing this alone can help us understand the importance of carbon storage within these systems and how changes in these relative distributions can impact the overall earth system. Inputting too much coal into the atmosphere, for example, can result in a warming of the planet that can have consequences for human well-being.

Beyond cycling between components of the system (like the atmosphere and biosphere example above), one can also have cycling within the same component of the system (Schlesinger 1997, 3–14). The ocean provides an example of this process. Nitrogen (N) and phosphorous (P) are both considered limiting nutrients in the ocean (Schlesinger 1997, 316–32). The reason they are considered limiting is these two elements are necessary for primary production, the growth of plants and plant-like organisms in the ocean, but both elements are in short supply.

As limiting nutrients, nitrogen and phosphorous tend to remain in the upper reaches of the ocean where light penetrates and photosynthesis can take place; this region is referred to as the photic zone of the ocean (Schlesinger 1997, 316–32). Because these elements are in short supply, they are constantly recycled in this upper layer of the ocean. They are used to help create the necessary fertilizer for marine plants and algae, which is then eaten by small animals who discard some of the nitrogen and phosphorous as waste product. The nitrogen and phosphorous are then recycled into a gaseous state by decomposers of the waste product, and this is all done in the upper region of the ocean. The available nitrogen and phosphorous

---

* In burning through a chemical reaction and in dying through the respiration of the organisms that will consume the wood, giving off carbon dioxide as we humans do.

are reused by primary producers and the cycle continues. In this way, these two elements continually cycle with the ocean component of the natural system.

In our summary review of cycling, we can see how movements of things within the system can vary. Some things will become an input and stay within the component they move into by cycling within the component or becoming stored within the component. Other things will move from one component to a different component. Yet other things will become "trapped" and stored within a component of the system.

We can generally tell what components of a system are major storage areas and which are not by looking at the distribution of concentrations of the constituent within the system. Those components that have the largest amount of the constituent tend to hold on to the constituent for the longest period of time. Conversely, those components with the lowest amount tend to hold on to the constituent for the shortest period of time. The amount of time a constituent stays within a component of a system is generally referred to as residence time (Lorenz and Lal 2010, 11–16). By looking at these numbers in our box model, we can get a sense of what each box component represents to the thing we are studying. We can also find major sinks and sources of the constituent through this same process. Let us now look at a real-life example of the carbon cycle in detail, and use the example as a way of expressing these concepts in practice. The carbon cycle is represented in Figure 2.8.

The earth contains approximately 1×10^{23} g of carbon (Schlesinger 1997, 359); this is the entire amount of carbon available for movement in the earth system. The vast majority of this carbon is buried deep in the crust of the earth, the lithosphere. The amount of carbon that is active for cycling between components of the earth system is approximately 4×10^{19} g of carbon (Schlesinger 1997). This means there is approximately 2,500 times the amount of carbon stored in the lithosphere as there is carbon actively moving throughout the earth system. Imagine if all of the carbon currently stored in the earth's crust became available for active cycling within the other components of the earth system!

The following is an attempt to describe the carbon cycle expressed in Figure 2.8. First, it is important to note the represented cycle is only describing the carbon actively available for cycling within the system; it does not include the 1×10^{23} g of carbon buried deep in the earth. Second, we can note the visual cues expressed in the figure to help provide us with additional insights on the cycling, or movement, of the carbon between system components. Boxes have been drawn around major components (the biosphere and hydrosphere, for example), but elements of these spheres are also represented in figures (such as trees and human manufacturing as part of the biosphere). The goal is to better link the ideas of the box model to something we are more visually attuned to viewing.

Finally, we need to recall that our box will show three things: inflows, outflows, and feedback mechanisms. The arrows identified in the carbon cycle model represent these three movements of energy (carbon being the energy flow under consideration here). Inflows occur when an arrow points into a system component

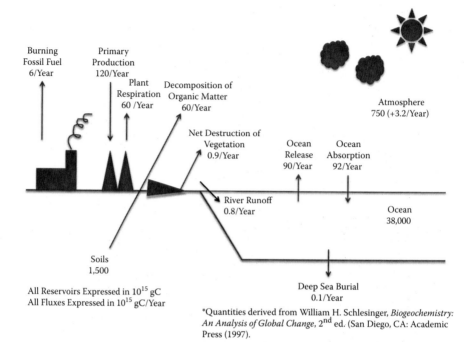

Burning
Fossil Fuel
6/Year

Primary
Production
120/Year

Plant
Respiration
60 /Year

Decomposition of
Organic Matter
60/Year

Atmosphere
750 (+3.2/Year)

Net Destruction of
Vegetation
0.9/Year

Ocean
Release
90/Year

Ocean
Absorption
92/Year

River Runoff
0.8/Year

Ocean
38,000

Soils
1,500

Deep Sea Burial
0.1/Year

All Reservoirs Expressed in 10^{15} gC
All Fluxes Expressed in 10^{15} gC/Year

*Quantities derived from William H. Schlesinger, *Biogeochemistry:
An Analysis of Global Change*, 2nd ed. (San Diego, CA: Academic
Press (1997).

Figure 2.8   Model representation of the carbon cycle.

(or subcomponent of the system), and outflows when arrows point away from the component. Feedback is sometimes represented by a cycling of the arrows where both an inflow and an outflow are observed within the same component, and other times the feedback must be interpreted by the observer of the model by close examination of the numbers and relationships observed. Now that we have these two qualifications out of the way, we can describe the box model of carbon cycling in detail.

We can begin at the very left of the figure and observe the industrial building in what appears to be a release from the burning of 6 units of carbon into the atmosphere.* We can see that this creates an outflow of carbon, with one arrow moving from the facility into the atmosphere. There is no arrow moving back into the industrial building, so we know that the carbon is a net increase somewhere else in the system (the carbon has to be dealt with somewhere else). We also should know that this carbon likely comes from coal, or some other source that has been

---

* *Units* is used here as a basic term. The actual numbers represented in the diagram are expressed in 10^{15} g C for all pools of carbon (where the carbon is stored in a component for a period of time), and in 10^{15} g C/yr for all fluxes of carbon (where carbon is moving between components of the natural system). As an aside, 10^{15} is the equivalent of a gigaton. Thus, the amounts represented may also be referred to as gigatons of carbon.

removed from the large sink of carbon in the lithosphere; we should not expect this carbon to be coming from another component of the system because there is no other source that is readily observable.

Where is this carbon ultimately going? We know from the arrow that the carbon is moving directly into the atmosphere. If we look at the atmospheric pool, we see a number of +3.2/year, meaning carbon is being added to the atmospheric pool; the atmosphere is acting like a sponge and soaking up some of the carbon. However, this still leaves 2.8 units of carbon unaccounted for (6.0 − 3.2 = 2.8). Looking around at the diagram, there are 92 units of carbon entering the ocean, but only 90 cycling out. The additional 2 units being absorbed by the ocean can account for another 2.0 of the remaining 2.8 being burned by humans. If this is true, it still leaves 0.8 units of carbon unaccounted for by humans every year. We will talk in more detail about this unaccounted carbon a bit later in this chapter.

Hopefully we can see how moving around the box to find potential sinks for the additional source of carbon can help us understand the impacts of the human activity. In this case, the mining and burning of carbon by humans is leading to the atmosphere absorbing about 3.2 units of carbon per year,* and the oceans absorbing about 2.0 units of carbon per year. Unless the atmosphere and ocean find places to put this carbon, the additional absorption of carbon by the atmosphere can lead to problems.

Remember our discussion of equilibrium, specifically where natural systems move toward equilibrium? In that discussion we mentioned thresholds, representing a maximum point in a system that, if moved beyond, can lead to significant shifts in the system resulting in a new equilibrium state. Consider the atmosphere and oceans as sponges that are continually absorbing additional amounts of carbon. A few relevant questions for inquiry include: Can carbon force an equilibrium shift in the earth system? (There is already evidence of this in terms of a warming atmosphere, and increased carbon in the ocean is leading to acidification.) If so, how much carbon can the components absorb before a threshold has been reached? If we do not know the limit, we can simply guess the limit is well beyond our understanding. As we will see in Chapter 4, a precautionary measure has often been used when we arrive at environmental uncertainly precisely because of not knowing when a threshold might be breached (from which we may not return to previous equilibrium levels). We will get back to the missing carbon (0.8 unit) later in this discussion.

Moving to land plants in our diagram, we observe storage of 560 units of carbon in the plant matter of the biosphere. We also see fluxes of carbon between the land plants and the atmosphere. There are 120 units of carbon being absorbed by the plants from the atmosphere annually, with 60 units being respired (R_p) by those same land plants back into the atmosphere. We might think this means land plants are a "net" sequester of carbon, taking in twice as much carbon (120 units) as

---

* The 3.2 being added to the atmosphere every year is just less than ½ of 1% of the total amount of carbon contained in the atmosphere (3.2/750 = 0.00426).

they give back (60 units) to the atmosphere. However, this is not entirely the case. The additional 60 units of carbon sources from the soils are shown by an arrow of outflow netting 60 units back to the atmosphere. Thus, the natural processes of the atmosphere and biosphere are in equilibrium with one another, at least when it comes to these 120 units of carbon under analysis. Since we assume systems are supposed to be in equilibrium, this matching makes sense and should draw no immediate concern. It is when we see mismatches, like in the 6 units of carbon being forced into the atmosphere through human interactions, that we must look at the issue with heightened scrutiny.

Briefly mentioned above, soils are both a storage and outflow for carbon. Approximately 1,500 units of carbon are stored in the earth's soils. Of this amount, 60 units of carbon are annually cycled into the atmosphere as an outflow. The way in which these 60 units of carbon are released by the soils has to do with the microbial breakdown of plant matter. Microbes in the soil eat away at dead and dying plant matter, respiring in the process (Schlesinger 1997, 161–63). It is the respiration of the microbes that results in the 60 units of carbon moving into the atmosphere.

While we might think these 60 units deduct from the 1,500 deposited in the soils, they actually do not because of the additional 60 units that are absorbed by land plants each year. The additional 60 units absorbed by the land plants account for the annual decay of existing land plants, which then results in microbial breakdown within the soils, ultimately leading to the 60 units respired back into the atmosphere. In this way, the interaction between the soils is in balance with the interactions between the land plants and the atmosphere, another example where the concentration of carbon (dC) in the soils (1,500) and the land plants (560) does not change over time (dT).

Moving to the immediate right of Figure 2.8, we now observe the net destruction of vegetation, which is a complete outflow of 0.9 unit of carbon every year; no carbon returns from this net destruction of vegetation. The causes of this destruction are both human and nonhuman in nature; forest fires caused by lightning strikes are one example of a nonhuman phenomenon, while clear-cutting and removing forest for development are examples of human-based causes of vegetation destruction.

Most of this net destruction is accounted for in the box model diagram as an input of DOC and DIC (0.4 + 0.4 = 0.8) into the oceans. The process for this is river runoff, where the deforestation leads to erosion of soils that then move the carbon from watersheds to the oceans. Of course, we already have more carbon going into the ocean than is coming out (or being buried), so the destruction of vegetation only exacerbates the problem of continuously increasing the amount of carbon in the ocean component of the system. We can likely look at destruction of vegetation as a problem in terms of an environmental management perspective; this includes all of the causes related to vegetation destruction.

To the right of the biosphere in Figure 2.8 we find the oceans. The oceans represent the largest pool of carbon (38,000 units) outside of the lithosphere; this should not be surprising based on the size of the oceans relative to the earth's surface. Beyond the already mentioned river influx of carbon into the oceans, there is also a flux of carbon coming in from the atmosphere (92 units), and a flux going out of the ocean (90 units). We've already identified that some of this imbalance (92 – 90 = 2 units) likely comes from the additional burning of carbon by humans (along with the river runoff). We have also mentioned the potential consequences of using the ocean as a sponge for additional carbon, another area of concern as we examine the fluxes between the system components.

The final box in Figure 2.8 is the atmosphere. It has a pool of about 750 units of carbon, but is increasing at a rate of about 3.2 units of carbon per year (Schlesinger 1997, 358–82). Major inputs of carbon into the atmosphere derive from respiration of the biosphere (collectively 120 units of carbon), and transfer from the ocean in an air-sea exchange (90 units). All of these inputs are balanced against outflows from the atmosphere in at least the same quantities (120 units to the biosphere, and 92 units to the oceans). The imbalance comes mainly from the human burning of carbon (6 units), with the majority remaining in the atmosphere (3.2 units), increasing atmospheric concentrations, with most of the rest being absorbed by the oceans (2 units). Science has not yet been able to conclusively determine where the remaining 0.8 unit of carbon is fluxing within the natural system, but it will undoubtedly be known in time.

We have now spent some considerable time detailing the inflows and outflows of this carbon system, but we have not yet discussed feedback mechanisms as they relate to the carbon cycle diagram. Recall feedback helps us understand a causal relationship between two or more parts of a system. Numerous feedback exists in our diagram of the carbon cycle, both obvious and inferred. For example, we see there is a constant exchange of carbon between the biosphere component of the system and the atmosphere; carbon is constantly flowing between these two components of the earth system. At equilibrium, the feedback is neutral, meaning there is no net change in the concentrations of carbon found within each component of the system averaged out over time. The same can be said for the exchange between the ocean and the atmosphere; there is a constant exchange of carbon between these two components.

There are numerous insights we can now make after our thorough review of the carbon cycle. For instance, consider the importance of the atmosphere as an intermediary between other system components. The atmosphere acts as an exchange, allowing carbon to constantly flux in and out of system components. We can see this clearly because the largest fluxes in the system involve the atmosphere. What this should tell us is that the atmosphere will likely be a key component of carbon movement throughout the earth system. If we know a human activity might generate additional carbon flow (say through mining and burning), then we can assume the carbon will interact with the atmosphere unless we directly intervene in the process (say by "capturing" the carbon before it gets to the atmosphere).

This becomes particularly important if we identify atmospheric increases of carbon concentration to a feedback that creates negative outcomes for humans. This brings us to another insight.

Our Figure 2.8 tells us that each component of the system, in addition to moving carbon between components, also stores carbon. This means each component of the earth system holds onto carbon for some period of time. Like other components of the earth system, the atmosphere has a reservoir of carbon, and this leads us to examine the impact this stored carbon has on other parts of the system. For example, what is the relationship between the amount of carbon in the atmosphere and the average temperature of the earth? If more carbon positively correlates to warmer temperatures, then this fact influences our understanding of the impact of increased carbon in the atmosphere. When we see the atmosphere absorbing additional carbon at a rate of 3.2 units per year, we see a potential feedback mechanism indicating that the additional carbon will result in warmer temperatures. If we link this additional carbon to human activities from the biosphere, then we can say the cause of the potential warming is the observed human activities.

Simple feedback correlations allow us to focus our attention on how to solve the problem; if we do not want a warmer planet through additional carbon in the atmosphere, then we can focus our attention on the human activities related to carbon forcing. The same insights can be made toward the ocean and its role in carbon uptake; if the oceans are getting more acidic over time because of increased carbon, we can look to the causes as a way of managing this result. If one cause is human behavior, then we have a choice about continuing this behavior, or otherwise adapting the behavior to protect ocean resources.

In summary, the feedback we observe is based on logical inferences from the data displayed on the box model itself. Of course, we have not discussed how these numbers were derived in detail, and we really do not have time to go into depth in this text. What we can observe is that the numbers are critically important in making the model accurate; if we are looking at incorrect numbers, then our assumptions are wrong and, therefore, our interpretations are wrong. The numbers themselves are derived through scientific inquiry. In environmental decisions, we rely heavily on the state of science. Since science is a process that evolves understanding over time (by constantly limiting our uncertainty about our environment), the numbers we place in our box models will likely evolve over time as well. This means we may create new boxes within the model, new inflows and outflows, new numbers within and between boxes, and as a result, identify new feedback mechanisms. In this way, we adapt our knowledge and understanding to the level of science that is available when we are making our decisions. However, environmental decisions must always be based on that science and should not deviate from scientific understanding without this being transparent. If we do deviate from science in our decision-making process, then the use of modeling is pointless because we are looking at a wholly unrepresentative picture of the interactions in our environment.

Conclusion

This chapter has attempted to review critical themes of science that underlie environmental decision-making. Only a few themes have been covered here, and none of them in ultimate detail. However, the themes that have been covered are representative of the basic scientific principles needed to inform environmental decisions, most importantly those who aid in or directly make such decisions. Although the treatment of each theme has been brief, there has been sufficient coverage to inform the reader of why these basic themes are important in environmental decisions and how to apply these themes to environmental problems. This base knowledge will be combined with principles of economics and values learned in the chapters of this text. In addition, the ability to apply these themes can be further examined by applying them to the case studies at the end of this book; other case studies undertaken, including real-life application, will also show the value of applying these basic concepts in practice.

The basic scientific concepts themselves cover two main areas: natural systems and systems thinking. Natural systems covered three topics: ecosystem principles, biodiversity, and ecosystem-based management. The goal of this natural systems section was to understand systems thinking from the natural environment perspective. Components of the natural system were discussed, as well as the services provided by natural systems. (The services identified here will be discussed in greater detail in Chapter 3, with a focus on how to properly value and account for these important ecosystem services.)

Biodiversity was also discussed from several viewpoints, with the goal being to expose the reader to the important natural role diverse life plays in maintaining a viable planetary habitat. Theories such as the Gaia hypothesis were mentioned as ways of understanding the importance of biodiversity. Finally, ecosystem-based management was introduced to help the reader place systems thinking within a management context. This is really the proposed method of managing environmental resources and, therefore, decisions, focusing squarely on the systems at issue and the environmental questions that naturally flow from such a focus.

Systems thinking took what we had discussed in terms of natural systems and mixed some underlying theory of specific scientific principles with a detailed discussion of box modeling. Box modeling is a way of engaging in ecosystem-based management, reducing the environmental question to component boxes that represent parts of the system under review, and then identifying the major inflows, outflows, and feedback mechanisms within that system so they can be analyzed. Fundamental assumptions about our environment were included in this discussion, including the understanding that mass and energy are equivalent and, importantly, the idea that our natural systems exist in a state of equilibrium, which means we should generally see no changes in concentrations of natural things in the environment over time. By focusing on the flows of energy between components of the system, we can decipher when something is out of whack with the underlying system; this can help us focus our attention on what may truly be an environmental problem, including potential causes and solutions.

To reiterate, this science chapter reviewed basic components of scientific theory most prevalent in many environmental decisions. Its value lies in how this chapter relates to the other two chapters of this text. For example, we may use ecosystem-based management ideas to get a sense of what really matters in an environmental context, but that alone does not tell us which decision between two alternative choices is superior. The economics chapter (Chapter 3) will help us with this question by having us internalize costs and consider trade-offs between alternative courses of action. The value chapter will delve deeper into how value might be perceived in an environmental setting, and when choices about environmental issues might go beyond more rational economic analysis. In this way, all three chapters relate to one another to establish a set of tools to apply to environmental decisions. The decisions that may be reached might not always be clear, but the way in which the decision was made will be. That is a primary goal of this text, to make whatever decision is reached fully informed by the principles discussed.

References

Bertaianffy, Ludwig. 1968. *General Systems Theory: Foundations, Development, Applications.* New York: George Braziller.

Bolsover, Stephen R., Elizabeth A. Shephard, Hugh A. White, and Jeremy S. Hyams. 2011. *Cell Biology: A Short Course*, 3rd ed. Hoboken, NJ: John Wiley & Sons.

Bryant, Edward. 1997. *Climate Process and Change.* Cambridge: Cambridge University Press.

Center, Ted, Roy van Driesche, and Mark Hoddle. 2008. *Control of Pests and Weeds by Natural Enemies: An Introduction to Biological Control.* Malden, MA: Blackwell Publishing.

Chapin III, F. Stuart. 2009. Managing Ecosystems Sustainably: The Key Role of Resilience. In *Principles of Ecosystem Stewardship: Resilience-Based Natural Resource Management in a Changing World*, edited by F. Stuart Chapin III, Gary P. Kofinas, and Carl Folke, 41. New York: Springer.

Convention on Biological Diversity. 2011. Convention on Biological Diversity. http://www.cbd.int/convention/text/ (accessed September 23, 2011).

Costanza, Robert, Ralph d'Arge, Rudolf de Groot, Stephen Farber, Monica Grasso, Bruce Hannon, Karin Limburg, Shahid Naeem, Robert V. O'Neill, Jose Paruelo, Robert G. Raskin, Paul Sutton, and Marjan van den Belt. 1997. The Value of the World's Ecosystems Services and Natural Capital. *Nature*, 387: 253–60.

Del Moral, Roger, and Lawrence R. Walker. 2007. *Environmental Disasters, Natural Recovery and Human Responses.* New York: Cambridge University Press.

Fagan, Brian. 2004. *The Long Summer: How Climate Changed Civilization.* New York: Basic Books.

Freeman, Jennifer. 2007. *Science 101: Ecology.* New York: Harper Collins.

Gagosian, R.B., and C. Lee. 1981. Processes Controlling the Distribution of Biogenic Organic Compounds in Seawater. In *Marine Organic Chemistry: Evolution, Composition, Interactions and Chemistry of Organic Matter in Seawater*, edited by E.K. Duursma and R. Dawson, 96–97. New York: Elsevier.

Gardner, Toby. 2010. *Monitoring Forest Biodiversity: Improving Conservation through Ecologically-Responsible Management*. London: Earthscan.

Gautier, Catherine. 2008. *Oil, Water and Climate: An Introduction*. New York: Cambridge University Press.

Gross, Joel M., and Lynn Dodge. 2005. *Clean Water Act: Basic Practice Series*. Chicago: American Bar Association.

Hemming, Brooke L., and Gayle S.W. Hagler. 2011. Geoengineering: Direct Mitigation of Climate Warming. In *Global Climate Change: The Technology Challenge*, edited by Frank Princiotta. New York: Springer.

Hill, Marquita K. 2010. *Understanding Environmental Pollution*, 3rd ed. Cambridge: Cambridge University Press.

Holling, C.S. 2010. Resilience and Stability of Ecological Systems. In *Foundations of Ecological Resilience*, edited by Lance H. Gunderson, Craig R. Allen, and C.S. Holling. Washington, DC: Island Press.

Hubbell, Stephen P. 2001. *The Unified Theory of Biodiversity and Biogeography*. Princeton: Princeton University Press.

Intergovernmental Panel on Climate Change. 2007. IPCC Fourth Assessment Report: Climate Change 2007 (AR4). http://www.ipcc.ch/publications_and_data/publications_and_data_reports.shtml (accessed September 23, 2011).

Katzer, James R. 2011. Coal and Coal/Biomass-Based Power Generation. In *Global Climate Change: The Technology Challenge*, edited by Frank Princiotta. New York: Springer.

Kremen, Claire. 2008. Crop Pollination Services from Wild Bees. In *Bee Pollination in Agricultural Ecosystems*, edited by Rosalind R. James and Theresa L. Pitts-Singer. New York: Oxford University Press.

Krishnamurthy, K.V. 2003. *Textbook of Biodiversity*. Enfield, NH: Science Publishers.

Lindenmayer, David B., and Joern Fischer. 2006. *Habitat Fragmentation and Landscape Change: An Ecological and Conservation Synthesis*. Washington, DC: Island Press.

Lorenz, Klaus, and Rattan Lal. 2010. *Carbon Sequestration in Forest Ecosystems*. New York: Springer.

Lovelock, James. 2000. *Gaia: A New Look at Life on Planet Earth*. Oxford: Oxford University Press.

Margulis, Lynn, and Dorian Sagan. 1995. *What Is Life?* Berkeley: University of California Press.

Millennium Ecosystem Assessment. 2003. Ecosystems and Human Well-Being: A Framework for Assessment. http://www.maweb.org/en/Framework.aspx (accessed September 23, 2011).

Millennium Ecosystem Assessment. 2005. Ecosystems and Human Well-Being: Policy Responses. http://www.maweb.org/en/Responses.aspx (accessed September 23, 2011).

Molles, Manuel C. 2008. *Ecology: Concepts and Applications*, 4th ed. New York: McGraw-Hill.

Moring, Gary F. 2004. *The Complete Idiot's Guide to Understanding Einstein*, 2nd ed. New York: Alpha Books.

Murray, David Ronald. 2003. *Seeds of Concern: The Genetic Manipulation of Plants*. New York: CABI Publishing.

Philander, George S. 2008. *Encyclopedia of Global Warming and Climate Change*. Thousand Oaks, CA: SAGE Publications.

Pierzyniski, Gary M., J.T. Sims, and George F. Vance. 2005. *Soils and Environmental Quality*. Boca Raton, FL: CRC Press.

Princiotta, Frank T. 2011. Global Climate Change and the Mitigation Challenge. In *Global Climate Change: The Technology Challenge*, edited by Frank Princiotta. New York: Springer.

Rice, Stanley A., ed. 2007. *Encyclopedia of Evolution*. New York: Facts on File.

Saunders, Thomas. 1973. *Ocean Resources and Public Policy.* Seattle: University of Washington Press.

Schlesinger, William H. 1997. *Biogeochemistry: An Analysis of Global Change*, 2nd ed. San Diego: Academic Press.

Suter II, Glen W. 1993. *Ecological Risk Assessment.* Boca Raton, FL: CRC Press.

Tennesen, Michael. 2008. *The Complete Idiot's Guide to Global Warming*, 2nd ed. New York: Alpha Books.

Worster, Donald. 2008. *A Passion for Nature: The Life of John Muir.* New York: Oxford University Press.

Chapter 3

Economics of Environmental Decision-Making

Introduction

This chapter is devoted to the topic of *economics* as it relates to environmental decision-making. Broadly speaking, economics is a subject derived out of an understanding for the need to manage one's household.* The household in the context of environmental problems is really the earth system, a natural system that is described in great detail in Chapter 2. If the earth is our household that we must manage, then economics defines the rules by which we choose to manage our earth house.

The purpose of this chapter then is to present and understand a set of economic tools to help in making informed environmental decisions. This chapter will attempt to categorize the different types of economic rule sets that tend to apply most directly to environmental decisions. Once these categories have been identified, some definitions of value as related to economic considerations of the environment will be highlighted. A relevant economic technique, *total valuation*, will be highlighted because it can be used to help make environmental decisions in context; this technique is mentioned in some detail in the other parts to this text.

---

* The term *economics* is derived from the Greek *oikonomia*, which essentially means customs or rules of the house.

Finally, this section concludes with a discussion of *benefit–cost* analysis, which is an exploration of how environmental decisions are made in context, weighing the relative benefits against the relative costs of a proposed action.

As indicated above, economics is about management of the household, and in environmental decisions the household is our natural environment, collectively referred to as the earth system. So economics is really a way of accounting for our management of the earth system; we account for the actions taking place in our natural environment, and how those actions relate to specific goals. An important element in this economic accounting process is a clear understanding of precisely what are the goals we are trying to achieve. We often think of goals in environment settings through a lens of what is best for human well-being in relation to the environment. Specifically in environmental management settings, this question will be referred to as best management practices (Erickson and King 1999).

Inherent in our choices of best management practices are assumptions about what is best.* For example, is the question of best answered from the perspective of a human? Or, should the question be answered from a different perspective, for example: What is best for the natural environment? And if we decide we want our determination of what is best to relate to the environment, then should this control our decision-making even when it results in harm to humans? Or, is the answer of what is best something in between? The point here is that we must focus on our assumptions when it comes to what we call environmental decisions, including the values we apply to evaluating our decisions. Understanding our assumptions will help us in answering environmental questions and therefore help us identify the framework of economics we might apply. We will attempt to decipher a few of the different types of economic frameworks that might apply to environmental decisions in the first part of this chapter.

As we move throughout the parts of this chapter, it is important to connect the economic principles discussed here with the other chapters of this text. For example, we have already mentioned that economics is a system of accounting that is driven by choices about what is best, leading to the achievement of particular goals. Inherent in this discussion is the question of *values*, specifically how do values

---

* This difficulty in choosing what is best is similar to the question of how reasonable people can differ on how best to manage personal finances. For example, some might believe any form of debt is bad, and thus living a debt-free life is the best possible way to manage one's finances. Others might see the value of managed debt in helping to establish credit while allowing the leveraged free cash to be invested elsewhere to create wealth. For example, rather than buying a house for $100,000 in cash, a mortgage is taken out for $100,000 at 4% interest. The $100,000 of cash is then invested in an instrument that earns 8% per year. Thus, by leveraging the cash with debt (the mortgage note), the person is making 4% net interest on the investment rather than 0% interest if he or she had paid for the house in cash (taking the liquid asset cash and transferring it into the illiquid asset of a house). Who is right here? It really depends on which method of management you believe is superior, for whatever reasons you would define *superior* in this case.

play a role in our decision-making? The values chapter (Chapter 4) goes into some depth to discuss how we go about creating, identifying, understanding, and applying our value systems to environmental questions. As we establish the framework for environmental decision-making in the following section, some of these considerations will be quickly summarized and cross-referenced with Chapter 4. Readers are encouraged to go to the relevant material in Chapter 4 for a more in-depth treatment on the subject.

Another example of connections between chapters is the *total valuation* part of this chapter. You may notice total valuation links directly with the *services* section identified in Chapter 2 under *ecosystem principles*. It may be helpful to reread the services materials in Chapter 2, either before or after you read the total valuation part of this chapter. As stated above, efforts will be made to cross-reference important principles discussed in the following section where indicated.

Finally, it is important to understand our discussion of economics here, like the other major topics covered, will necessarily be incomplete. In order to offer a text that highlights the major principles associated with environmental decisions, I give less than full exploration to topics as a necessity of space and other constraints. You are encouraged to seek additional insights in any topic that is identified or discussed in this chapter. In particular, I would recommend some additional review of basic economic principles, both micro and macro, to accompany a more detailed treatment of topics such as ecological economics. For the subject of ecological economics itself, there are a number of excellent resources available for deeper exploration by those with or without a background in the subject.* Now we begin our exploration of economics principles in earnest, beginning with a summary of the different categories of economic study relevant to environmental decision-making: natural resource economics, ecological economics, and the role of discounting and substitution in economic analysis.

Categories of Economics Relevant to Environmental Decision-Making

In this section, we explore several categories of economics that are relevant in environmental decision-making. The first two categories, *natural resource economics* and *ecological economics*, are different in both the scope of environmental topics

---

* For example see the following: *Ecological Economics: The Science and Management of Sustainability*, edited by Robert Costanza (New York: Columbia University Press, 1991); *Valuing the Earth: Economics, Ecology, Ethics*, edited by Herman E. Daly and Kenneth N. Townsend (Cambridge, MA: MIT, 1993); Gareth Edwards-Jones, Ben Davies, and Salman Hussain, *Ecological Economics: An Introduction* (Oxford: Blackwell Science, 2000); and Michael Common and Sigrid Stagl, *Ecological Economics: An Introduction* (New York: Cambridge University Press, 2005).

they cover and the techniques they use to analyze those topics. Where natural resources economics focuses on the market-based direct values of environmental assets, ecological economics takes a broader view of environmental assets, looking at the full range of values that might be associated with the asset in question, including nonmarket values. The third topic in this section is not really a category of economics applied to environmental decisions, but rather a discussion on the role of two economic principles, *discounting* and *substitution*, and how they might be used when making environmental decisions.

I have referred to parts of the environment as assets in the preceding paragraph when describing the different categories of economics to be discussed in the following pages. Why might I use this term to refer to the environment? Isn't an asset something that we agree has value? For example, we consider gold an asset because people have generally agreed it has value. In fact, there is a commodity market for gold, a place where people from all over the world can buy and sell gold by the ounce (Schaeffer 2008). The value of the gold is based on the relative supply and demand of the commodity, and it changes all the time. While not in vogue in most developed nations today, gold has traditionally been used as a means of currency to buy things. What can be said for sure is that gold is almost universally seen as something of value among humans. In this sense, one can understand gold to be an asset.

Like gold, can parts of the environment also be considered assets? Can air be considered an asset? It seems water can, especially when it is bottled in small plastic containers and sold in convenience stores; people will show a preference for this kind of water by paying money to purchase it. There are many things from the environment that we find direct value in because of how we use the thing; trees for paper and wood products, corn for consumption, land for development.

What about environmental services, say the ability of trees to "scrub" carbon dioxide from the atmosphere (Lorenz and Lal 2010). Is this an asset as well? Note we are not talking about the tree itself, but rather the ability of the tree to consume carbon dioxide. A wetland may be valuable for its capacity to filter water, making the water safe for consumption by humans, but I'm not sure how I can trade this water filtering process like I can gold.

As you may see here, what we define as an asset has much to do with how we value the components that make up our economic analysis. Economic analysis can take two broad approaches to its management of value, one objective and one more subjective. Let us summarize these two points of view now so we can have an understanding of how they apply in the context of the categories we will be discussing.

Positive economics is a form of economic analysis that relies heavily on objective information, meaning the analysis focuses on objectively based facts while dismissing clearly subjective variables from consideration (Friedman 1953). A primary source of objective information in environmental issues is scientifically derived information. Positive economic frameworks can be a favorable way of accounting for scientific information in environmental decisions, allowing the scientific information to drive the economic analysis. One of the problems with positive economics is the relative equal weighting of objective information; sometimes it is hard for decision-makers to determine a superior course of action when presented with equally weighted alternatives (Seager et al. 2006, 236–40).

Normative economics differs from positive economics by instituting a more subjective framework from which to make decisions (Camerer 2008). Stated simply, normative economics begins with a premise or assumption. If we begin with the premise that maintaining current levels of biodiversity on earth is critical to our survival, then biodiversity will be weighted highest in our economic analysis; we will tend to conclude that the protection of biodiversity is the best alternative to a set of proposed actions. Conversely, if we determine economic output as defined by gross domestic product (all of the goods and services produced by a nation in a given year) is of upmost importance, then economic analysis weighting our economic output will likely prevail over other considerations.

In a mathematical sense, positive economics tends to weight each factor considered equally, while normative economics alters the weights of factors based on preexisting assumptions. We could also say positive economics discusses what is, while normative economics discusses what should be (Tietenberg and Lewis 2010). It is important to consider which economic theory being discussed in this chapter focuses on more positive forms of analysis, and which focuses on more normative viewpoints. Ultimately, we can connect the different methods to values, and environmental decision-making is a value-laden process.

As we explore these materials, we will find examples where physical environmental goods (like a tree) and nonphysical environmental processes (trees taking up carbon from the atmosphere) are both treated as values. We will see this particularly when we begin to discuss *indirect values* (regulating services of natural resources). It may help if we now begin thinking of the entire environment as an asset, specifically with reference to the entire earth system. Borrowing from our discussion of systems thinking in the science section, we can accept the premise that the earth is a closed system, meaning all of the potential values of the earth can be known (they are not changing). Another way of saying this is we can assume no new capital will be allowed into our earth system for valuation purposes. What we are trying to do is establish all of the values that actually exist in the natural environment.

To summarize, what we are trying to do in parts of this chapter is to quantify what values actually do exist in the earth system, and this includes both current values that exist today and future values as *option values* and *legacy values* that are impacted by our actions today. Consideration of future value can cause some complications in our analysis, and these complications will be highlighted and mitigated when possible to allow us to understand the major concepts being expressed.* However, our goal is simply to get a good accounting of our earth "house" so that we can use an economic framework as a way of making environmental decisions. With these foundational considerations out of the way, let us begin by exploring *natural resource economics*.

Natural Resource Economics

Natural resource economics is a subfield of economics that focuses on the earth's natural resources (Field and Field 2006, 23). A goal of natural resource economics is to understand the connections between natural systems and human economies. Often, the environment is seen as a constraining factor, meaning human society and institutions are seen as existing within the natural environment and are thus constrained by the broader environment. A representation of this relationship is shown in Figure 3.1.

The term *natural resource economics* itself is often taken to apply to a variety of disciplines. For example, some like to place ecological economics as a subcategory of natural resource economics (Asafu-Adjaye 2005, 10). While the nomenclature varies, our use of the term is meant to differentiate from ecological economics in one main way; natural resource economics is defined to represent traditional economic analysis of components within the natural system as applied to some direct human use. The direct human use is the kind of use that is defined through market forces, meaning humans have actively identified a market value with the resource and the resource can be valued based on current market prices.

Natural resource economics is differentiated from ecological economics in this section. Ecological economics will be defined as an economic discipline that goes beyond direct market uses of natural resources, and looks to other services and values provided by these resources, or in conjunction with other resources (Common and Stagl 2005). Like the term indicates, ecological economics focuses

---

* Sometimes for simplicity we will have to evaluate a proposed environmental issue with the assumption that all value of the earth system (and thus subsequent subsystem under consideration) is known. While the assumptions might not actually be true (we likely will not know all of the value at stake, for example), they can help simplify the process so that what is known can be evaluated. As an example, consider we know the total value of the environment under consideration is $10 (just imagine we can actually determine this value). If we know there is a maximum of $10 available as value, then we can determine the *relative* (and that is a key term here) benefit and costs of a particular policy approach. Say we want to take an action that will have $3 worth of net harm to the environment. Knowing the total value is $10, we can relate the net harm caused ($3) to the total value ($3 out of $10 is 30% of the total, so it gives us some idea of total harm to the environment). We can then compare this choice against other choices, which may create less of a net harm to the environment. However, we must remember that while the alternative action chosen may indeed create less harm toward the environment, it may also create less benefit for humans as well. Benefitting one variable under consideration (say the environment) while harming another (say human well-being) highlights the idea of *trade-offs* in economics, a topic we will cover under the benefit–cost analysis section below.

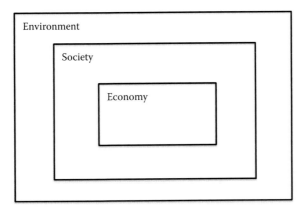

Figure 3.1   Representation of the relationship between the environment, society, and the economy.

on a systems-based approach to identifying values within a natural system; we can link this ecological approach to the systems discussion in Chapter 2.

Natural resource economics focuses on direct uses of natural resource components (Kopp and Smith 1993). What is meant by direct use is traditionally based on the extraction and consumption of the resource. For example, precious metals like gold, silver, and copper have often been mined for either their direct value (gold as a source of inherent value) or some applied value (copper for use in conducting electricity) (Schaeffer 2008). These kinds of natural resources are extracted and possibly refined to provide humans with direct uses.

Trees are another example of a natural resource that has direct uses; the wood fiber of trees is often used as an input for paper, furniture, and other associated uses (Conrad 2010, 1–10). The raw material provided by nature is the wood fiber. Effort is then added to the wood (via human work of milling, sawing, cutting, shaving, sanding, etc.) to produce a finished product. Natural resource economics focuses on the ore or wood as a provision from nature that is then meant to provide humans with some degree of comfort (food, shelter, clothing, etc.).

One question that often arises in natural resource economics is how the extraction and use of resources will impact human well-being over time. For example, what happens if all of the copper available on earth is mined for current human use? What will this mean for future generations of humans? We will discuss these questions in greater detail when we talk about discounting, substitution, and trade-offs in a later section below. For now, let us identify a main difference between types of resources, those that are capable of being *depleted* because of the nature of the resource, and those that are capable of being *renewed* because of their inherent characteristics. The relevance of a nonrenewable resource versus a renewable resource has to do with how economics treats these different types of resources, and the assumptions that are built into each category of resource.

A nonrenewable resource is one that does not regenerate itself within a reasonable period in human timescales (Asafu-Adjaye 2005, 4). For example, oil is a type of hydrocarbon that results from carbon-based life-forms slowly degrading in particular conditions of heat and pressure over geologic time. Since it takes so long for oil to be created under natural processes, it is said to be nonrenewable because we will use up available resources of oil before any more can be made.*

Renewable resources differ in that they "renew" themselves on a regular basis and in a time interval that is manageable by human standards (Liu 2005, 13). Trees are one example; essentially all agricultural activity (both plant and animal based) is another. The key characteristic of renewable resources is they regularly replicate themselves over a short period of time. Issues that arise from questions about the use of renewable resources are different than resources we classify as nonrenewable; we must take greater care with nonrenewable resources because once they are used up, there is no more available for use. This is not the case with renewable resources, which can theoretically last indefinitely, depending on the rate of use.

The assumed rate of use in natural resource economics is a key assumption in making sure a natural resource will remain available for use over time. It is usually determined by looking at the rate of extraction, and comparing this rate to an assumption about how fast the trees will regrow (Keohane and Olmstead 2007, 98–108). This relationship is represented in Figure 3.2.

If renewable resources are harvested faster than replacement rates, then the resource will likely be depleted even though it has the capacity to renew itself; in essence, the resource becomes nonrenewable because it has been used at an unsustainable rate. Conversely, if the same resource is being harvested at a rate below its replacement rate, then the resource will likely maintain a healthy population over time, remaining available for prolonged human use.

Natural resource economics focuses on the extent to which resources support human well-being (Kopp and Smith, 1993). This focus primarily assumes extraction and use of natural resources is for some human-centered purpose. Because natural resource economics focuses on the availability of resources to support direct human uses, one important question to consider is whether the resource is renewable or depletable. If a resource is depletable, then rates of extraction matter and long-term planning is essential because the resource will one day become unavailable. Planning on how to best use this kind of resource is essential. If the resource is renewable, then less planning may be required because the resource has the capacity to renew itself over time. Of course, things like rates of extraction still matter because a renewable

---

* I am not suggesting humans would actually find every last ounce of oil that exists on earth. It is understood that some reserves might never be discovered, and the costs associated with reaching the more difficult deposits of oil would likely lead to alternatives prior to actually exhausting the resource. The comment here is to identify that oil has a nonreplication characteristic to it within timeframes and variables important to humans from an economic management perspective.

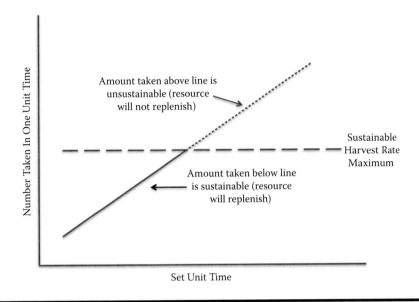

Figure 3.2   Representation of rates of resource extraction in a given unit of time.

resource can be overexploited by taking too much of it too fast. In environmental management, a key variable in making decisions is to determine the underlying characteristics of the resource (renewable versus depletable), and then to also consider the impact that a proposed plan will have on the longevity of the resource. These types of considerations occur in natural resource economics analysis.

For depletable resources, consideration is given to understanding how much of the resource is available for use, and how much of that resource is actually being used over time (the rate of use in relation to the overall supply of the product) (Anderson 2010, 333–46). In this linear type of evaluation, it is pretty easy to make recommendations because as long as the total amount is known, and no more of it will be made, then it is relatively simple to determine a time when the supply will run out based on current and future use predictions. Additional factors that can complicate this process include the price of the product itself. If the product is in high demand, then decreasing supply might result in higher prices. Higher prices can lead to alternatives, if they exist, because in a free market consumers are allowed to find the best deals. This will be discussed in greater detail when we talk about substitutes later in this chapter.

Renewable resources management considerations focus more on rates of extraction and regrowth for the reasons identified above. These resources require a greater deal of active management because they are capable of lasting in perpetuity so long as the rate of extraction never exceeds the ability of the resource to regenerate itself (Tietenberg and Lewis 2010). Managers of renewable resources also tend to worry about gaining efficiency over the resource. For example, in forestry management, a good deal of emphasis is placed on harvesting trees at a point when they offer the greatest amount of wood over the shortest period of time (Keohane and Olmstead 2007, 98–108). To meet demands for wood product, certain species of tree that are fast growing but still offer a viable wood product tend to be preferred from a management standpoint. Without going into too much detail, it is interesting to consider how management decisions about environmental resources can differ based simply on whether the resource is seen to have renewable characteristics as opposed to depletable characteristics.

Our definition of natural resource economics is limited; it focuses almost entirely on the extractive value of the resource in question. Trees are important in natural resource economics analysis because they offer a source of wood that is then made into things valuable to humans. What we have not considered in our review of natural resource economics is the nonmarket values associated with natural resources. What other values might trees have that are not constrained to wood inputs for human welfare? Well, as has been mentioned, trees also offer an important filter for our atmosphere, converting carbon dioxide into oxygen that is necessary for our survival. Trees also sequester additional carbon in the atmosphere,* absorbing the carbon as additional growth within the parts of the tree itself (Lorenz and Lal 2010). Trees also provide important soil stabilization through their root systems directly, and because of their ability to diminish the strength of wind gusts (Binkley and Menyalio 2005).

Trees purify our air, mitigate warming of the climate, and ensure the stability of important organic soils for agriculture; in a word, trees are amazing! Should we not consider these additional attributes of trees when we think about value of natural resources? Do we not benefit from these things trees do, and aren't these benefits just as important (and maybe more so) than the products we create from the wood fiber of trees? These are the questions entertained by ecological economics as a discipline; it goes beyond direct extractive market-based valuations of natural resources, begins to look at the other services provided by these resources, and analyzes the nonmarket aesthetic values associated with resources. We now turn to an examination of ecological economics to better understand these additional values offered by nature.

Ecological Economics

Ecological economics takes a broad view of the interrelationships between humans and the environment (Common and Stagl 2005). It focuses on all aspects of the natural system, and includes humans as a component of natural systems (Ehlers and Frafft 2001, 7). For our purposes, we can differentiate ecological economics from natural resource economics by widening our definition of value. While natural resource economics focuses on the extractive value of natural resources as applied

---

* Refer to the carbon cycle example in Chapter 2 for more on this point.

to human use, ecological economics considers resources for what they provide humans; how resources help to regulate for the overall health of the environment, and how they help support cultural services. Ecological economics goes beyond a focus of the physical resource itself (say the tree as wood fiber to input into some human use), and extends its analysis to the interactions between system components, for example, how trees also help to clean the air we breathe and also sequester carbon from the atmosphere. In short, we differentiate ecological economics as a system of economic analysis that more fully embraces the systems approach to understanding the environment.*

Accounting for interactions between system components is a critical part of what makes ecological economics fundamentally different when we consider the two categories of economic approaches; the reason why is because understanding how energy flows between the system components helps us to identify where potential problems exist from an environmental standpoint. This is not done in traditional natural resource economic analysis.

Not including the regulating services provided by natural systems results in important environmental values being missed. For example, the burning of fossil fuels has been shown to produce some undesirable impacts. Early in industrialization, England documented cases where the burning of coal led to strong buildup of soot in the air, which was then deposited around the local communities (Reible 1999, 11). Burning gasoline from auto emissions also impacted the local air quality of communities like Los Angeles (Johnson 2007, 188). Countries like China are currently dealing with fossil fuel emissions impacts on air quality as they continue to industrialize (Casper 2010, 159–61).

The examples mentioned in the preceding paragraph identify directly observable causes of the burning of fossil fuels. The observation is linear and only requires a most basic level of inquiry and attention to see the causal relationship.† A more indirect (less observable) impact of burning fossil fuels occurs at the chemical level, and must be analyzed from an energy budget standpoint. We know today that the carbon being burned is moving from one component of the natural system (the lithosphere) to another component (the atmosphere). This has resulted in increasing amounts of carbon being absorbed by the atmosphere, which is creating a greenhouse effect, allowing heat to be trapped by the earth and thus leading to a change in the dynamics of the earth system itself (Intergovernmental Panel on Climate Change 2007). This more indirect impact requires an assessment style that is systems based, because such an assessment style will allow for an understanding

---

* The systems approach is more fully discussed Chapter 2.
† One can watch the emission of soot from the burning of coal; it can be visibly seen as black smoke. This smoke can then be seen to accumulate in the immediate area of the burning, and the residue (soot) can be seen to accumulate on the surrounding buildings, trees, etc. The connection between the burning of coal and the soot buildup is linear because it is direct; the cause and effect can be clearly discerned.

of cause and effect between these interactions. Ecological economics encourages this kind of relationship thinking because it incorporates the relational energy flows between system components.

Another difference between ecological economics and natural resource economics has to do with the belief that different forms of capital (value) can be freely interchanged, specifically, the presumption that natural capital and human capital are completely substitutable for one another (Chapin 2009, 19). Ecological economics does not believe natural capital can be substituted for human capital, but rather sees natural capital as a necessary prerequisite for human survival. This leads to a conclusion that natural capital should be preserved over human-based considerations in most instances. Implied in this statement is a preferential judgment in ecological economics that favors intergenerational considerations, the idea that future generations are just as important as the current generation of humans (Asafu-Adjaye 2005, 305). Thus, in order to ensure equity among generations, natural capital should be maintained, and a primary way to maintain this capital is through a management of the resources that employs a systems thinking perspective (Asafu-Adjaye 2005, 13–18).

Beyond valuing energy flows and questions of equity, ecological economics also values cultural connections between humans and natural resources (Jenkins 2005, 501–2). Nature provides a variety of benefits to humans without any physical extraction of the resource; consider how national parks and wilderness areas in the United States are often defined by their breathtaking beauty and opportunities for solace and reflection (Crawford 2004). There is a spiritual component inherent in nature, and many humans (individuals, cultures, etc.) place a significant value on its very existence (Kopp and Smith 1993). These are not the kind of values that can be easily replaced according to main views in the ecological economics field (Kopp and Smith 1993).

To summarize, we can see some main differences between a natural resource economics perspective and an ecological economics perspective, at least in the way we have decided to define these two terms for our purposes in this text. Natural resource economics tends to focus on natural capital as an input for humans to be made into something else. In this way, the "thing" from nature is completely substitutable for human capital (a tree becomes a chair with some additional input by human ingenuity). Most things that are considered under a natural resource economics framework can be identified in a market, meaning a value can readily be determined. Ecological economics expands this view of value to a wider, systems-based approach. Not only do physical natural resources have direct or market-based values, but they also have indirect and nonuse values as regulating and cultural services. In addition, ecological economics emphasizes the flow of energy between system components as an important additional framework for analytical purposes. We can summarize these main differences between the two economic approaches in Figure 3.3.

Characteristic	Natural Resource Economics	Ecological Economics
Valuation Based on Market Forces?	Generally Yes	Generally No, Especially Indirect and Non-Use Values
Direct Values Considered?	Yes	Yes
Indirect Values Considered?	No	Yes
Non-Use Values Considered?	No	Yes
Emphasize Natural System Interactions?	No	Yes

Figure 3.3 Major characteristic differences between natural resource economics and ecological economics.

Environmental decisions made under an ecological economics framework generally require significantly more information and analysis than might be required in a more traditional natural resource economics-based framework. This is because ecological economics embraces systems thinking, which requires additional insight into cause and effect when analyzing the environmental impacts of actions (White, Mottershead, and Harrison 1992, 585–88). Thinking systematically can allow an analysis that comprehensively examines all environmental values at stake in a particular decision, ensuring choices are being made on the best science available.

Ecological economics, as a framework, also has its problems as a framework for decision-making. There is a greater likelihood for error in this type of analysis because there is often insufficient information to make informed decisions. For example, how would one know ahead of time that the burning of fossil fuel would lead to additional carbon being trapped in the atmosphere? There was really no reason to understand this connection when we first began to burn fossil fuels. Further, even if that could be known beforehand, how could the connection between increased carbon and increased global temperatures be known beforehand? Imagine the kind of mental forecasting that would be needed to accurately make such a connection?

We can see the difficulty with this kind of systematic analysis in preventing environmental harm before we engage in actions that can lead to the harm (simply because we do not know). However, even though this analysis might not be able to predict certain harms before they occur, it allows us to consider those harms as they arise, and to properly balance our decisions by creating more informed valuation techniques to aid in deciding how to best respond to those harms; this is the value ecological economics offers in environmental decisions. A direct application of this is discussed in other sections of this text under *adaptive management* techniques.

The Role of Discounting, Substitution, and Trade-Offs

Discounting, substitution, and *trade-offs* are all terms used in economic analysis. Each term represents a specific concept related to economic valuation, including assumptions about how the value of things changes over time. In this section, we will identify and explain each term individually. We will then tie the concepts together and show how they collectively impact our understanding of environmental decision-making, specifically, how values can change over time, and how the very process of valuation is a function of the assumptions we make about resources under consideration. The goal is to begin understanding how economic tools impact the way in which we value natural resources, and by consequence environmental decisions related to natural resources. These economic tools build upon one another, and each step in the process creates values that form the basis of an overarching evaluation framework. In this way, it is important to understand how these specific values are derived because they ultimately drive the environmental decision-making process.

As you read through this section, consider how each concept discussed can impact environmental analysis. See if you can determine how the application of the opposite concept expressed can have a different outcome in the analysis. You might be surprised just how powerful these concepts can be at creating opposing conclusions simply based on small adjustments to the assumptions being used in the analysis.

Discounting is a technique used in economics to acknowledge the idea that the value of something can change depending on a set of circumstances (Conrad 2010, 11). For example, the value of a dollar is discounted over time; a dollar is worth more today than it is worth ten years from now (Taylor and Weerapana 2009, 478–88). This assumption is supported by the concept of inflation; over time economies grow in size, causing greater demand for currency (the supply of money). As money supply grows, the marginal value of a dollar increases simply because there are more dollars available in the supply chain. Thus, the relative value of the dollar decreases over time. Discount rates are often used to establish assumptions in economic analysis, so the results of those assumptions can then paint a picture of the resultant output based on different discount rates (Conrad 2010, 11–17).

The term *discounting* may be used as a way of expressing preference for one set of criteria over another, and this is particularly true when considering the value of natural resources. We can borrow our example of fossil fuel burning above as a means of explanation. Consider the burning of coal to produce electricity. Even if we do not consider the impacts of climate change, we know burning coal releases compounds into the atmosphere, and some of these compounds have negative consequences for humans. Examples include the soot that dirties the air and can create respiratory illness, as well as the sulfur that can mix with molecules in the air to create acid rain (Chhetri and Islam 2008, 101–2).

Let us further say the coal is primarily burned for the production of electricity. If consumers of that electricity are only paying for the actual cost of producing the electricity (the costs of mining the coal, transporting it, and burning it to produce the electricity) along with a margin for the company's profit, then we can say the coal is being purchased at a discounted price. The discount in this case comes at the expense of the air, which is polluted as a result of burning the coal. The discount also comes at the expense of the water and plants, which suffer from the acid rain. If these costs are not included in the price of the electricity purchased, then the environment is acting as a subsidy for the price of electricity.* If we include some analysis of climate change in our discussion here, then the additional carbon that is being forced into the atmosphere through the burning of coal becomes an additional discount because of its role in affecting climate change, if those costs of climate change impacts are not also priced into the cost of electricity generated by coal.

Some of the associations and differences between natural resource economics and ecological economics should be seen here through the lens of discounting. In natural resource economics, the focus is on the use of the coal as a means to a human end. By only looking at the direct use of the coal, one can support a cost structure that does not account for the impacts of the coal on the larger natural system. However, application of an ecological economics framework would have us look at the impact of coal burning on the entire earth system. In this way, we should see how the two types of economic theories would respond differently using the concept of discounting.

Substitution in economic theory deals with finding an alternative to the current use or practice that yields the same or very similar results (Anderson 2010, 42). In natural resources, substitution means finding one thing to replace another in achieving a particular goal. For example, consider the use of hydrocarbons to produce electricity; they are not the only source of energy to create electricity. Current substitutes include hydropower, wind power, nuclear power, solar power, geothermal power, and others (Anderson 2010, 155–66). Each one of these other inputs and methods of producing electricity can be considered a substitute for the use of hydrocarbon; they all achieve the result of producing electricity (albeit in various different ways, and with correspondingly different levels of efficiency based on current technology, etc.).

When a substitute exists for a good, then we have choices about which goods we can use to achieve the same goal. In our example here, natural resources are combined with technological innovation to create the inputs from which the desired

---

* Those who live near coal-burning power plants also pay for some of these costs, including higher incidence of respiratory illness in the local population. This leads to higher health care costs, lost work productivity because of illness, and other associated costs. In this way, we can say all of the individuals and businesses that are impacted negatively by the burning of coal also subsidize the lower cost of electricity.

output (electricity) is produced. If we only had one known natural resource that could accomplish the goal of producing electricity, then we would be limited in our ability to make choices about how we could make electricity. Since electricity seems to be an absolute necessity for human advancement and well-being, we can see the importance of having a variety of ways to produce this essential resource. From an environmental standpoint, we can think about the overall benefit of choosing one form of electricity production over another. Let us now consider that question in more detail.

Consider all of the ways of producing electricity. We can call each way of electricity production an alternative, and then develop criteria to choose among the alternatives presented. For example, electricity production must be relatively consistent in order to respond to changes in demand. So, whatever source we use to produce the electricity, we would want to make sure it was capable of providing us with a sufficient quantity of electricity output at any given time (Anderson 2010, 167). Beyond the need to ensure a constant sourcing of electricity, another important consideration would likely be the overall cost per unit of electricity to the consumer. Cost is an important consideration from a public standpoint because electricity is seen as a public good,* and has become a basic necessity for human well-being in an advanced society (Anderson 2010, 155). So, if we decided the main two criteria for determining which natural resource to use for producing electricity were cost and control over quantity produced, we would have a framework for evaluating the several alternatives available to produce the outcome.

Control over quantity produced is very much tied to technology and the manner of production. Considering coal, the only unknown is ensuring that a facility has sufficient supply of the input (coal) in order to produce the desired amount of electricity. Otherwise, assuming sufficient supply on hand, a facility can make the choice to simply burn more coal to produce needed electricity, subject to the limits of the facility itself in how much electricity can be generated within a particular time span, as well as the system in place to deliver the electricity to the areas where demand is high. Aside from these limits, human decision is the only factor, meaning there is a great amount of control in electricity production using coal.

Other sources of electricity production, like wind, water, and solar, offer potential problems with control because there are natural limits and natural variability that place additional constraints on the ability of humans to control the production process. Sometimes the water stops flowing in a drought, leading to lower hydroelectric production. Sometimes the wind does not blow, leading to lower output from wind power; you get the idea. Technological advances can limit the amount of unknown with these other sources of power generation; solar power, for example, has developed significantly over the past decade, allowing power to be produced in very low ambient light conditions (Jha 2010, 1–5).

---

* Refer to Chapter 4 for a definition of *public goods*.

Cost as a consideration in choosing alternatives is a good example to show how natural resource economists and ecological economists differ in their analytical approaches. Natural resource economics would look at the extractive costs of harvesting the coal, and then the production costs of transporting and burning the coal to produce electricity. Ecological economists would look at these direct costs, but also consider costs associated with indirect and nonuse values of the natural system that are impacted by the use of coal as a source of electricity production.

The costs associated with burning carbon (climate change, dirty air, acid rain, etc.) would be part of the analysis in an ecological economics framework. The costs derived from a natural resource economics framework would tend to be lower than one derived from an ecological economics analysis. The point here is that even with a good understanding of substitution as the theory, the actual factors that go into evaluating the relative benefits and costs of a particular substitute are equally relevant. Coal may be a cheaper substitute under a direct value analysis, but it may be a more expensive substitute under a total value analysis. This point suggests that in environment decision-making, one has to make sure he or she identifies clearly what framework for analysis he or she is using (for example, determining production control and costs as the main criteria), and also how he or she is conducting the analysis (how are costs being determined and judged for comparison?).

Trade-offs is the final topic to discuss in this section. A trade-off occurs when one choice is made that commits resources, preventing other choices to be made for the commitment of those same resources (Anderson 2010, 99–100). A simple example is how we choose to spend our time. Knowing our time has an upper limit (our individual life span is not infinite), each unit of time spent doing one thing necessarily means that same unit of time cannot be spent doing another thing; one cannot be spending the same unit of time doing more than one thing, multitasking aside. So, the trade-off is the choice one makes when deciding to do one thing versus another.

Say I have a choice of either watching television or writing a term paper over the next hour, since I cannot do both of them at the same time; at least I cannot do both of them well simultaneously. I must choose one or the other. If I choose to watch television for the hour, then I have made a trade-off between television and writing; television has taken priority over the writing for that hour. Some might even argue I have discounted the writing of the paper in making the trade-off to watch television. One interesting question that might arise is to decipher why I have chosen television over writing the term paper, and whether the decision is the most beneficial use of my time; this gets into questions of value that will be discussed at greater length in Chapter 4.

Trade-offs are an important consideration in the environmental arena because any decision that impacts the environment for the benefit of human well-being includes trade-offs. Conversely, a decision that benefits the environment at the expense of human well-being also contains trade-offs. The ability to properly recognize and account for the trade-offs being made in a particular action allows decision-makers to more accurately evaluate the relative costs and benefits of a proposed action; we discuss benefit–cost analysis at the end of this chapter. In theory, this more accurate accounting allows for transparent decisions where the relative benefits of an action are internalized against corresponding costs. Of course, judging what is a benefit versus a cost is a value-laden process; was the decision to watch television over writing the term paper a good decision overall? The answer largely depends on the criteria one uses to judge good.

Trade-offs are often termed opportunity costs in economics, the idea being that when one engages resources in one thing (watching television), he or she has lost the opportunity to engage those same resources in something else (writing a term paper) (Anderson 2010, 111–16). Applying this to environmental questions, we can see how trade-off analysis is impacted by a number of considerations. When it comes to actions that can have long-term impacts—climate change—the question of trade-offs can become increasingly difficult because of intergenerational issues. Consider a hypothetical situation where one is faced with making a choice that will supply the current generation of humans with a substantial benefit, but this benefit may have a substantial cost for future generations. Should the action be taken? Who should be considered in the decision, the current generation of humans only? Or should a nonexisting future generation also be considered? Is there some threshold probability that is required to aid the decision, like anything above a 50% likelihood requires one to consider the future generation, but below 50% means the future generation can be completely disregarded? These are difficult questions that lead us back to value judgments; the answer really depends on how we feel about our responsibility to future generations.

Many environmental decisions today require the consideration of intergenerational issues because evidence suggests that the impacts of current activities will have effects that last for generations, at the very least (Bowersox 2002). Climate change is probably the best example, where our manipulation of the carbon cycle (see Chapter 2) may result in an intergenerational change in the average temperature of the earth. This change in temperature can lead to significant changes in how the earth's natural systems function, resulting in bigger storms, greater frequency and duration of droughts, sea level rise, and other phenomena (Stern 2008, 65–103).

Trading off these impacts to future generations creates a basic fairness question. Some economists believe this question cannot be answered adequately today because, even if these natural shifts occur, we cannot currently perceive of the capacity of future generations to deal with these issues. They argue that the best we can do is create as much wealth as possible today so these future generations are left with that wealth as the foundation from which to deal with these problems. Julian Simon is one economist who has often argued substitutes will readily exist in the future through scarcity, and this includes the ability of humans to find new ways of dealing with their natural environment (Simon 1996). The best way to create this wealth is to keep current prices as low as possible, allowing economies to grow. Others, like Paul Ehrlich (a scientist and not an economist), argue that the earth system has limits and there is an upper limit from which human activities will cause a shift in the system. Thus, there is no indefinite level of substitutes for natural capital through human ingenuity as an economist like Simon believes (Ehrlich 1997).

We will leave the value-laden questions to Chapter 4. For now, it is enough to understand how the three economic principles (discounting, substitution, and trade-offs) apply to environmental decisions. They are assumptions used to help us understand an environmental problem in context. These assumptions are not always correct, but they can help us frame an issue in a way that allows for a reasoned and more complete analysis. How we end up weighting different factors—like inter-generational equity, for instance—depends on our set of basic values we apply to the question. In the next section, we broadly discuss the question of value from a macro-perspective of societal goals. For example, is wealth maximization the primary function of government and society? We will explore existing paradigms and alternatives to this question.

Defining Value: Linking Environment and Human Interactions

Although the concept of value is discussed in much greater detail in Chapter 4, an overview of several different economic models of valuation is given here in order to understand how economic analysis impacts environmental decision-making. Specifically, how is value generally defined in economic terms, and how does this definition impact the weighting and analysis of environmental factors?

We discussed above how natural resource economics and ecological economics can take different views on the valuation of natural capital, with ecological economics expanding what is deemed a value applied to natural resources. Underlying the answer to what is valuable about natural resources are assumptions we carry both individually and as a society. So let's examine some of these assumptions below and see what they mean in context. As we do, consider how value is being defined in each category below, whether the definition ascribes more closely to a natural resource or ecological framework, and also whether you subscribe to any portions of the definitions offered.

Measurements of Well-Being and Progress

What exactly does it mean to do well? How is wellness measured? Assuming a society judges itself to be doing well, should it strive to do better than well? These are the kinds of questions that drive the goals associated with public policy; decisions governments make about how to measure progress are important indicators that help to frame the definition of well-being (Gerston 2010). In this section, we review the traditional dominant form of measuring progress—gross domestic product

(GDP)—and then look to some alternatives to this progress indicator. Remember, we are trying to understand the framework from which economic analysis occurs. For example, if the goal is to increase the amount of goods and services produced in a system (without considering anything else), then the extractive value of natural resources should be a primary consideration. However, if our goal is to increase intergenerational equity through a principle like sustainability, using resources today, without diminishing the capacity of the earth to provide resources for future generations (Bell and Morse 2008, 10–12), then we might apply other considerations to our use of natural resources (rate of use, impact on natural system, etc.).

Gross Domestic Product

One of the main roles of modern government is to help create prosperity for its citizens. In a capitalist system, this is generally done through the development and support of free markets (Smith 1904). Markets support economic activity by allowing for the free trade of goods and services by individuals. Governments can help to support market activity by legitimizing markets, providing a basic set of rules to support the legitimacy of market transactions, and provide a forum for the resolution of disputes between private parties (Anderson 2010, 69–76).

Beyond the role of government in supporting the creation and legitimization of markets, market activity is generally left in the hands of private individuals. The basic premise of the free market system is that it allows for an efficient exchange of goods and services, and this form of exchange is an efficient—and therefore superior—means of creating overall individual and societal well-being (Smith 1904). Supporting this basic proposition, most developed nations that engage in market-based transactions use a similar indicator to measure well-being, and this is the gross domestic product of a country.

Gross domestic product is a measure of all of the goods and services that are produced by a country in a given year (Baumol and Blinder 2011, 546–50). GDP is made up of the following variables: private consumption, gross investment, government spending, and net exports (exports minus imports). It is meant to measure overall standard of living within a country, again linking overall capital expenditure of the country to the amount of transactions occurring within the country; the more transactions occurring within a country, the greater the overall well-being that is presumed to exist.* This is particularly true where the GDP is divided by the population of the country, which yields the amount of goods and services being

---

* Remember, the assumption here is that market-based activities are the most efficient way to create well-being. Thus, the more market transactions presumed to exist in a country, the more likely that country is engaging in activity that represents preferences of the citizens, as well as the means to achieve those preferences (wealth). So under such an assumption, it makes sense to assume that GDP would be a rough measure of overall well-being of the citizens of a particular country.

provided per person per unit of time (often referred to as GDP per capita) (Baumol and Blinder 2011, 546–50).

The validity of GDP as a measure of overall well-being within a country has its criticisms.* One critique is how *government spending* is considered part of GDP (Baumol and Blinder 2011, 546–50). Governments can often spend large sums of money well beyond what they take in (deficit spending), and this is rarely argued to be a superior form of managing government affairs (Wheeler 2004). Even so, under a traditional definition of GDP, government spending is considered part of the product produced by that country. Of course, deficit spending cannot go on indefinitely, and repeated and long-term deficits would lead to unsustainable outcomes for future generations, including a likely lowering of GDP (Organization for Economic Cooperation and Development 2010, 270–77). This is one example where the measure of GDP can be shown to be problematic in accurately identifying overall well-being.[†]

There are other criticisms of GDP. For example, GDP does not accurately account for income distribution over the populations as a whole; rather, it simply divides total GDP by population to get a GDP per capita rate (Grant and Vidler 2000, 126–27). This means GDP does not show how the wealth of the nation is distributed among the population of nation. By not identifying disparity between incomes, GDP can offer an invalid picture of overall well-being within a country.[‡]

GDP also does not measure future directions of growth for a country; it simply measures the current state of economic activity (Grant and Vidler 2000, 126–27). So, a country with a high measured GDP can actually be experiencing a downward trend where quality of life is decreasing. However, this trend would not necessarily be identified in a straight GDP measurement. Thus, the nation might not be doing well, even though it represents a high GDP.

GDP can also be increased in socially perverse ways, like engaging in war (creating a war economy) or responding to natural disasters (rebuilding) (Anderson 2010, 111–13). The tsunami that struck Japan in the spring of 2011 is an example of

---

* Can you immediately think of any based on our definition and previous discussions thus far? For example, can you image situations where GDP might not actually yield better well-being for those living in the country?

† It should be noted that debt of any kind is not necessarily a bad position for a nation. However, there is general agreement that continually spending more than a nation takes in will ultimately lead to premiums being paid to service debt. These premiums will lead to greater burdens being placed on the citizens of a country (likely through tax increases), and result in a reduced investment in the country. All of this tends to have a negative impact on the growth prospects of that country, at least when we consider the traditional market presumptions that we are using for discussion in this section.

‡ For example, a country can have a high measure of GDP, and even a high measure of GDP per capita. However, in a hypothetical situation of a country with 100 members, it is possible for 99% of the wealth of the country to be held by one member of the country, and the remaining 1% to be divided among the remaining 99 members. In such a case, we can hardly say the high GDP measure likely reflects the overall well-being of that country as a whole, can we?

a natural disaster that will, ultimately, increase GDP because of the rebuilding that will be needed in the area (Baumol and Blinder 2011, 89–93). These are not prime examples of activities that tend to be directly associated with human well-being. In this way, there are a number of critiques that challenge GDP as a proper measure of human well-being and prosperity.

The most relevant criticism of GDP to environmental issues is that of how externalities, specifically environmental damages, are handled. GDP does not present a net accounting of the total goods and services produced by a national within a year. In other words, it does not subtract environmental harms as a by-product of economic activity from the economic activity itself; GDP simply measures the economic activity and does not account for any damages that activity caused to the environment (Grant and Vidler 2000, 128–29).

From a natural resource economics perspective, this kind of accounting method might make sense; economic activity is really about focusing on market-based interactions, and not necessarily the impacts of those actions. In contrast, an ecological economics framework would tend to focus on the externalities because the environmental harm would need to be accounted for in order to understand the overall impact of the activity on the natural system. This is because ecological economists believe the environment is necessary for economic activity to exist and continue to thrive (Hardin 1991). By not accounting for negative externalities, GDP fails to give an accurate picture of how our economic activity is impacting our capacity to engage in economic activity.

It would be difficult for environmental managers to use GDP as a means of understanding environmental welfare for the reasons identified above. Remember, it is generally recognized that a healthy environment is a key component to healthy humans (physically and spiritually) (Norton 1991). As such, economic frameworks that support environmental decisions may need alternative ways of determining human well-being beyond GDP. Since there have been a number of criticisms aimed at GDP as a measure of human well-being, alternatives have been offered in its place. These alternatives tend to focus on variables and criteria that directly address generally accepted principles of human well-being; a few of these alternatives are offered for contrast in the next section.

Alternatives

The purpose of this section is to highlight a few alternatives that have been suggested and, in some cases, put into practice. Prior to reviewing these alternatives, it may be beneficial to consider what criteria one would deem important in measuring overall human well-being. Should the criteria seek to be as objective as possible so that there is the ability to compare between indicators? Alternatively, should the criteria allow for more subjective means of establishing well-being, such as a criterion for happiness? If more subjective forms of criteria apply, then how would you propose to evaluate those criteria in practice? For example, could you accurately compare happiness between cultures? It may be that happiness in one culture is derived through very different means than in another culture. Remember, we are looking in some depth at economic frameworks, including the assumptions used in these frameworks. We are trying to determine how well some of these assumptions apply to environmental decision-making, and if alternative assumptions may be more appropriate when applying economic frameworks.

Assumptions are often found in the criteria used to measure environmental goals. For example, government spending was mentioned as one criterion used to measure GDP. However, we determined a potential problem with this criterion: government could continually deficit spend, and this would be calculated as a positive in GDP. It is hard to see how continually deficit spending can result in long-term human well-being. One way to solve this issue is to remove government spending as a criterion for evaluating overall happiness. We might alternatively suggest net government spending as a better criterion, meaning we look at how much the government has taken in for income versus how much the government has spent. If the government has spent more than it has taken in, the overall spending can be one factor (for the amount of activity), but we would also account for the deficit incurred as a penalty (negative) toward the overall spending.

If we were creating ecological criteria for analysis, we might want to establish some kind of criterion that measures the environmental impact of the total goods and services produced by a country. If the environmental impact is negative, this hurts the overall analysis. If the environmental impact is net positive, then this would be seen as beneficial toward overall human well-being (especially if we decided to include a criterion that required well-being to be maintained for future generations). The point is criteria can be established to better meet the goals of the measure; of course, how we choose to define well-being will make a significant difference in our overall analysis, as will our decision to allow more subjective (normative) measures alongside objective measures of analysis.

Two alternative ways of measuring well-being are offered below; one alternative is more subjective in form, while the other is more objective. As you review the different examples, consider them in light of any criterion you have developed in your own mind to meet the objective of overall human well-being. You may find neither example meets your personal definition, but some aspects of each come closer than GDP as discussed above. You may also find that GDP is a fine measure overall based on your personal values and the role you see of government in defining such terms. Just remember, however it is defined, well-being as a measure certainly impacts our understanding of environmental decisions in context.

Gross National Happiness

Gross national happiness (GNH) is offered as an alternative measure of human well-being over that of gross domestic product (GDP). Its main difference lies in its focus on different criteria than GDP to measure happiness. Specifically, it attempts to measure well-being (via a complementary term, *happiness*) through a more holistic approach that focuses on slightly different assumptions about the role economic wealth alone plays in overall social welfare (Daly and Farley 2011, 274). The underlying principles upon which GNH is based are found in the philosophy of Buddhism, as well as in some areas of psychology (mostly positive psychology). The main emphasis is on the kinds of underlying circumstances that reinforce individual and group happiness within a society. These underlying circumstances are concerned not so much with the accumulation of wealth (although wealth is considered a criteria in GNH), but how that wealth serves as a catalyst for providing a minimum living standard for the members of a country (Folbre 2010, 316–20).

The four main goals of GNH are sustainable development, preservation and promotion of cultural values, conservation of the natural environment, and the establishment of human-centered governance systems. Criteria to help determine these four goals of GNH include physical, mental, and spiritual health; time balance; social and community vitality; cultural vitality; education; living standards; good governance; and ecological vitality (Folbre 2010, 316–20). Most of these criteria are qualitative in nature, meaning they are more subjectively based, and hard to compare with other forms of measurement. This is one criticism of GNH as an indicator over GDP; while GDP may be unrefined between more normative aspects of good and bad types of production and consumption, the measurements themselves (goods and services) can be objectively quantified numerically.

More objective quantification allows for a number that can be compared to other countries regardless of the manner and circumstances in which the goods and services are produced. However, the ability to quantify results does not, in itself, establish meaningful results.* In fact, some more objective indicators have been established to suggest that the qualitative measures of GNH are being met; infant mortality is one indicator that has been suggested as an objectively based

---

* Of course, some would argue the benefit of the number becomes limited when it does not have sufficient refinement to explain anything of substance. For example, miles per gallon is often depicted as an important goal of automobile fuel economy standards because it is a quantifiable number that helps us identify a potential level of efficiency within cars offered by manufacturers. However, turning this number into a more meaningful evaluation of impact on gasoline consumption is difficult to do. The more interesting query has to do with what behavioral reactions people are having to automobiles that get better gas mileage. Say the average person drove 12,000 miles per year with an automobile that achieved 20 miles per gallon. If that same average person now has an auto that gets 40 miles per gallon, but now drives 30,000 miles per year, then he or she is actually consuming more gasoline per year than when he or she drove the less fuel-efficient model (anything over 24,000 miles per year would equal using more gas). So, focusing only on average fuel economy does not tell the entire story; it shows a capacity, but really nothing more. The real question arises when we evaluate how driving behaviors change in response to higher fuel economy.

measurement that identifies whether or not the criteria of GNH is being met.* So while there are disagreements between qualitative and quantitative forms of measurement, there are arguments to both support and critique GNH as an accurate indicator of overall societal well-being.

The concept of GNH has progressed since first offered as an alternative by the King of Bhutan in the early 1970s (Daly and Farley 2011, 274). For example, efforts have been made to utilize GNH as an indicator of well-being based on more objective measures (International Institute of Management 2006). Additional work has been done to find ways of quantifying GNH in a variety of settings. These efforts reinforce a desire to more rigorously define human well-being through measurements that connect market transactions and government actions, collectively determining the impact of this connection on basic notions of justice, equity, and sustainability. These concepts are certainly related to environmental decisions, especially when we consider how environmental management is moving toward a more ecosystem-based approach.† As such, it seems the desire to consider the impacts of human activities is beginning to be called for when we calculate our overall progress as a global community through the measurement of prosperity.

We can pause here to reflect on the general dissatisfaction of some with traditional models of calculating well-being (like GDP), resulting in efforts to design additional measures that more meaningfully tell the story of how we are progressing as a nation, culture, and humanity. Consider our earlier discussion of natural resource economics and ecological economics; one discipline, natural resources, focuses most clearly on the extractive aspects of our interactions with nature; the other, ecological economics, takes a more holistic approach by thinking systematically and attempting to account for our actions as they relate to a net impact, considering, for example, whether we have taken more from the system resource than what we have gained for ourselves in the bargain. If we take these admittedly rough definitions of our two categories of environmental economics as accurate, then which one would you ascribe to GDP and GNH most specifically? If you could only choose one measurement (either GDP or GNH) to ascribe to each category of economic analysis, which would go where, and why?

It seems, at least on the surface, that GNH and ecological economics share a desire to get at a more complete accounting of the goal (human well-being/happiness)

---

* If infant mortality is decreasing, then there is obviously some indication of an increased capacity for keeping children. This increased capacity can be due to a variety of factors, including increases in medical capacity (a sign of economic and industrial advancement), as well as social factors (increased prosperity, better family planning, women's rights through equality, etc.). No matter which factors are influencing the decrease in infant mortality, all of the potential factors contribute to GNH. In addition, the result (less infants dying) undoubtedly speaks to increased overall happiness, as it is generally assumed that most infant mortality experiences are negative, both individually and from a societal standpoint.

† Ecosystem-based management is discussed in detail in Chapter 2.

when it comes to our interactions with our environment. Both GNH and ecological economics seem to embrace the notion of complexity, and both seem to identify the connection between human prosperity and a healthy environment. Some might even go so far as to suggest that GNH, like ecological economics, embraces a systems approach, connecting the many components of the human system (physical, spiritual, social, etc.) in order to determine an accurate measure of overall happiness (International Institute of Management 2006).

Natural resource economics seems to correlate more closely with GDP because they both seem to view the environment as a source for extraction and human use. The resultant production that is yielded by the process results in activity that is measured and roughly correlated to human wellness. Its simplicity allows for fewer qualifications, which can be of great value when one is considering macro-level decisions. However, it may have limits when we are considering some of the more intricate problems facing our environment today. Let us now look at a different alternative, the genuine progress indicator, to see how it attempts to measure overall human well-being, and to compare its methodology with that of GDP and GNH.

Genuine Progress Indicator

The genuine progress indicator (GPI) is an attempt to create a net gross domestic product (GDP) reading by differentiating between economic activity that improves human welfare (both today and in the future), and economic activity that degrades human welfare (Lawn and Clarke 2006, 17). Recall, GDP measures all economic output—all goods and services produced by a country within a given timeframe, generally 1 year. GDP does not try to decipher between good and bad types of economic output; it simply measures the total economic output as an indicator of total economic activity. GPI measures total economic output in the same manner as GDP, but it also attempts to give a picture of net economic output based on a sustainability criterion (Parker 2002, 32). Thus, the goal of GPI is to be a more accurate representation of net GDP, trying to link economic output to what it deems to be true human progress.

GPI states a goal of linking a country's actual growth through increased production of goods and services to the improvement of well-being of the people living in that country (Parker 2002, 32). Where growth does not correlate to improved well-being, GPI would find fault with portions of economic output that are not leading to growth. GPI mirrors many of the critiques identified above about GDP, essentially suggesting GDP is a blunt measure that provides little useful information about overall impact of economic activity on well-being. Of course, in order for GPI to give a more accurate picture, it must give some definitional structure to its conception of human well-being, as well as show how it is being measured. For example, GPI can have the same issues identified under gross national happiness, specifically the need to relate the goal back to some objective criteria from which the goal can be judged.

The merits of GPI as an indicator tend to focus on a standard that is more like GDP, but deciphers between positive and negative types of economic activity. In this way, GPI is different from GNH, at least in the sense that it does not try to incorporate specific principles of happiness (say through Buddhist teaching) as a primary goal. It does, however, incorporate the goals of sustainability into its measurement of progress; this is more in line with the basic goals outlined in the GNH indicator. In essence, GPI attempts to create a more accurate view of how economic activity is impacting overall human well-being. For example, development away from urban centers—often called urban sprawl—contributes to overall economic activity through the building of roads, buildings, utilities, etc. Such expansion converts land, increases commutes, creates pollution, and has other impacts that might be considered negatives from a well-being standpoint (Soule 2006). GPI aims to quantify the different types of economic activity expressed here based on overall impact; in this case if the negative impacts outweighed the positive impacts, then the overall project would be deemed to be negative from a GPI standpoint. In contrast, this same activity would likely be lumped into all positive economic activity from a GDP analysis, resulting in a net positive.

Let us now sum up the major points discussed in this section on defining value by first stepping back to look at value through an economic lens, and then comparing the three different indicators offered as ways of measuring well-being and progress. Recall from the very beginning of this chapter that economics is a system of managing one's house. Related to this literal definition, economics is a sophisticated kind of accounting system that attempts to understand the forces that influence economies: production, distribution, and consumption of goods and services. From an environmental decision-making standpoint, economics serves an important role by helping us measure the interactions of economic activity, giving us some indication of how these interactions impact our overall life. This is especially true when the tools of economics can aid in our making connections between human actions and the environment.

The purpose of discussing the macro-scale measures of well-being and progress is to see how current measures of economic progress jibe with environmental considerations. Gross domestic product (GDP) has been the basis for measuring economic output in industrialized nations and continues to be the measure of choice in most nations today (Grant and Vidler 2000, 126–27). By focusing only on the total goods and services produced by a nation within a given timeframe, GDP is an admittedly blunt instrument for measuring human well-being; the connection it makes to well-being is rough, correlating growing economic activity with human happiness and overall satisfaction. Even where actual human satisfaction is not presumed, the increased overall wealth produced through increasing GDP is argued to contain the capacity to produce happiness; it is a necessary prerequisite for happiness based on such indicators as access to quality food (Hassan, Scholes, and Ash 2005, 237).

Presumptions of increased economic output positively correlating to happiness and well-being can be seriously critiqued, and one major critique is in the environmental arena, where examples have been provided that show increased GDP can lead to serious environmental harm. What this tells us, at a minimum, is that the criteria used to determine GDP might not be very useful when making environmental decisions. Thus, an increase in GDP cannot presume an increase in environmental health.* Rather, environmental managers likely need to look beyond GDP if they are looking for some kind of aid in these macro-level progress indicators when making environmental decisions.

Gross national happiness (GNH) and the genuine progress indicator (GPI) are both alternative indicators to GDP, and are meant to offer a more realistic interpretation of how our economic activity matches core human values of well-being and progress. Both GNH and GPI explicitly include environmental issues into their accounting methods for determining well-being, as well as connecting principles of sustainability to a natural systems analysis where they try to determine the economic activity's impact on the environment.

Both GNH and GPI offer a potentially powerful measure for environmental managers, as they can help match the overall economic activity to goals that align closely with environmental considerations. The major difference between the two approaches is that GNH tends to focus on more normative measurements, although there have been efforts to make this indicator more objective in recent years, and GPI tries to more objectively establish a net GDP measure where "good" economic activity is measured against "bad" economic activity. The key in using any of these measures is to understand their limitations; none of them are perfect measurement tools, and all contain assumptions that can lack validity under certain circumstances.

Beyond the practical use of these different measures in environmental decisions, we should also connect the basic goal of economics to environmental considerations. Again, if we assume a more natural resource-based stance in our scientific thinking, then we see natural resources as mostly there for extractive purposes, and our role in management is limited. However, if we see natural resources as more of a systems-based process, then we would likely be apt to find values outside of the traditional market values identified in classical economic analysis; in such circumstances, measures like GNH and GPI are more attuned to this systems-based way of thinking.

In keeping with a systems-based theme, we now turn to a technique used in economics to determine the *total value* of a resource. Total valuation is one way to incorporate all of the values associated with environmental resources, including systems-based values, and then compare these values in a rigorous methodology (cost-benefit analysis), which will be discussed in the last part of this section.

---

* In fact, an increase in GDP might as well signal a decrease in environmental health.

Total Valuation Technique (Tv = Dv + Iv + Nuv)

In Chapter 2, we discuss the kinds of services described under ecosystem principles; these services include provisioning, regulating, and cultural services. In this section, we take the different services identified in our natural systems analysis and apply economic valuation terms to those services. The goal is to use economic terminology to help create an accounting system for these different services. The value of this process will be seen when we consider a major economic technique often used in environmental decision-making, *benefit–cost analysis*.

The total valuation technique is derived, in large part, from the Millennium Ecosystem Assessment (Hassan, Scholes, and Ash 2005, 55–63). The purpose of total valuation is to ensure a full accounting of ecosystem services when making environmental decisions. This technique embraces ecosystem concepts; it includes the extractive-based market values that often focus on natural resource economics (under *direct values*), but goes on to include the other services offered by the environment, to include regulating and cultural services. The principle behind total valuation is to allow for consideration of all forms of value in natural resources, including the value of processes between components of natural systems. Through this consideration one is capable of making informed decisions.

The manner of decision-making depends on the framework used; for example, we will be applying total valuation to the economic framework of benefit–cost analysis at the end of this chapter. However, total valuation can be easily applied to other frameworks, like cost-effectiveness analysis as one example.* Whatever framework is being used, total valuation offers a methodology that encourages the consideration of all natural resource values. It does not require a weighting of these values, and those working with this valuation technique can apply different weights based on varying circumstances.

Total valuation is comprised of three distinct categories of value: direct, indirect, and nonuse value. A representation of the total valuation as an equation is shown in Figure 3.4.

Total value is the dependent variable in the equation, meaning the value derived here is completely dependent on the values of the variables sitting on the other side of the equation (the other side of the equal sign). Direct, indirect, and nonuse values are the independent variables of the equation; their value is not dependent on consideration of the other variables. For example, direct value

---

* Cost-effectiveness analysis is often used when one is comparing things that do not have a monetary value as the sole means of comparison. For example, the choice between purchasing two types of washers can include price as one variable, but may include other nonmonetary factors, such as size, displacement, washing efficiency, settings, electricity utilization, etc. Cost-effectiveness, although not specifically discussed in this chapter, can be applied to a variety of environmental problems, especially where values are hard to determine for certain environmental components.

$$Tv = Dv + Iv + Nuv$$

Tv = Total Value
Dv = Direct Values
Iv = Indirect Values
Nuv = Nonuse Values

Figure 3.4 Total value equation.

is not determined by what the indirect values are, and vice versa; the same goes for nonuse values—they are all independent of one another. If you are trying to understand the total value associated with a particular ecosystem under study, then direct, indirect, and nonuse values must be determined. However, if you are only trying to determine a subset of indirect values within that ecosystem, then you would not necessarily need to know the direct and nonuse values for this purpose.

What is powerful about total valuation is the need to determine all three independent variables if one is seeking to understand total value, which is at the heart of an ecosystem-based analysis of valuation. By only looking at direct market values (say the provisioning services of trees as wood fiber), one can easily miss the total value of a mangrove forest. However, by engaging in total valuation of the resource, additional values will be considered in the process.

Not all values may be capable of being defined in a total value analysis. For example, there may be insufficient information from which to obtain total value of a resource. This is especially true when nonmarket values (indirect and nonuse) are being considered. Also, nonmarket values are hard to quantify accurately into monetary units.

One of the main goals of using a total valuation approach is to create a monetary accounting so that apples can be compared to apples; it is much easier to compare $100 dollars of direct value to $100 dollars of indirect value than it is to compare wood fiber to carbon sequestration potential of a forest. Thus, various valuation techniques have to be used in certain instances (contingent valuation, willingness to pay) where markets are absent; the assumptions built into these alternative valuation techniques can impact the overall validity of the final number established. This is an important fact to consider when contemplating environmental decisions. Let us now discuss the different categories of value—the independent variables—in the total valuation technique.

Direct Values (Dvs)

Direct values relate to provisioning services of natural resources; they represent the types of values associated with market-based systems. From an environmental standpoint, these values are usually identified as natural resource goods. Our previous example of identifying the wood fiber in a tree stand as a basic natural resource for extractive purposes is a prime example of a direct value associated with trees. We can look to commodity markets to determine the kinds of natural resources, and in what particular form, that often represent direct values (Kopp and Smith 1993).

The direct valuation method is relatively straightforward, mainly because direct values are known through market transactions and based on fair market value. Fair market value can be defined as an estimate of what a willing buyer would pay for something and at what price a willing seller might allow the something to be purchased. In an open market with many buyers and sellers, like a commodity market, the ongoing fair market value of the product—generally referred to as the spot price*—is available for purchase during the hours of the market's operation (Brealey and Myers 2003, 312–13). The price reflected at a given moment is based on a current demand or willingness to pay for a set amount of the product. So, for example, a bushel (a set unit) of corn can have a spot price that changes from moment to moment in a commodities market. The fair market value of the bushel is based on what buyers are willing to pay for that bushel. The assumptions contained in that willingness to pay are that the buyers have perfect information about the product, including the reasons the product might be worth what they are willing to pay. Sellers of the product are assumed to have equal access to this information, although this assumption of equal information is often inaccurate (Bradfield 2007, 29–31).

Fair market value is meant to reflect the overall value of a thing as applied to the purposes of the thing. For example, a bushel of corn is generally valued as a source of food whether for human consumption or animal feed (Chiras 2009, 65–66). A bushel of cotton is generally valued as a source (input) for clothing, linens, and other associated manufactured goods (Riello and Parthasarathi 2009). A barrel of oil is valued as an input for fuel generation, whether through direct burning or as an input for further refinement into gasoline and other forms of distillate (Yeomans 2004). The common factor is that there is a presumption about the value of these different goods, and that value is generally based on the use of the good as a direct input for human consumption.

Direct values are generally identified alongside provisioning services because we tend to use natural resources in market-based transactions as a means of providing something other than their natural state. We grow corn for consumption, but we consume the corn in a refined state—a cereal, for example. We grow cotton to harvest and extract the cotton fiber as an input into the manufacture of textiles. We extract oil from the ground and refine it for use as a source of energy in a variety of applications, as well as using it to provide us with petroleum-based manufactured products such as plastics. The price we place on the value of these goods in market transactions is directly related to how they are used for human consumption.

---

* The spot price is the price quoted for an immediate purchase and sale of a given quantity of the good being sold.

Although fair market value dominates the way in which natural resource value is determined in an open market-based transaction, it is not the only means of determining value. *Intrinsic value* is another way of determining value, and it is based on the preferences of an individual in determining the value of a thing (Beardsley 2005). For example, consider a house for sale in an open market. The house may have a generally accepted fair market value based on objective criteria (condition, location, size, prices paid for comparable houses in the community); all of these factors can be used to establish a generally accepted fair market value for the home. An individual who grew up in that home might feel differently; he or she might have a special connection to the home because of his or her past experience with the home. He or she might be willing to pay a price outside the fair market value in order to express his or her unique preferences in relation to the home. In this case, the intrinsic value of the home for this individual is probably greater than the fair market value of the home to the general public; this is because the individual is adding an additional criterion (personal connection) to the valuation of the home that is increasing his or her willingness to pay for the property. Through this example, we may begin to see how a slightly different perspective on valuation can change what is considered a fair value for the thing being considered; we will see how additional insights into the value of the thing being considered can impact a determination of fair market value for the thing.

Market-based valuation works particularly well when there is a lot of the thing being sold within the market (Granovetter 1993). For example, there is a lot of gold available by the ounce, and thus a market price can be established for gold at this unit price. Market valuations do not work so well when the thing is unique or one of a kind because there is really no way to determine a fair market value by price alone (Smith 1993, 187–88). An example of this kind of problem occurs often in the world of art where a particular painting is a one-of-a-kind unique item. Because there is only one of these items, it is hard to judge a fair market price for the item; there is insufficient buying and selling of the item in order to discern a generally accepted willingness to pay. Because of the unique nature of the thing being sold, the market cannot offer a price prior to the sale with confidence; usually an auction is required to determine a price, and the price paid can reflect values outside of fair market, including the intrinsic values of the highest bidder.

One of the benefits of direct valuation methods through an open-market system is the legitimacy of pricing; the market helps to create a transparent pricing notification to potential buyers by showing what others are currently paying for the product (Kopp and Smith 1993). Transparency is important when we consider a fair and just society; people are capable of assuring themselves a price that is within boundaries of what others are paying for the product (Burt 1993). Direct valuation also gives us good information on how to actually value the product under consideration. For example, if we want to know the direct value of a stand of trees, we can look to the commodity market for the current price of similar wood fiber. Once we calculate the total amount of wood fiber in the stand, we can do some simple calculations to achieve the approximate direct market value of the wood fiber in the stand. Further, our final number would be supported by objective information; we could show a clear methodology on how we calculated the per-unit value of the wood fiber.

The amount of clarity added to direct valuation is still limited because direct valuation does not include values represented outside the market transaction; for example, a stand of trees has value beyond the wood fiber that is contained in the stand. Limits to direct valuation methods are tied to the market in which the valuation is derived; the value given to the product is based entirely on the market price, which itself only reflects the values that are being considered during the buying and selling of the product at hand.

If I am a purchaser of wood fiber, I am not concerned with where the wood was harvested or the impacts the harvesting of that wood has on the ecosystem of the area; I am simply interested in the use of the wood fiber as an input in some manufacturing process (if I am a direct purchaser). Alternatively, I am interested in the potential increase in value of the wood fiber because of speculation on future willingness to pay (if I am an investor). The market system itself does not ensure the consideration of other values in the process. We have to look outside direct valuation methods in order to find some of these other values.

Indirect Values (Ivs)

Indirect values represent values of natural resources outside traditional market-based direct values (Kopp and Smith 1993). Specifically, indirect values relate to the *regulating services* discussed in Chapter 2. Recall that regulating services include the kinds of benefits provided by natural resources when viewed from a systems perspective, particularly the kind of services provided by processes (energy flows) occurring between components of the system. For example, a wetland provides important water filtering functions that are not inherent to the physical wetland itself. What is meant by inherent here is that if we cut out the wetland, we would not be able to capture this filtration function; the function is really a by-product of the interaction between the wetland plants, soils, and the water flowing through the wetland (Cronk and Fennessy 2001, 29–34). Thus, the function is a process between two components of a natural system. Indirect values represent these kinds of regulating services between ecosystem components, and in order to understand indirect values, one needs to understand basic principles of systems analysis, specifically ecosystem analysis in the context of environmental issues.

Indirect values are different from direct values in one important way associated with valuation; it is difficult to have a market-based system for determining indirect values. Using our example of the wetland above, let us consider how traditional methods of extraction and fair market valuation would apply to the wetland resource. Imagine the wetland consists of a variety of grasses, shrubs, and water-loving (hydrophilic) trees along a large body of water. The wetland provides a number of system regulation functions that are not necessarily part of the wetland itself (like the water filtration services mentioned above). What would be the value of the wetland under a direct value analysis? What kinds of values could we represent in a free market as described above? Certainly the wood fiber contained in the wetland might have a market-based value. Also, the land itself might have a development value that could be determined under fair market analysis. However, the regulating functions, and thus the indirect values of the system, would not be represented in these transactions.* This leads to two problems: determining the dollar value of the indirect services provided by the resource, and having those values represented in a market transaction setting.

There are ways of determining indirect values of natural resources. For example, if the wetland is known to naturally filter a certain amount of water, making it potable for human consumption, then we might look to the costs of potable water within the local community to get an idea of this value. If the community has its water treated for consumption purposes and is charged for the cost of this treatment (construction, maintenance, and operation costs), then a correlation could be made between the cost per unit of water treated and the value of filtration per unit of water treated by the wetland (LePage 2011, 12–13). The correlation here would be pretty linear, meaning not a lot of additional assumptions or calculations would need to be done to make this value determination.

If the wetland also served as a habitat for young fish that are part of a larger commercial fishery, then with some basic science determining the number of fish nursed within the wetland habitat (along with natural mortality rates and other factors), a measure of the wetland as a replacement for fish farming could be determined. If the wetland was in an area where hurricanes and other large storms were prevalent and the wetland served as a barrier to inland human populations, then the value of the wetland as a barrier to storm damage could be determined (although with less precision on actual value) (Wilson and Liu 2008, 133–34). These are just some of the methods that could be employed to determine a market-based value of the wetland resource.

There are other problems with indirect valuation of natural resources beyond determining a value for the regulating services. This is because it is hard to see people freely deciding to add the regulating services provided by natural resources

---

* It is certainly conceivable to have a market based on the regulating services of wetland resources. However, the market itself would be established for this particular purpose, the buying and selling of wetland regulating services. In order to do this, a number of legal and regulatory mechanisms would have to complement the establishment of this market. Some examples include creating markets for environmental harms, like sulfur as a pollutant in the air, and then allowing a restricted trading of sulfur permits with a cap on the total amount of sulfur allowed in a particular airshed. This kind of cap-and-trade program incorporates a partial regulation (cap) and partial market scheme (trade) in order to accomplish environmental goals. What is being described in this part of the text is the difficulty in creating classical market mechanisms for indirect services provided by natural resources.

to market transactions, either by creating a market for these services or by incorporating the value of these services into the direct value aspects of the resource itself. Doing so would be almost like self-imposing a tax on the value of the products being bought and sold in the market (Field and Field 2006, 30–32, 110–33). For example, wood fiber harvested from wetlands would cost more than wood fiber from elsewhere because it would include the value of the water filtering services lost by the wetland when the wood was harvested.* The land upon which the wetland exists would have a higher market cost because it would have to include the value of the regulating services that would be lost upon development of the land. Because higher costs generally make a product less competitive in an open market (the basic theory of markets is that competition will reduce costs because buyers will naturally desire the lowest-cost competitor), internalizing these indirect values in a market transaction voluntarily seems unlikely.

As just mentioned, one way to internalize indirect values in markets is for the government to require the internalization of these costs; taxing is one way to accomplish this goal.† Government intervention is generally considered necessary in many environmental issues because the background environment has traditionally not been part of voluntary market activity (this is simply a way of saying markets have focused on direct values while externalizing indirect values, using the vernacular we have chosen for our current discussion). Governments can impose all kinds of mechanisms (regulatory, market based, taxing, etc.) as ways of trying to incorporate indirect values into traditional economic considerations (Field and Field 2006, 193–270).

We have already discussed how a government might adopt measurement of well-being and progress, moving beyond a GDP-based definition. Consider the reinforcement of indirect values where a government chooses to determine its overall progress based on these factors (say by choosing a GPI standard), and then also adopting mechanisms within market-based transactions (such as taxes, for example) to further internalize the environmental costs associated with degradation of ecosystem regulating services; the reinforcement from both the macro- and micro-levels would make it much easier to incorporate values for these kinds of services. If they were automatically incorporated into pricing structures, then

---

* This assumes the nonwetland wood does not contain regulating services equal to or exceeding the regulating services of the wetland wood.
† A Pigovian tax is often argued as a way of internalizing undesirable market outcomes. An undesirable market outcome in this case is one that has negative externalities, or conditions that lead to inefficiencies. In our example, the loss of regulating services of the natural system through wetland loss is a negative externality because it leads to a social cost (a reduced capacity of the natural system). A tax equal to the amount of the negative externality is added to the price of the product in order to internalize this cost, making the overall cost of the product reflect the true value in the market (benefits-costs). If the tax makes the product less desirable because of price, then this is simply a reflection that the product is too costly (social costs included) in comparison to similar products that do not carry the same social costs.

environmental decision-making would not need to engage in additional value analysis when presented with an environmental problem; the expressed market values would be sufficient information because they would include the indirect values associated with natural resources.

The benefits of indirect values are directly related to the ecosystem-based management principles discussed in Chapter 2. Indirect valuation helps to incorporate the processes between system components into our understanding of value, and internalize the social costs that occur when these kinds of values are not considered in market transactions. The difficulties associated with indirect values include the fact that it is hard to come up with a specific monetary value for these services. However, this difficulty can be mitigated by using similar direct values where appropriate, for example, by matching the costs of treating water for human consumption with the same service provided by a wetland. Actually incorporating indirect values into a market system is difficult to contemplate on a voluntary basis, but government intervention in the process (like through placing a tax on the good equal to the indirect values lost) can properly increase the direct value of the good, incorporating these indirect values into the market system. The remaining variable in our equation is nonuse values, which is discussed next.

Nonuse Values (Nuvs)

Nonuse values represent the third category of value provided by natural resources we are discussing in this section. Nonuse values are linked to the cultural services further discussed in Chapter 2. If you recall, *cultural services* is a term that tries to encompass the values we derive out of nature that are not extractive (direct values), and also not necessarily tied to a function of the natural system (indirect values). Rather, cultural services focus on the more aesthetic aspects of natural resources (Daly and Farley 2011, 106). In this way, nonuse values are very much a human-based system of valuation because the value that is being identified is based on our unique cultural and social norms as related to a part of nature.

The type of value we apply to natural settings varies by individual and group. For example, I may look at the Grand Canyon in the United States and find in it aesthetic pleasure because of its large scale and beautiful vistas, finding a personally rewarding experience of contemplation and reflection. A member of a Native American tribe who sees the Grand Canyon as an important spiritual source might look upon it as a place of worship, finding religious value through this particular natural setting (National Research Council 1996, 138–46). Other individuals and groups might find yet additional meaning and value that is different from what has been mentioned.

Nonuse values are different than direct and indirect values because they are not attached to a market-based system of trading among these values; one would be hard-pressed to find a willing buyer of an individual's sense of calm and reflection that is brought on by the natural resource. Similarly, it would be hard to "purchase" the spiritual identity of a particular person or group; what would be the price and how would the transaction be consummated—can you imagine?

Nonuse values represent nonmarket, human-based valuations of natural resources. In a way, nonuse values prove a human capacity to internalize nonmarket values associated with natural resources and the environment. A national policy of setting aside public lands for wilderness and national parks, including the strong visitation rates seen at these places, is a testament of our capacity to value nature for nature's sake. It should not be too difficult for us to imagine that nature has value attached to it that exceeds extractive, direct valuations; the hard part is not necessarily accepting this principle, but determining how to act in light of this understanding.

Nonuse valuation provides a tool to identify the value of nature as a thing unto itself. Like a unique piece of art, we can see intrinsic value in natural things. However, when trying to monetize the value of a natural resource, we run into similar problems as those found in valuing unique pieces of art; what is the actual value of the resource from an intrinsic standpoint? Like some arguments in the arts, unique pieces of nature like the Grand Canyon are seen as irreplaceable and therefore are often argued to be priceless. This may be true for unique natural areas like the Grand Canyon, but it likely cannot apply to all areas of nature, for if it did we would have a real problem of engaging in any extractive use of nature, even responsible extractive use.

In some cases, extraction of resources does little to disturb the nonuse value at stake. An example is an unobstructed view of the ocean from the shore. Intermittent fishing of the ocean's waters does little to impact the view from the shore. However, obstructing that view permanently, say by placing a large number of wind turbines in the water, can significantly impact the overall aesthetic of the view. If the view has special meaning to certain groups, like having a religious significance to a group of Native Americans, then the issue can become increasingly thorny. Further, even though the fishing might not impact the view, it may impact the indirect value of ecosystem services within the water, depending on how the fishing activity is carried out.

Without delving too deep into the difficulties presented in some of these issues, we can certainly see that direct uses of resources does not necessarily have to always impact nonuse values as the example above provides. However, mountaintop removal, where mountains are actually blown apart to extract coal, is a kind of extractive practice that can lead to significant aesthetic changes to the area, impacting nonuse values directly (House and Howard 2009). Removing mountains through explosions can also significantly impact indirect values associated with the local ecosystem. The point here is that the relationship between nonuse and other types of values must be closely examined on a case-by-case basis.

Not all nonuses are priceless, and they likely cannot be treated as such when making environmental decisions. A generic stand of trees within the larger White Mountains of New Hampshire does not have unlimited value by itself, but its marginal value depends on a number of factors that include a consideration of its value in relation to the larger ecosystem. Focusing solely on nonuse value connections, the stand of trees, when aggregated, becomes important in establishing the overall value of the area. However, assuming it was the only stand of trees to be extracted in the entire mountain region, its relative impact on nonuse value considerations would be minimal.

If we add additional facts to our tree example, like the stand sits immediately on top of important Native American burial grounds and removal of the trees represents a serious violation to the rest and well-being of the spirits buried, then we have special facts that change our analysis. Further, if the stand of trees is a unique habitat for an endangered species of animal, then we have additional facts that change the overall importance of that stand. Still, under normal circumstances, the stand alone might be rightly judged to have minimal indirect and nonuse values; when this happens, the extractive value of the stand can exceed other considerations, and it makes sense to cut down the stand for direct human use. If it did not, then we would have a hard time engaging nature in ways that maintain and improve our human well-being on earth. Recall that in most rational ecosystem-based analyses, including ecological economics, humans are considered *part* of the ecosystem, not separate from it. The real question here is, because we have the capacity to judge our actions against other considerations, how should we approach out interactions with nature?

The difficulty in valuing nonuses of natural resources becomes problematic when we consider the total valuation technique as a whole. However, recall that nonuse value is an independent variable, meaning knowing its absolute value is not necessary in order to determine direct and indirect values. While the value determined for nonuses does impact our determination of total value (the dependent variable), it does not have to be a perfect number; simply beginning to develop ways of creating values for this variable sheds more light on total value than disregarding it in total. Even giving a nominal value to nonuses associated with a resource brings us closer to incorporating the total value of the resource when making environmental decisions. We will discuss how to incorporate total valuation as a technique below when we review benefit–cost analysis.

There are a variety of nonuse valuation techniques that exist in economics to try and place a monetary number on this variable. Probably one of the more widely used methods is referred to as *contingent valuation* (Field and Field 2006, 149). Contingent valuation is similar to the replacement method described above under the discussion of indirect values; the point is to find a replacement of value, like where water filtration of wetlands was valued by finding out how much it costs to filter water through human-made technologies. However, contingent valuation goes further, often searching out less directly associated means of valuation. For example, if one is trying to find out the existence value of the California sea otter (an endangered species), one might look at how much people spend to vacation in a California coastal town (flight, lodging, meals, rentals, etc.), and then try and determine what percentage of their decision to vacation was based on seeing the California sea otter in the wild. Armed with this information, a likely value within a range might be possible for determining how much certain persons might value a California sea otter's existence, or similar environmental values that do not have direct market valuations (Field and Field 2006, 151–54).

A slightly different way to do contingent evaluation is through a survey asking people what they are willing to pay to protect the existence of some resource. For example, a survey might ask people if they are in favor of protecting a natural area. If protection requires paying more for the cost of energy (say because protection of the area means less coal can be extracted), then the survey might ask just how much people are willing to pay extra in their energy costs. If the survey has a large enough set of responses, some monetary amount can be calculated to show nonuse values for the resource are being considered. Of course, as indicated by the Grand Canyon example, people and groups can find different forms of nonuse value in the same resource. The accuracy of the value depicted is dependent on whether the survey is taken by a wide swath of different people representing the different kinds of nonuse values that can be attached to the resource (Field and Field 2006, 155–56). Sometimes people or groups with strong nonuse values are missed in these surveys, and that can have some impact on the final determination of value.

Collectively, direct, indirect, and nonuse values help to make up some form of *total valuation* of a natural resource. However this final value is determined (and the methodology used to derive this value is critical!), it must then be placed into a framework for making an informed decision about how to interact with the resource—what kind of decisions to make about environmental impacts in light of this information. We now turn to an examination of benefit–cost analysis, a powerful tool often used in economics to judge between different possible alternative choices. This kind of framework is similar to the way decisions are often made in an environmental framework. After describing the process and applying it to environmental decisions, there will be a summary tying together the major points expressed in this chapter; we now turn to an examination of benefit–cost analysis.

Benefit–Cost Analysis

Benefit–cost analysis (BCA) is a technique used in economics to help guide decision-making. The essential idea behind the approach is to compare the total expected benefits of an action against the total expected costs to see if the proposal is worth doing. The action can be either proposed (BCA occurs before the action) or already undertaken (BCA is used as an evaluative tool of the action) (Anderson 2010, 18–20). A representation of BCA is shown in Figure 3.5.

An action or activity is generally considered worth doing when the expected benefits are shown to exceed the expected costs. The process of engaging in a BCA not only allows for an assessment of the overall merits of engaging in a particular

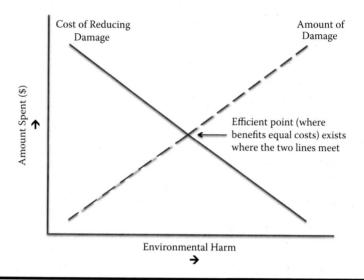

Figure 3.5   Representation of benefit–cost analysis.

action, but also identifies a variety of alternatives to the proposed action (Anderson 2010, 18–32). Alternatives to the proposed action are determined during the process of identifying the proposed benefits and costs of the action; for example, a number of expected costs identified may be mitigated under an alternatives analysis to make the proposal a net benefit. The removal of certain costs tends to change the characteristics of the proposal, making the new proposal an alternative from the original proposed action.

Benefit–cost analysis uses monetary units to express its evaluation of an action, meaning it reduces benefits and costs to monetary units so they can be compared to one another. Sometimes it is hard to compare, for example, the benefits and costs of a new manufacturing plant to the environmental and social impacts that might occur as a result of building and operating the plant. While the economic benefits of the plant can be easily monetized because they are already defined in monetary units, other benefits cannot immediately be monetized: social integration of the community, the impacts of increased employment on family wellness, etc. In addition, most costs that are not immediately economic in nature, including many environmental costs, are difficult to classify in monetary terms. BCA creates a framework by which all variables under consideration are reduced to monetary terms; this way the comparison is dollars to dollars.

The conceptual process of BCA is pretty straightforward. On one side of a sheet of paper, benefits of a proposed action are calculated and added up. Costs are calculated and added on the other side of the paper. One of three mathematical signs is placed in between the two sums; an = sign if the benefits and costs are equal, a > sign if the benefits (on the left in this example) outweigh the costs, and a < sign where the costs outweigh the benefits. Of course, the process is not entirely this easy, as deriving the benefits and costs to be evaluated can be complicated and subject to interpretation. Consider that the discussion of the *total valuation technique* above provides an accounting system for determining all values associated with natural resources: direct, indirect, and nonuse values. These valuations can form the basis of a BCA, where the values derived can be placed in either the benefit or cost category of the analysis, depending on what proposal is being considered, and how the person engaging in the BCA (the analyst) determines which value is a benefit and which is a cost. As we will see, just how benefits and costs are chosen depends largely on the methodology employed by the analyst.

There are a variety of factors that can be used to include the final determination of benefits versus costs. One of the most influential factors is the use of a *discount rate* in the analysis. Discount rates help us understand that by applying capital to one thing, it is no longer available to be used for a different thing. In benefit–cost analysis, discount rates make a difference because they can lead to countervailing conclusions about the overall net benefits of a proposed project (Anderson 2010, 100–16). Where a discount rate is close to zero, then the actual monetary units presented should be used to calculate benefits and costs. Where the discount rate moves away from zero in a positive direction (is higher than 0), the overall benefit of a proposed project is changed; the higher the discount rate, the larger the net benefit needs to be in order for the project to be viable. A discount rate is a difficult concept, and we do not spend significant time on the concept in this text. It is enough to know it exists, and it impacts the overall analysis of BCA depending on the extent of the discount applied to the analysis.

Beyond some of the difficulties provided in BCA due to valuation techniques (discussed earlier), and the issue of discounting, which is particularly prevalent in environmental issues, BCA has been shown to provide a rough calculation of the relative merits of an environmental action (Anderson 2010, 18–20). One area where BCA has been used extensively in environmental decisions in the United States has been in the implementation of the National Environmental Policy Act (NEPA), a federal statute passed in 1970. A quick explanation of NEPA follows along with application of BCA principles to NEPA-related issues.

In 1970, the National Environmental Policy Act was passed by Congress and signed into law by President Richard Nixon. The purpose of NEPA is to ensure that all major federal actions that have the potential to significantly impact the environment are reviewed prior to the taking of action. The environmental review conducted is to determine if the proposed action would significantly impact the environment (Caldwell 1998, 23–72). If there is the potential for a significant impact, the review must conduct an alternatives analysis, which must include a "no action" alternative (meaning the proposed project is scrapped).

The preferred method by which an environmental review is conducted is through benefit–cost analysis (BCA). Experts are hired in the various disciplines necessary to review potential environmental impacts and they submit their reports, which contain detailed findings of any potential environmental impacts. These impacts are then aggregated to determine an overall environmental impact. While actual monetary values are not required under NEPA, they are often used to give some indication of the costs in light of the value estimated from the proposed project (Caldwell 1998, 48–72). This is especially true when the alternatives analysis is discussed, explaining in detail how different alternatives can be used to mitigate the impacts of identified environmental harms and how these alternatives will change the perceived costs and benefits of a proposed project.

NEPA is a statute that focuses on understanding potential environmental impacts of a proposed action; it is very similar to the kinds of goals and questions asked in environmental decision-making: What are the environmental impacts of this project? Are there alternatives? What are the costs and benefits associated with different choices among the alternatives? BCA is the framework by which these questions get answered. Of course, sometimes the questions and answers cannot be framed in monetary terms; sometimes the question is one of how to do the least amount of harm, rather than focusing on the assessment of a proposed direction. The other variants of analysis that can be applied, however, include the same kinds of principles and accounting techniques described in this section. One seeking additional insights on different methods of decision-making outside BCA should consult environmental economics texts for further examples. A few of these texts are provided in the notes section of this text.

BCA is not a perfect framework for analyzing environmental questions, and it certainly has its shortcomings. As indicated above, determining values for environmental goods (at least those outside of market-based valuation systems) can be difficult. If one cannot determine an appropriate value, then can we say BCA is an accurate way of measuring the environmental merits of a proposed activity? Direct values have a proven market system that incorporates a vast amount of purchases and sales to identify an accurate spot price for the natural resource being traded. Add up all of these transactions, and they can count in the millions to billions. With that great number of transactions to review, one can be relatively assured the value being given to the commodity is a close approximation of the actual value (as it is being expressed in direct value terms).

There is no such sample size for indirect valuations of natural resources. The value actually given to the natural resource will depend on the techniques for valuation employed, as well as the skill of the individual actually doing the valuation. There can be wide fluctuations in actual valuations determined, especially depending on the methodologies used. Consider the example of a wetland's indirect value as a water filtration mechanism, which was discussed earlier in this section. It was said that wetlands naturally filter water, and this function often is carried out artificially (by humans) when wetlands are removed from the natural system. A more accurate statement is lands that abut water bodies used for human consumption can act as an important buffer of the water resource; the buffers can certainly include wetlands that help to filter water, but also the near-shore uplands that help to create a barrier between the water resource and human activities. Trees, shrubs, and grass all help to hold the soils in place, and also help to absorb any runoff from nearby roads and other human developments. If this buffer did not exist, it would be easier for pollutants to reach the water resource through pathways like runoff (especially if a road is built adjacent to the water).

The natural flora help to ensure the integrity of the water in a variety of ways; the question is how much is this buffering worth? The answer is not so simple. If the buffer lands exist near a large reservoir that serves as the major drinking water supply of a large city, then the indirect value of the land as a buffer is likely a large sum per unit of land (because it serves a large population) (Korhnak and Vince 2005, 184–85). If the land is near a natural water source feeding groundwater that is then used by a small rural population through individual wells, then the value may be less; the land is not protecting solely potable water, and the groundwater goes through sediments that also act as filters (as well as individual filters that may be purchased by each homeowner).

Not only does the proximity to drinking water and size of the population served matter, but also considering what process will replace the filtering functions of the land is equally important. If a municipality is looking to build a large water treatment plant as an alternative to the natural land buffer, then that cost can be considered part of the indirect use value. However, if the governing body might simply require individual filters for each household (like in our well water scenario), then the indirect value of the buffering land will likely be lower. The point is that indirect values can vary; not all of the same natural resources will yield the same indirect values. The land per unit area in the Amazon Rainforest probably holds a lot more biosphere value per unit area than does the same unit area located in a desert climate (although this should not simply be presumed in every case).

Nonuse values are even harder to determine with accuracy across resources than indirect values. The unique nature of many nonuse values has already been identified previously in this chapter. The Grand Canyon contains a variety of aesthetic, cultural, and spiritual values; the extent of those values varies from person to person, culture to culture. Native Americans might find great spiritual value in an otherwise unremarkable piece of land. An old homestead can have great historical importance. The tools used to decipher these values are dependent on the person conducting the analysis, and the choices made by that person in coming to a final determination of value need to be closely scrutinized to understand the limits placed on that valuation.

For the reasons set forth above, benefit–cost analysis (BCA) is an imperfect measure for evaluating a proposed environmental action based on a total value approach. It is not that BCA lacks sufficient rigor, but rather, obtaining accurate value amounts of environmental resources is imperfect. This leads to the application of these values in a BCA analysis also being imperfect. Still, BCA is a foundational method any environmental decision-maker will observe being used again and again in the environmental management context. Having an awareness of how it operates is an important part of understanding how environmental decisions are made.

Conclusion

The purpose of this section has been to cover basic economic theory as applied to environmental decisions. Economics is an important consideration in environmental decisions because it helps us determine how our valuation of natural resources impacts the decisions we make about those resources; this is why economics is covered as a subject in this text.

In this section, we reviewed two major categories of economics relevant to environmental decision-making: natural resource economics and ecological economics. We also reviewed the role of three important concepts in economics and how they apply to environmental decisions: discounting, substitution, and trade-offs.

Natural resource economics helped us understand how environmental goods are viewed from an extractive standpoint and how markets aid us in determining a fair market value for environmental goods. Ecological economics showed us how environmental goods, viewed from a systems standpoint, can have more than an extractive value; coinciding with our discussion of the earth system in Chapter 2, we identified additional values that include regulating and cultural services provided by the environment.

The economic concepts of discounting, substitution, and trade-offs were explained because they are important factors to consider when understanding the impacts of decisions on environmental resources. Often, we can discount certain values associated with natural resources. The question of substitution is important when understanding alternatives analysis in environmental decision-making. Trade-offs are inherent in any kind of environmental decisions; something is always being given up in order for something to be gained elsewhere.

In the *defining value* section, we attempted to link the interactions between the natural environment and humans. To do this, we reviewed the macro-economic indicators that are often used as measurements of human well-being and happiness. These included the traditional measurement of gross domestic product (GDP), and the more nontraditional methods of gross national happiness (GNH) and genuine progress indicator (GPI).

GDP, the traditional measure, was defined as all of the goods and services generated by a governmental unit (country) within a given timeframe (generally 1 year). The main critique of GDP from an environmental standpoint is that it fails to differentiate between economic activities that contain environmental harms. In so doing, human well-being and progress can be assumed to be occurring in instances where GDP shows positive gains, even when those gains include economic activity that harms the natural environment, including the resilience of the natural system.

GNH and GPI were offered as alternative ways of measuring human well-being, with GNH focusing on socially orientated goals of happiness, and GPI being like GDP in measurement but differentiating between economic activities that harm the environment and economic activities that do not. Suggestions were made for the reader to sense when a different model of value definition in economics might be warranted based on environmental considerations. Also, GDP was linked more closely with natural resource economics as a discipline, while GPI was linked more closely with ecological economics.

This section also discussed the *total valuation technique* as a way to express the several categories of values contained in natural resources. Total valuation was expressed by the equation Tv = Dv + Iv + Nuv, or total value = direct value + indirect value + nonuse value. Direct values are those values that relate to the provisioning services found in natural resources, generally those kinds of values of natural resources represented in markets such as the commodities oil and corn. Indirect values are those values that relate to the regulating services provided by and between natural resources; examples include the filtering capacity of wetlands and the storm surge protection offered by barrier islands. Nonuse values are based on the cultural services one finds in natural resources; these can include personal aesthetics from an unobstructed view of nature, to religious and cultural relationships with certain natural resource areas. The goal of obtaining a total value for the natural resource is to aid in balancing the interests between human activities and environmental harm. When the true value of a resource is known, a more informed decision can be obtained during this balancing of interests.

Benefit–cost analysis (BCA) is the final subject discussed. BCA is the major analytical tool used in economics to make informed decisions about the relative benefits and costs associated with an action. Since most environmental decisions occur during the planning stages of human activities, BCA is an oft-used analytical framework in the environmental management world. BCA can be a powerful and insightful tool, but its overall function is dependent on the accuracy in which costs and benefits are determined. The assumptions and techniques used in identifying values in the total valuation approach were identified as a possible problem when using BCA in the context of environmental decisions. Special care must be taken to ensure that the methodology of analysis being employed is capturing a reasonable interpretation of value; this includes some close scrutiny on any discount rates being used in the analysis of valuation.

Overall, economics is a foundational accounting system that provides a "language" in which we "speak" our justification for making informed decisions. It is a powerful tool that can offer important insights into environmental decisions, but it must be used in the right context. We have identified a variety of issues with traditional economic theory as it relates to valuing environmental resources. These critiques have noted alternative ways of viewing values associated with our natural resources, and these techniques should be understood so that they can be used when necessary in properly evaluating the merits of any action that impacts our environment. In conjunction with the other two sections of this text, economics offers a promising set of tools and analytical frameworks that offer hope in the future of our environmental decision-making capacity.

References

Anderson, David A. 2010. *Environmental Economics and Natural Resource Management*, 3rd ed. New York: Routledge.

Asafu-Adjaye, John. 2005. *Environmental Economics for Non-Economists: Techniques and Policies for Sustainable Development*, 2nd ed. Singapore: World Scientific Publishing Co.

Baumol, William J., and Alan S. Blinder. 2011. *Economics: Principles and Policy*, 12th ed. Mason, OH: South-Western, Cengage Learning.

Beardsley, Monroe. 2005. Intrinsic Value. In *Recent Work on Intrinsic Value*, edited by Toni Ronnow-Rasmussen and Michael J. Zimmerman. Dordrecht: Springer.

Bell, Simon, and Stephen Morse. 2008. *Sustainability Indicators: Measuring the Immeasurable*. Sterling: Earthscan.

Binkley, Dan, and Oleg Menyalio. 2005. Gaining Insights on the Effects of Tree Species on Soils. In *Tree Species Effects on Soils: Implications for Global Change*, edited by Dan Binkley and Oleg Menyalio. Dordrecht: Springer.

Bowersox, Jow. 2002. Sustainability and Environmental Justice: A Necessary Connection. In *The Moral Austerity of Environmental Decision-Making: Sustainability, Democracy, and Normative Argument in Policy and Law*. Durham, NC: Duke University Press.

Bradfield, James. 2007. *Introduction to the Economics of Financial Markets*. New York: Oxford University Press.

Brealey, Richard A., and Stewart C. Myers. 2003. *Financing and Risk Management*. New York: McGraw-Hill.

Burt, Ronald S. 1993. The Social Structure of Competition. In *Explorations in Economic Sociology*, edited by Richard Swedberg. New York: The Russel Safe Foundation.

Caldwell, Lynton Keith. 1998. *The National Environmental Policy Act: An Agenda for the Future*. Bloomington: Indiana University Press.

Camerer, Colin. 2008. The Case for Mindful Economics. In *The Foundation of Positive and Normative Economics: A Hand Book*, edited by Andrew Caplin and Andrew Schotter. New York: Oxford University Press.

Casper, Julie Kerr. 2010. *Fossil Fuels and Pollution: The Future of Air Quality*. New York: Facts on File.

Chapin III, F. Stuart. 2009. Managing Ecosystems Sustainably: The Key Role of Resilience. In *Principles of Ecosystem Stewardship: Resilience-Based Natural Resource Management in a Changing World*, edited by F. Stuart Chapin III, Gary P. Kofinas, and Carl Folke, 41. New York: Springer.

Chhetri, Arjun B., and M. Rafiqul Islam. 2008. *Inherently-Sustainable Technology Development*. New York: Nova Science Publishers.

Chiras, Daniel D. 2009. *Environmental Science*, 8th ed. Sudbury, MA: Jones and Bartlett Publishers.

Common, Michael, and Sigrid Stagl. 2005. *Ecological Economics: An Introduction*. New York: Cambridge University Press.

Conrad, Jon M. 2010. *Resource Economics*, 2nd ed. New York: Cambridge University Press.

Crawford, Donald W. 2004. Scenery and the Aesthetics of Nature. In *The Aesthetics of Natural Environments*, edited by Allen Carlson and Arnold Berleant. Mississauga, ON: Broadview Press.

Cronk, Julie K., and M. Siobhan Fennessy. 2001. *Wetland Plants: Biology and Ecology*. Boca Raton, FL: CRC Press.

Daly, Herman E., and Joshua Farley. 2011. *Ecological Economics: Principles and Applications*, 2nd ed. Washington, DC: Island Press.

Ehlers, Eckart, and Thomas Frafft. 2001. Understanding the Earth System—From Global Change Research to Earth System Science. In *Understanding the Earth System: Compartments, Processes and Interactions*, edited by Eckhart Ehlers and Thomas Frafft. Heidelberg: Springer.

Ehrlich, Paul. 1997. *The Population Bomb*. Cutchogue, NY: Buccaneer Books.

Erickson, Steven L., and Brian J. King. 1999. *Fundamental of Environmental Management*. New York: Wiley.

Field, Barry C., and Martha K. Field. 2006. *Environmental Economics: An Introduction*, 4th ed. New York: McGraw-Hill.

Folbre, Nancy. 2010. *Greed, Lust and Gender: A History of Economic Ideas*. New York: Oxford University Press.

Friedman, Milton. 1953. *Essays in Positive Economics*. Chicago: Chicago University Press.

Gerston, Larry N. 2010. *Public Policy Making: Process and Principles*. Armonk, NY: M.E. Sharpe.

Granovetter, Mark. 1993. The Nature of Economic Relationships. In *Explorations in Economic Sociology*, edited by Richard Swedberg. New York: The Russel Safe Foundation.

Grant, Susan, and Chris Vidler. 2000. *Economics in Context*. Oxford: Heinemann Educational Publishers.

Hardin, Garrett. 1991. Paramount Positions in Ecological Economics. In *Ecological Economics: The Science and Management of Sustainability*, edited by Robert Costanza and Lisa Wainger. New York: Columbia University Press.

Hassan, Rashid M., Robert Scholes, and Neville Ash. 2005. *Condition and Trends Working Group, Millennium Ecosystem Assessment*, Vol. I. Washington, DC: Island Press.

House, Silas, and Jason Howard. 2009. *Something's Rising: Appalachians Fighting Mountaintop Removal*. Lexington: University Press of Kentucky.

Intergovernmental Panel on Climate Change. 2007. IPCC Fourth Assessment Report: Climate Change 2007 (AR4). http://www.ipcc.ch/publications_and_data/publications_and_data_reports.shtml (accessed September 23, 2011).

International Institute of Management. 2006. The American Pursuit of Unhappiness: Gross National Happiness (GNH)—A New Economic Matrix. http://www.iim-edu.org/grossnationalhappiness/ (accessed September 24, 2011).

Jenkins, T.N. 2005. Socio-Cultural Dimensions of Ecological Economics and Sustainable Rural Development. In *Dimensions of Environmental and Ecological Economics*, edited by Nirmal Chandra Sahu and Amita Kumari Choudhury. Hyderabad: Universities Press (India) Private Limited.

Jha, A.R. 2010. *Solar Cell Technology and Applications*. Boca Raton, FL: Auerbach Publications.

Johnson, Barry Lee. 2007. *Environmental Policy and Public Health*. Boca Raton, FL: CRC Press.

Keohane, Nathaniel O., and Shelia M. Olmstead. 2007. *Markets and the Environment*. Washington, DC: Island Press.

Kopp, Raymond J., and Vincent Kerry Smith. 1993. Understanding Damages to Natural Assets. In *Valuing Natural Assets: The Economics of Natural Resource Damage Assessment*, edited by Raymond J. Kopp and Vincent Kerry Smith. Washington, DC: Resources for the Future.

Korhnak, Larry V., and Susan W. Vince. 2005. Managing Hydrological Impacts of Urbanization. In *Forests at the Wildland-Urban Interface: Conservation and Management*, edited by Susan W. Vince, Mary L. Duryea, Edward A. Macie, and L. Annie Hermansen. Boca Raton, FL: CRC Press.

Lawn, Phillip A., and Matthew Clarke. 2006. *Measuring Genuine Progress: An Application of the Genuine Progress Indicator.* Melbourne: Nova Science Publishers.

LePage, Ben A. 2011. Wetlands: A Multidisciplinary Perspective. In *Wetlands: Integrating Multidisciplinary Concepts,* edited by Ben A. LePage. New York: Springer.

Liu, Paul. 2005. *Energy, Technology, and the Environment.* New York: ASME.

Lorenz, Klaus, and Rattan Lal. 2010. *Carbon Sequestration in Forest Ecosystems.* New York: Springer.

National Research Council. 1996. *River Resource Management in the Grand Canyon.* Washington, DC: National Academy of Sciences.

Norton, Bryan G. 1991. Ecological Health and Sustainable Resource Management. In *Ecological Economics: The Science and Management of Sustainability,* edited by Robert Costanza and Lisa Wainger. New York: Columbia University Press.

Organization for Economic Cooperation and Development. 2010. Making Reform Happen: Lessons from OECD Countries. http://www.oecd.org/publishing/corrigenda (accessed September 24, 2011).

Parker, P. 2002. The Potential for Integrated Assessment and Modeling to Solve Environmental Problems: Vision, Capacity, and Direction. In *Understanding and Solving Environmental Problems in the 21st Century: Toward a New, Integrated Hard Problem Science,* edited by Robert Costanza and Sven Erik Jorgensen. Oxford: Elsevier Ltd.

Reible, Danny D. 1999. *Fundamentals of Environmental Engineering.* Boca Raton, FL: CRC Press.

Riello, Giorgio, and Prasannan Parthasarathi. 2009. *The Spinning World: A Global History of Cotton Textiles, 1200–1850.* New York: Oxford University Press.

Schaeffer, Peter V. 2008. *Commodity Modeling and Pricing: Methods for Analyzing Resource Market Behavior.* Hoboken, NJ: Wiley.

Seager, T.P., S.H. Rogers, K.H. Gardner, I. Linkov, and R. Howarth. 2006. Coupling Public Participation and Expert Judgment for Assessment of Innovative Contaminated Sediment Technologies. In *Environmental Security and Environmental Management: The Role of Risk Management,* edited by Benoit Morel and Igor Linkov. Dordrecht: Springer.

Simon, Julian Lincoln. 1996. *The Ultimate Resource 2.* Princeton: Princeton University Press.

Smith, Adam. 1904. *An Inquiry into the Nature and Causes of the Wealth of Nations.* London: Methuen & Co.

Smith, Charles, W. 1993. Auctions: From Walras to the Real World. In *Explorations in Economic Sociology,* edited by Richard Swedberg. New York: The Russel Safe Foundation.

Soule, David C. 2006. Defining and Managing Sprawl. In *Urban Sprawl: A Comprehensive Reference Guide,* edited by David C. Soule. Westport, CT: Greenwood Press.

Stern, Nicholas. 2008. *The Economics of Climate Change: The Stern Review.* New York: Cambridge University Press.

Taylor, John B., and Akila Weerapana. 2009. *Economics,* 6th ed. Boston: Houghton Mifflin Company.

Tietenberg, Thomas H., and Lynne Lewis. 2010. *Environmental Economics and Policy,* 6th ed. New York: Pearson.

Wheeler, Graeme. 2004. *Sound Practice in Government Debt Management.* Washington, DC: The World Bank.

White, I.D., D.N. Mottershead, and S.J. Harrison. 1992. *Environmental Systems: An Introductory Text,* 2nd ed. Cheltenham: Stanley Thornes.

Wilson, Matthew, and Shuang Liu. 2008. Non-Market Value of Ecosystem Services Provided by Coastal and Nearshore Marine Systems. In *Ecological Economics of the Oceans and Coasts*, edited by Murray Patterson and Bruce Glavovic. Cheltenham, UK: Edward Elgar Publishing Limited.

Yeomans, Matthew. 2004. *Oil: A Concise Guide to the Most Important Product on Earth.* New York: The New Press.

Chapter 4

Values of Environmental Decision-Making

Introduction

Values are about choices. When we freely make a choice about something, we are showing a preference. The preference exhibits itself through action. Actions reflect our choices. In environmental decisions, values are embedded in the decision-making process itself; we can discern values by looking at the decision as the physical manifestation of value choices. Many times these choices reflect compromises between competing values, and this is especially true in a democratic governance system, where values compete among individuals and groups to gain the attention of decision-makers (Perrin 1994).

In this chapter, we look at the term *value* mostly from the perspective of risk assessment (Suter 2007). While values certainly go beyond an immediate relationship to risk,* this chapter focuses on the process by which values are incorporated into environmental decisions (for example, policy decisions). Thus, for the reminder of this chapter, the question of values will be discussed using the proxy term *risk*; whenever you see the term *risk*, you should immediately correlate it to the underlying values (assumptions, etc.) that are being used to define risk. Values are part of assessing risk in this context, while perceptions of risk can aid in understanding values being applied to a particular environmental problem.

---

* See, for example, *The Deep Ecology Movement: An Introductory Anthology*, edited by Alan Drengson and Yuichi Inoue (Berkeley, CA: North Atlantic Books, 1995).

Most decisions centered around environmental questions focus on the question of risk (Crawford-Brown 1999). The goal of environmental management often is to find ways to limit risk for the benefit of human beings (Barrow 2006, 23–26). Of course, people can differ on what activities they believe are *risky*. Is risk defined solely by scientific assessment? If so, what do we do when science has not yet reached a consensus on the question or risk? Can risk be defined outside of an objective scientific basis? What if a community perceives the development of a wind farm nearby as a risk to their well-being—even where objective scientific analysis finds no significant risk?* Is this a valid form of risk? Should such community ideas be accepted as part of a risk assessment in environmental decisions?

Risk is important to consider because it is an *indicator* (measurement) to determine a level of harm, actual or perceived. For environmental issues, it helps to form the basis of decision-making.† A high-risk, perceived or actual, will result in a strong policy response. Consider nuclear reactors; one has not been built in the United States since the 1970s, when the Three Mile Island incident occurred (Walker 2004). Many other countries, including France and Canada, use nuclear power to supply much of their energy needs.‡ This must be some evidence that the overall probability of risk is low. However, there is a strong perception of risk that remains in the United States over the development of nuclear energy.§ So, it might be said that nuclear energy policy in the United States is being driven by a perception of risk rather than an objective assessment of risk. Knowing how risk is being defined and incorporated into environmental decisions is important for our overall understanding of how different kinds of values impact our overall assessment of risk. Sometimes those values are based on objective information, and sometimes they are based on more subjective perceptions of risk.

In this chapter, the subject of risk will be discussed from two major categorical perspectives. The first deals with a more objective means of quantifying risk, what might be referred to as the more scientific approach. The second will focus more on subjective bases for identifying and categorizing risk; the focus is more on emotional aspects of human interactions with risk, identified through worldviews and public perception. Our goal in this section is to better understand how a variety of elements go into the process of identifying and quantifying risk, and how these various elements impact overall environmental assessment and decision-making. We begin with an overview of objective forms of valuation.

---

* See Wendy Williams and Robert Whitcomb, *Cape Wind: Money, Celebrity, Class, Politics, and the Battle for Our Energy Future* (New York: Public Affairs, 2007).

† From a government perspective, risk is the main factor used in determining a policy response to an environmental issue.

‡ At the time of writing this book, France produces over 90% of its domestic electricity from nuclear power.

§ The 2011 tsunami in Japan, and the resultant damage to a nuclear facility in that country, helps us to understand that even a low probability of risk still provides a real risk.

Objective Values

When thinking about values (interpreting the term operationally through risk assessment), we can broadly decipher between *objective* forms of value and the more *subjective* forms of valuation (discussed in depth later in this section).

Objective forms of valuation in the environmental field rely on subfields of science, spanning from traditional use of the scientific method to more social science-related disciplines such as economics. The main idea behind objective valuation is the separation of personal bias—as much as possible—from the question of value (Suter 1998, 184). When we place objective valuation in the context of risk assessment, it generally takes the form of limiting an assessment of risk to objective facts, and the logical extension of those facts (usually through close reasoning). Broadly speaking, we tend to connect facts to our current state of knowledge about a particular thing and apply a specific methodology to this current state of knowledge in determining an overall *risk assessment*. For example, our current knowledge of thermodynamics can give us some measurement of the risks involved with nuclear power generation. The facts discerned from this knowledge become the basis by which we quantify a particular risk associated with the development and operation of nuclear power facilities (Walker 2004).

This section on objective values is broken down into two parts: *risk assessment* and *quantification methods*. In the risk assessment section, we look at how science is used to objectively identify potential risks. In the quantification methods section, we see how this information is then used to set a limit on the amount of risk we are willing to accept in a particular decision-making context.

Risk Assessment and the Role of Science

Broadly speaking, an objective view of risk draws a relationship between the *probability of harm* and the *magnitude of harm* (Ricci 2006, 36). This is represented in Figure 4.1.

The first thing we might notice about this figure is that there is an inverse relationship between the two lines; as the probability of harm increases, the magnitude of harm decreases. Conversely, when the probability of harm decreases, the magnitude of that harm increases. Economists might argue the efficient (or optimal) level of risk occurs where the probability of harm line intersects with the magnitude of harm line. Said another way, the most efficient outcome for evaluating risk is where the probability of harm and the magnitude of harm are equal. A few questions we might ask here is whether this relationship is always true, and whether the relationship makes sense? Let's deal with the second question first, whether the relationship makes sense in an ideal situation.

In looking at the figure, we can discern a major assumption implicit in the objective quantification of risk; the probability of harm is always set to correspond, inversely, to the known magnitude of harm. So, if we think the magnitude of harm

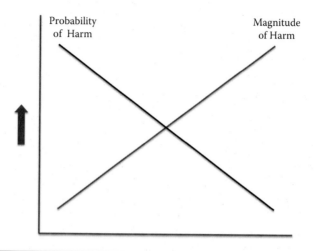

Figure 4.1 Relationship between probability of harm and magnitude of harm.

is really high, then we will only engage in that activity if the probability of that harm occurring is correspondingly very low. What exactly makes the probability of harm low? This is a good question that will be discussed in further detail within the quantification section below. For now, it is important to understand this basic assumption in the way objective forms of value are expressed. Consider the assumption that things with high magnitudes of harm will only occur infrequently; we can apply this assumption to an example and then change the assumptions to see what occurs.

Let us assume that the current state of science indicates the generation of nuclear power is safe using certain technologies and standards to limit the potential for exposure to nuclear radiation. Under this current state, nuclear power is deemed to have a high potential magnitude of harm, but a corresponding low probability of harm. Under these assumptions, government policy allows a number of nuclear facilities to be built and placed into operation. Now, at some point in the future, scientific information changes to suggest our initial impressions about the probability of harm were wrong (for whatever reason), but the magnitude of harm is still high. What does this mean in terms of our objective identification of risk? Well, for one thing, we should be able to see that even "objective" statements about risk can be wrong. Moreover, if they are wrong, then we must acknowledge that decisions have been made based on incorrect assumptions about risk, and we must likely be willing to change our decisions to match this new information.

Often, the extent of our objective knowledge is limited. This limit makes assumptions subject to being found invalid, or at least not as valid as once believed. This is the nature of objective information based on science; because of the incremental nature of science, our understanding of what is known or knowable changes with time. If this understanding includes assumptions about risk, then we must be willing to update our assumptions of risk at the same time we refine our scientific understanding of risk.

A second point to consider is how we should treat environmental issues that show, initially, a potential for a high magnitude of harm. As we can see, our limits of knowledge may alter our analysis regarding the probability of harm in a particular instance. (Over time, what we see as a low probability may change to a higher probability because of new evidence, better science, whatever.) However, we are (generally speaking) more likely to get the *magnitude* of harm correct (Ricci 2006, 36). Even if it is not correct, if we begin assuming a high magnitude of harm based on present evidence, and then the magnitude of harm is shown to be lower than expected because of new information, we really are not placing ourselves in greater danger by basing our policy decisions on the assumption of a high magnitude of harm.* Some argue such an approach (sometimes referred as a *precautionary approach*) is the appropriate kind of framework from which risk should be identified.†

A precautionary approach assumes information about the issue at hand is incomplete. Thus, ultimate policy directions should assume incomplete information and therefore be precautionary in application. For example, if we assume a particular activity might pose minimal probability of harm to the environment, the precautionary approach would suggest this assumption is based on incomplete information and may not be true. Thus, the decision-making process should leave room for this potential error in calculating probability of harm. This may be represented in a choice not to engage in the particular activity, or otherwise to limit the amount of engagement pending further information.

If we stop and think for a moment, the precautionary approach is really a value judgment that influences the way in which we view the assessment of risk from an objective standpoint. It alters our reliance on objective information because it assumes the objective information is incomplete; therefore, our actions need to account for this uncertainty in practice. The precautionary approach is of particular relevance to environmental decisions because of the dynamic nature of the environment itself. Of course, our need for precaution is limited if we simply assume the worst in most cases, or as hinted above, assuming the magnitude of harm is always high for almost any activity. However, making such assumptions may prove to limit or even prevent progress, especially when the assumption is ultimately proven

---

* There may be some costs associated with a faulty determination of a higher magnitude of harm than actually exists. These costs are usually present in the manner in which the higher magnitude is handled. For example, costs can occur from actions taken to prevent against the after-the-fact determined erroneous high magnitude of harm assumption. These costs may be found to be unnecessary to protect against human life, for instance, and thus resemble an overcapitalization. This can be of special concern when the costs are public funds and incurred by governments who must account for the expenditure from a political standpoint.
† See *Implementing the Precautionary Principle: Approaches from the Nordic Countries, The EU and USA*, ed. Nicholas de Sadeleer (London: Earthscan, 2007).

wrong. One hypothetical example to highlight this point is the use of wind turbines to generate electricity.

Although we have been engaged in wind power generation for centuries, the magnitude and scale of wind power generation that has been proposed in recent years is unprecedented (Tong 2010). Technologies for power generation using wind are rapidly advancing, which means some of the newer advancements are unproven (Tong 2010, 33–42). Applying precaution to the development of wind power, policy makers might go with a default assumption that the magnitude of harm is high (or at least higher than any current information suggests). In doing so, the public may be protected against unknown dangers associated with wind turbines. So, rather than permitting the development of the turbines, the government denies them (or otherwise limits them in scope). Let us now consider the alternative ways of producing electricity now that we have ruled out wind because of unproven technology and unknown potential for harm.

Since advanced societies need power, we must look to an alternative to wind for power generation because we have ruled out wind due to the perceived risk of an unproven technology, and are taking a precautionary approach as a result of this perceived risk. The alternative is to remain with the status quo, which in the United States, for example, consists primarily of coal as the source of electricity production (Miller and Spoolman 2010, 305–6). We might ask ourselves whether the precautionary approach was appropriate in limiting the development of wind, whether the magnitude of harm was actually capable of being as high as assumed. The use of precaution has relevance here because the current status quo alternative (coal in the case of the United States) carries its own risks. The point here is that while science may be limited in the sense that information is rarely complete on any subject, there are other factors besides incomplete information that arise when making an objective assessment of environmental risk. These other factors become important considerations themselves when they are placed in the context of the particular issue being decided. It may be true that wind technology is unproven (especially newer forms of the technology), but does that fact alone suggest the current known risks of using coal as an energy source automatically outweigh the unknown of wind energy production?

Beyond providing information about magnitude and probability of harm, science offers additional insights when making objective decisions about risk. For example, science can help determine when new information is incapable of helping alter a current assessment of risk. Consider the situation where science helps in understanding (quantifying) the level of danger associated with a particular substance, radioactive uranium, for instance. We know radioactive uranium poses a significant health risk to humans (Cooper, Randle, and Sokhi 2003, 127–28). No matter what new information is provided by science about uranium, nothing will alter the fact that it is toxic to humans.

In this case, science offers an understanding that we have a *lack of choice* about some things; no matter how much we might want to, for whatever reasons, we can never choose for uranium to be harmless to humans. While this might sound obvious, the knowledge of what we cannot change (choices we cannot make) is incredibly useful when we consider making decisions based on risk assessment. Objective scientific evidence, while incomplete, can offer substantial insights by limiting the unknowns, one unknown being that we have a lack of choice when it comes to how harmful some things are to us.

Just as objective information can help us understand that we lack certain choices, the same kind of information can work in the opposite direction, making the unknown apparent, thereby giving us too many choices. Recall the discussion of the precautionary approach above; we move toward precaution in our decisions precisely because we lack complete understanding on the topics surrounding a particular choice. When objective information is lacking to help us create context, we sometimes have too many choices available, and thus fail to make a clear decision. In this way, the incomplete scientific information drives us away from a clear choice or set of choices.

An example often used about the use or nonuse of incomplete scientific information is our current societal stance toward climate change. There is certainly good evidence supporting the existence of climate change, but the evidence is incomplete (Intergovernmental Panel on Climate Change 2007). It is even more incomplete when we try to determine whether human activities are the sole factor in causing climate change. This is mainly due to the dynamic nature of the environment, and thus the inability to account for all the variables that might be impacting climate change within our current models.* The point here is that just as objective information can help to remove choice through a strong degree of certainty, it can also inhibit choice when there is a degree of uncertainty in the evidence presented.

This discussion on the use of objective information in assessing risk (making choices) is not trivial. Much of our decision-making processes in the public arena (and especially environmental issues) are driven by scientific information. Public environmental laws demand that decisions be made, in many cases, by *best available science*. But exactly *how* this information informs our decisions and how it relates to our determination of objective value are key elements in understanding environmental decision-making. The answer to this how question is explained in further detail in the next section, as we explore the manner in which objective information provides the foundation by which risk is quantified, forming the basis of decision-making.

---

* Note that a perfect experiment to account for various influences of climate change would require a control earth, meaning one would need a complete and accurate model of the earth that could be controlled (like in a laboratory). We could then compare what we see in our real earth with the control earth (controlling for things like fossil fuel burning), and then make a better assessment of causal relationships. Of course, we cannot re-create an entire earth, and thus we must rely on incomplete forms of experimentation, including computer models that will tend to lack *all* variables of the natural system.

Quantification Methods

There are two main categories of topics to discuss when we consider the quantification of risk and the methods used to quantify risk. Remember, this discussion is really about how objective information is used as a framework for making environmental decisions. The two main topic areas include developing a *set of priorities* for environmental decision-making, and the actual steps (process) taken in *risk assessment*. As a side note prior to discussing priority setting and risk assessment, it should be mentioned that we will be discussing subjective aspects of valuation in detail later in this chapter. Some subjective aspects of valuation (like what judgments go into setting priorities) will be touched upon in this section, but the reader should understand a more rigorous handling of subjective valuation will be reserved for the next section. Still, it is important to connect the information gleaned from this section with the more detailed treatment of subjective values discussed below. Environmental decisions are not made in a vacuum, and both objective and subjective measures of value are incorporated in the process of making value judgments. The two categories here are necessarily separated as a judgment of the author, so that we might understand the inner workings of the two categorical processes in valuation.

The first step we undertake here in understanding quantification methods of risk is to realize there are *standards* that exist to help us know what is a priority when engaging in a risk assessment process. It is crucial to know these standards are not defined by some enlightened source, but rather exist based on generally accepted principles in some cases, and social mores in other cases, which are themselves constantly changing.* So, what does this tell us about objective quantification methods in practice? Specifically, we must understand that while risk is objectively measured in many instances, the actual answer to "What is a risk?" can change based on changing attitudes and standards. Some call these standards *worldviews* (Layzer 2011). Now that we have placed the notion of standards into context, we can look at what generally falls into a normal priority list for risk assessment purposes.

Environmental risk assessment priorities generally follow something like this: priority 1, human health; priority 2, human well-being; priority 3, ecosystem

---

* It is important to recognize that generally accepted principles and social mores are both subject to change with time. Generally accepted principles are usually based on standards such as best available science. As noted elsewhere in this text, our acuity of scientific understanding is in constant flux, changing all the time. As such, what is a generally accepted principle today may be unacceptable tomorrow. For centuries, it was common practice in medicine to "bleed" individuals who showed particular symptoms, with the thinking being the bleeding helped to alleviate the symptom—some often caused by viruses. Obviously, this accepted practice is no longer considered valid today for the majority of ailments because we know the cause of the ailment is not related to bloodletting. The same can be said for social mores. Approximately 75 years ago, it was common acceptable practice for many parts of the United States to have a separation of citizens based on race. Obviously, this practice is no longer tolerated as acceptable in any shape or form by government or the populace.

well-being; and priority 4, aesthetic considerations (Suter 2007). We will review each priority in turn. As we review each priority, try and think about the assumptions that are being used in establishing this order. For example, do you think humans should be given greater priority when thinking about risk than any other species on the earth? Should ecosystem well-being be a lesser priority than human well-being? What if an argument can be made that healthy ecosystems are a necessary prerequisite to healthy humans?

This list of priorities is a general statement; it does not necessarily reflect the way in which priorities are set in every environmental decision. For example, the U.S. Endangered Species Act is a federal law that establishes a clear priority for the preservation and rehabilitation of threatened and endangered species, without consideration of their genetic proximity to humans.* The U.S. National Environmental Policy Act (NEPA) is another federal environmental law that arguably gives about equal weight to the environment as it does to human welfare and well-being. Actually, some would argue NEPA is an example of a law that properly identifies the importance of a healthy environment as a necessary prerequisite to human health and well-being. Thus, by focusing on the environment, NEPA simply ensures human activities are not counterproductive to human welfare (Caldwell 1998).

In our prioritization of risk, priority 1 focuses on human health (Crawford-Brown 1999). There are both historical and practical reasons for placing human health as the top priority in risk assessment standards. Historically, environmental laws in the United States developed as measures to prevent disease outbreaks in urban areas (mostly from the discharge of waste products into nearby alleyways and local watersheds) (Lazarus 2004, 43–67). Since early sanitation laws became the basis for later environmental laws, human health is at the heart of the early development of environmental regulations.

Later on, as human population increased along with scientific advancements, the environment's impact on human health extended beyond sanitary issues. While water pollution issues continued and expanded, air pollution, hazardous waste, and dangerous land uses all contributed to increasing the need for environmental protections. Even so, these protections were still primarily geared toward human health issues. While federal laws passed primarily in the 1970s have mitigated dangers related to human health, it remains a top consideration when thinking about prioritizing risk (Lazarus 2004, 43–67).

Priority 2, human well-being, is really an extension of human health without carrying the urgency associated with immediate health considerations. Said another way, if human health is about basic survival, then well-being is about quality of life. To place this in the perspective of establishing a risk threshold, one would want to establish a limit of risk under human health standards that prevents a swath

---

* For example, see *Endangered Species Act: Law, Policy, and Perspectives*, 2nd ed., edited by Donald C. Baur and William Robert Irvin (Chicago: American Bar Association, 2010).

of immediate hazards from death to seriously debilitating ailments; from a human health standpoint, the margin of acceptable risk is narrow.

For human well-being, the focus is more related to public welfare. Well-being can be distinguished from human health in looking at differences in two factors, context and intensity. For example, disease vectors might be a major indicator of public health concerns. Meanwhile, education, quality of life, and general happiness may all be indicators of well-being. Of course, the two are certainly related, as in the case where the well-being of those suffering from the plague in the Middle Ages was undoubtedly diminished because of the direct risks to human health the plague caused.

In environmental decisions, human health and human well-being are distinguished for priority purposes because actions can impact the one without necessarily impacting the other. For example, a nuclear power plant may pose unnecessary human health risks in an area that is geographically unstable and subject to earthquakes. The risk is to the immediate health of the public from nuclear radiation fallout. In focusing on human health as the priority in risk assessment, a choice might be to build a coal burning power plant instead of the nuclear power plant. The coal power plant might actually harm the well-being (quality of life) further than the nuclear plant because it will emit a variety of pollutants into the atmosphere, degrading the local air quality. However, the choice of a coal burning power plant is superior to the nuclear power plant from a risk assessment standpoint because the choice will protect human health over well-being; people will be assured of a livable area should an earthquake destroy the coal burning power plant, where the danger to human life is much greater with the destruction of a nuclear power plant.*

Priority 3 can be considered as ecosystem well-being. This concept is connected to the *total valuation technique* described in Chapter 2. Science has evolved to a point where the association between human well-being and human health is related to environmental health; a healthy environment supports healthy humans (Johnson 2007). This association is rooted in the discipline of ecology, which focuses on interactions between the physical environment and the species that inhabit that environment.

These ecosystem principles help us understand how the environment creates the necessary setting for sustaining human existence and prosperity. This is referred to elsewhere in this text as *indirect* or *provisioning service* values provided by the environment. It is through these connections that ecosystem well-being becomes a consideration for risk assessment. However, being a lower priority, we can see how objective decisions about risk can devalue this connection, focusing more on the immediate needs of human beings rather than taking a more holistic approach that fully internalizes the relationship between environmental health and human health. Concepts of sustainability often explicitly make this connection as a means

---

* This was seen directly in 2011 with the impact on livability of the Japanese earthquake.

of fostering value choices that are grounded in more long-term visions of human health. What is required to maintain a healthy human population over generations?*

The last stop in our rank order of priorities for establishing risk quantification is aesthetic considerations. Use of the term *aesthetics* here is meant to identify a general category where the risk is not to the immediate (or even remote) sustenance of the human species, but rather speaks more toward the aspects of life that make it more appealing. This includes such things as the maintenance of view sheds, areas that are considered naturally beautiful but might not be absolutely necessary for other functional purposes (Suter 2007, 542).

When all other risk factors have been considered in objective aspects of environmental analysis, the aesthetic questions become relevant as a potential tipping variable, potentially moving a questionable decision regarding risk in one direction or the other (Suter 2007, 542). An example one might consider is the impact of offshore wind farms on the view shed of a particular region. Some might argue that the location of a wind farm can impact tourism in an area because an unobstructed view is one of the values associated with choosing a particular location for vacationing purposes (and economically this value could be derived through indirect methods of what is spent on vacationing in the area and proposed loss of income from impacted views, etc.). Assuming a risk analysis to the proposed offshore wind farm was low in both human health and well-being categories, and low to moderate in ecosystem well-being, then a high risk value associated with aesthetics might sway the project far enough to be considered risky overall.†

Taken together, these categorical risk factors are important to our understanding of how risk is quantified, and further how this quantification relates to an objective assessment of valuation in environmental decisions. Let us now move on to the actual steps of a formal risk assessment exercise, so that we might better understand how these categorical factors are used to assess risk.

There are three main steps to a generalized risk assessment process: *hazard identification, dose-response assessment,* and *exposure assessment* (Suter 2007, 1–13). Once these three steps are completed there is a final output, the *risk characterization*

---

* The Brundtland Commission definition of sustainability in its 1987 report, entitled "Our Common Future." In the report, the commission defined sustainability, via development, as follows: "Sustainable development is development that meets the needs of the present without compromising the ability of future generations to meet their own needs."

† This depends largely on the weighting given to each of these risk factors. The rank order suggests human health would be given the highest weighting, while aesthetics would be given the lowest weighting. Still, a project that received an overall risk factor of 0.45 out of a 1.0 total risk (meaning it would be acceptable) might be driven to 0.55 with an aesthetic rating of risk at a weight of 0.10. The lesson here being that even a low-weighted risk category like aesthetics can still make a difference in an overall objective assessment process. This is telling, especially considering what can be defined as aesthetically positive or negative can easily fall into subjective considerations, showing us yet again the oft-blurred line between subjective and objective aspects of valuation.

(Smrchek and Zeeman 1998, 40–41). At each stage of the process, three main questions are attempted to be answered: (1) What is the *nature* of the risk? (2) What is the *likelihood* of the risk? (3) What is the *extent* of the risk? A visual representation of this risk assessment process, including the priority listing in environmental decisions, is shown in Figure 4.2.

At each stage of a risk assessment process, assumptions are made based on what is known, what is knowable, and what is unknown about the particular risk being quantified. As an example, we might determine a particular agent causes cancer in a certain animal (say a lab mouse)—this is what we know. However, we do not know whether the agent also causes cancer in humans—this is the unknown. It may be that we can determine whether the agent causes cancer in humans (the knowable), but we are unwilling to subject humans to a potentially deadly test for moral reasons.* Thus, for all intents and purposes, the effect of the agent in causing cancer in humans is unknown.

After an evaluation of what is known, unknown, and knowable, we can make a variety of choices about the risk. For example, we can take a precautionary approach and simply assume the agent causes cancer in humans by relating its cancer-causing qualities from the animal to humans (assuming a positive relationship in cancer-causing effectiveness). Or, we may make other assumptions based on additional analysis and considerations; we might decide to test other animals (primates) to determine if the cancer-causing qualities exist between species. Let us explore this question in a bit more detail using the three-step process identified above for characterizing this risk.

Let us refer to the cancer-causing agent described above as cancergen for simplicity purposes. Our job is to quantify the amount of risk posed by cancergen based on our priority listing identified earlier in this section (human health, human welfare, ecosystem welfare, and aesthetics). In the quantification process, our first step is already met, identifying the hazard. We know cancergen does cause cancer in certain species. However, we do not whether cancergen causes cancer in humans. Still, we are suspicious. The ability to put our suspicion to rest has limits; ethically we cannot engage in direct trials on humans. So, we may look to other methods for identifying a potential risk to humans. We do this through a dose-response assessment.

Dose-response assessment is similar to how organizations like the Food and Drug Administration (FDA) determine the relative safeness of proposed

---

* There are ample examples throughout human history where humans have been subjected to exposures that are known to impact human health. The Nazi testing done on concentration camp victims is a well-publicized example. The use of chemical weapons by Sadaam Hussein on Iraqi people is a more recent example. However, the U.S. government has a history of engaging in similar tests. A stark example is the purposeful placement of enlisted members in the U.S. Navy during nuclear weapon development. Navy ships full of sailors were placed near shore of nuclear test explosions, part of the reason being to determine the extent of exposure of radiation on military members.

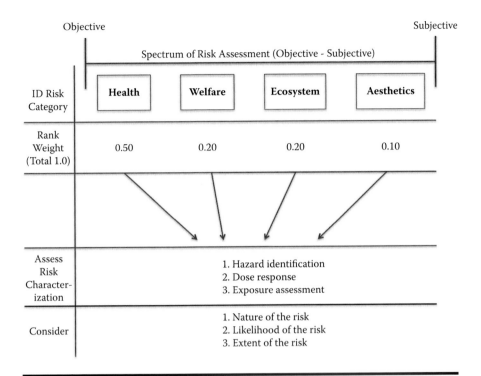

Figure 4.2   Visual representation of a risk assessment process.

pharmaceutical drugs (in conjunction with the testing of the drug manufacturers). In a dose-response, a surrogate for humans is chosen (usually lab mice but also sometimes chimpanzees and other apes due to similarities in genetic structure). The surrogates—many are used—are then given a variety of doses of the agent under study. The response to the doses is noted for any known risks (in our case development of cancer). The dose is then correlated to a particular response (Rodricks and Burke 1998, 234–37). The relationship identified in a dose-response may look something like that shown in Figure 4.3.

There are four types of responses that can be noted on the graph. The first is a *linear* response, where there is an equal response to the incremental increases in dose given. There is also a *threshold* response, which indicates the dose must pass a certain threshold before a response is noted. The third type of response is a *hermetic* response, where incremental small doses actually lessen the impact of the response, meaning small doses can actually be good for the test subject, until a certain threshold is reached where the response then tends to follow a linear relationship with the dose (Hammit 2007, 1697–703). The fourth and final type of response is an *exponential* response, where there is a doubling effect of response for every incremental increase in dose given; one unit of dose yields 2 units of response, 2 units of dose yields 4 units of response, and so on (Fazil 2005, 40–41).

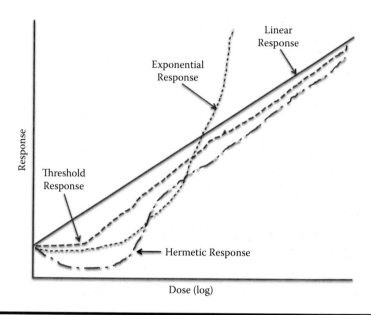

Figure 4.3 Examples of several dose-response curves.

An observed relationship of dose-response sets the stage for understanding *exposure assessment.* In this phase of analysis, the goal is to link the observed dose-response relationship done in experimental phases to larger questions of actual likelihood of experiencing certain doses in the real world (Fazil 2005, 5–6). This is where the objective analysis gets a bit tricky.

Consider how we might determine the *actual* likely dose in the environment (under natural conditions). We could focus empirically on the data itself, trying to determine what kind of exposure levels actually exist in the environment. However, in order to get a statistically significant set of data, there would have to be substantial data collection occurring on background rates of cancergen in the environment. In order to be thorough, we would also need to know in which areas the rates of cancergen might be higher, and whether cancergen has the capacity to accumulate in the environment to higher dose levels. We would then have to consider the ways in which cancergen might be transmitted in the environment. Is it diluted during transmission to human beings? If so, by what mechanisms? The point here is that getting actual data on the fate and effects of cancergen in the environment would be time-consuming, expensive, and difficult.

The alternative of determining an exposure assessment is to use a mathematical maximum exposure or a most at risk situation (Johnson 2007, 34–37). This ends up being a kind of worst-case scenario assessment based on probability analysis. It is not *based* on real data, but it is *informed* by real data (insofar as the laboratory testing represents real data). Whatever numbers are used, a final value is determined and this value becomes the basis for "drawing a line in the sand" when it comes to an acceptable exposure. Well, this is mostly true. In many cases, this number is tweaked a bit based on a further evaluation of what is known and unknown about the subject agent, in our case cancergen. If you recall, we know cancergen causes cancer, but we do not know whether it causes cancer specifically in humans.

At this point, we need to make a value judgment about how to set the maximum acceptable exposure rate to cancergen. For example, do we set the rate exactly at the number indicated in our final value determination, whether by actual data or mathematical calculation? Or, do we assume a cause-effect relationship between humans and cancergen, and because we do not know the precise relationship (because we did not test directly on humans), we assume a strong positive relationship and thus take a precautionary approach by setting the maximum exposure number lower than what our final value determination indicates? By setting the number lower, we are making a *value judgment* about how we want to approach risks that we do not fully understand. However, this is not the end of the story.

What if we decide to set the risk at a low rate, just above background levels of cancergen in the environment? We might choose this because we value human life and we do not want to take a risk in causing cancer by allowing high levels of cancergen in the environment (by whatever mechanisms we can control cancergen). But there are definite consequences to our actions here. For example, by setting the maximum amount of cancergen low, we have likely increased the costs associated with keeping exposure rates low. Simply put, less of the product is available for use.* If cancergen was widely used for economic activity and there is no readily available alternative, then the cost can be substantial in setting the maximum exposure rate so low (especially when we are not certain of its impact on humans).

We may choose to review the dose-response information obtained from our lab experiments in order to better inform our maximum exposure setting. What if the dose-response results show a hermetic response, meaning small doses actually showed a benefit to the test subject? What if this relationship also occurs in humans? Setting a low rate might be inappropriate because the data suggest little negative impact (assuming the relationship between the lab mouse and humans is positive), and the costs of limiting cancergen to this low amount will be high on society. Our conclusions might be the opposite where an exponential response is noted in the dose-response analysis. Recall that an exponential relationship suggests the response doubles for each incremental increase in exposure. So, where

---

* Our example here of cancergen has no immediate application. However, we can imagine instances where the agent is used for a variety of industrial and manufacturing purposes. One corollary in our industrial history might be asbestos. Asbestos was used expansively in both manufacturing and industrial applications, mostly because of its insulation and fire-retardant characteristics. It was only after its widespread use that asbestos was found to pose significant risks to humans (via the small particles that adhere and accumulate in lung tissue). Asbestos was ultimately deemed to pose a significant risk to human health, and it was banned for most applications.

an exponential relationship is shown, the choice may be to set a very low rate of cancergen (maybe background rates), and the costs would be justified by the potential harm to human health, our number one priority when setting risk standards.

Another consideration involves other factors identified above under risk assessment: human welfare, ecosystem welfare, and aesthetics. For our example agent, cancergen, the risk is directly related to human health, and also indirectly related to human welfare, as increased rates of cancer in a population can impact public health in a variety of ways.* We may wish to also consider the example of an agent in the environment that is not found to pose a significant risk to human health, but still impacts the other risk factors in some way; consider the building of a new landfill as an example.

A new landfill might have some probability of risk to human health, but generally this probability is very low, to make it almost nonexistent.† For our illustrative purposes, let us simply assume there is no significant risk to human health. However, the landfill can cause risks to human welfare (depending on how welfare is defined), ecosystem welfare, and certainly the aesthetics of an area (Petts 1998, 428–30). How might these risks be calculated? We would have to develop factors to analyze the risk of the landfill under the circumstances. So, what might those other factors be?

Categorically, we might begin identifying risk factors by understanding that the factors will likely break down into two general areas of risk: risks that can be described as more objective in nature, and risks that can be described as more subjective in nature.‡ For example, current surrounding land use patterns might be one basis for judging the risk of siting a landfill in a particular area. There can be both objective and subjective means for judging risk within this context. An objective basis might include a determination that a densely populated area with high proportions of residential use might be a factor that increases the risk associated with building a landfill in the area. The reasons might touch upon public health considerations that are more aligned with public welfare (smells emanating from

---

* Consider the costs associated with an increased rate of cancer among a human population. There are direct costs associated with treating the cancer (medical costs). However, there is also decreased productivity from days missed at work, as well as potential increases in social instability say, for example, from a parent who is no longer fully capable of handling social interactions within the family unit because of his or her medical condition. One could imagine other costs than those that have been identified here.

† Here we are not considering the inclusion of hazardous materials, but rather the more traditional landfill for nonhazardous waste.

‡ The difference between subjective and objective in this context can be difficult to discern. However, we can generally say that criteria that fall into a more objective description have the following characteristics: (1) there are established criteria; (2) the determination of whether or not the circumstances meet the criteria are based on a direct application of the facts to the established criteria; and (3) this process can be replicated to achieve the same results. Subjective forms of risk are those that do not meet the aforementioned criteria, especially the replicability prong described above.

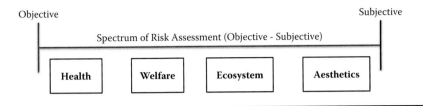

Figure 4.4 **A spectrum of risk assessment identifying objective to subjective measures.**

the landfill), while others are more economic (effect on property values). There may also be impacts on the local ecosystem, which can also be objective if supported by scientific evidence.* Subjective reasons for increasing risk might include the impact on aesthetic considerations of the area, often referred to as a locally undesirable land use (LULU) (Wallis 2008, 93).

As you may already be seeing, our movement away from immediate human health considerations changes the way in which risk is determined; a landfill for nonhazardous materials might pose some human health risk, but none more than other manufacturing and industrial operations that may also be occurring in a particular community. This change in how risk is determined is even more obvious as we move into lower-priority areas, such as ecosystem welfare and aesthetic considerations. One way of representing this general theme is shown in Figure 4.4.

When we consider the lower-priority risk factors, our analysis generally becomes less objective to a more subjective view of determining risk. As we move into a more subjective view of the world, our ability to find common ground on issues tends to decrease, from person to person and group to group (Zurawicki 2010). This means it is harder to come to a consensus on environmental issues when our criteria for judging the value of environmental questions become more subjective. This is probably the most important reason to differentiate between objective and subjective ways of determining value in environmental issues. We will now move into the section on subjective values to gain a better insight as to how our subjective nature impacts the way in which we value environmental issues—how we define risk, and how that definition influences our actions related to the environment.

Subjective Values

Subjective values make environment decisions less predictable, at least when compared to more objective forms of valuation. In the context of risk assessment,

---

* Some laws, like the federal National Environmental Policy Act (NEPA) in the United States, require an assessment of ecological impact of a proposed development such as a landfill where the action is federal in nature. Even where there is no federal action involved, many states have adopted similar environmental assessment statutes prior to permitting the development of projects like landfills.

objective measures of risk are generally based in a scientific type of methodology; chief among these characteristics is the ability to replicate the underlying information helping to formulate the opinion of risk. A clear example is the dose-response method used to determine the risk presented by a certain substance. This risk is generally defined in terms of human health standards; will exposure to a lot of this stuff result in human illness and even death? The risk can be measured by observing the dose-response relationship in a controlled environment. Also, this relationship can be replicated by employing the same methodology on different subjects, with the resultant risks being averaged out over multiple repetitions of the experiment. The resulting risk can then be correlated with the identified values at stake. If human health is considered an important value and the risk indicates a high potential for harm to human health, then the objective evidence demands action be taken.

Subjective risk determination is different in both process and outcome. Importantly, a subjective risk may be determined through measures that are not objective; one may not be capable of replicating the basis of risk that is determined through subjective measures. The reason why is that we tend to use different ways of determining risk with a subjective lens.* For example, I might have a worldview that is different from another person's worldview. I might have a more conservative slant to my beliefs, while someone else might hold a more liberal stance on similar issues. Our difference of opinions can impact the way we perceive an issue, and this is certainly true in the context of environmental issues.

It is interesting to consider how the subjective nature of personal views can inhibit an agreed upon foundation from which an issue can be rationally discussed, at least in relation to more objective means of quantifying a particular value judgment. Say we focus our attention on ecosystem welfare as the risk priority under consideration. A proposed action may post an impact to habitat of an endangered species. It has to be decided if the project should move forward. Person A might value human prosperity through economic development more than the welfare of a particular species, especially if that species is not of immediate known value to humans (say a salamander, for instance). Thus, person A is willing to discount the

---

* Judith Layzer outlines the influence of subjective risk assessment nicely in her book entitled *The Environmental Case: Translating Values into Policy.* Layzer indicates the following when describing how ordinary people perceive and identify risk: "Ordinary people do not assess risk based on objective analysis of statistical evidence; rather, they employ heuristics, or inferential rules" (p. 8). She goes on to explain how psychologists have, for example, identified an availability heuristic, where people will associate an event as low risk where the event is likely or frequent if instances of the event are easy to recall (say spilling insect repellant on the kitchen floor). These same people will tend to overestimate the risk of rare events that do not occur often, such as a train derailment or plane crash. This is an interesting insight into risk definition through the use of heuristics. If this relationship is true, then might effects of a warming climate (category 5 hurricanes, heat waves, etc.) become perceived as less risky over time as the occurrence of these events increases?

harm to the species, and place a higher value on the development. Person B may be the opposite, placing a high value on keeping the species alive, even though doing so might hinder the progress of human development. Person B is not willing to discount the value of the species like person A is, and therefore finds as much value (or more) in keeping the species alive than in the development of the project.

So how is it that person A and person B can come to opposite conclusions about the overall merits of the proposed project? The answer lies in the relative worldviews of each person, and how these views influence their individual values related to the question at hand. Person A might not identify value with the salamander, having a worldview that excludes this potential value. Person B might have a more expansive worldview, incorporating this expanded sense of value into his or her decision about the overall worthiness of the project.*

Now that we have some understanding of how worldviews can influence decisions on an individual level, let us expand our exploration by looking at the impact emotion has on subjective valuations (Zurawicki 2010, 99–103). When we talk of emotion in this context we are looking through a group setting, something we will refer to as public outrage, using the term in the context as explained by Peter Sandman (1993). This concept of risk that includes the subjective variable of community outrage will be explained in greater detail below.

It is important we distinguish between subjective forms of valuation that occur at different scales or levels of human dynamics (individual and group), which will be discussed in more detail below. However, we begin by understanding a generalized method for evaluating risk by adding the subjective context. In this process, risk is defined through what is known objectively (collectively termed hazard), and also including subjective sentiment of the individual or community (collectively termed outrage) (Sandman 1993, 34). We should take note of how the subjective components interact with the objective components of risk assessment, adding to our understanding of how environmental decisions are made, and maybe creating an initial complication of our understanding in the process.

Emotion and Public Outrage

Emotion is a subject unto itself, well discussed in the behavioral sciences.† Our usage of the term *emotion* here is to highlight perceptions of risk, specifically how risk is identified and quantified by humans when the assessment being made is not assisted solely by objective scientific-type information. As will be discussed in further detail below, we can view this emotional kind of risk assessment through various lenses of human perception, the largest distinction being between individual

---

* We will see how different values can be accounted for in the economic section of this text under the total valuation technique explained in that section.
† See, for example, *Emotions, Cognition, and Behavior*, edited by Carroll E. Izard, Jerome Kagan, and Robert B Zajonc (New York: Cambridge University Press, 1984).

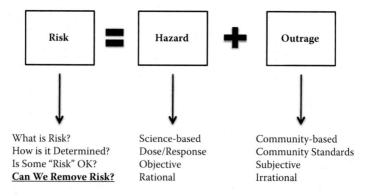

| Risk | = | Hazard | + | Outrage |

What is Risk?
How is it Determined?
Is Some "Risk" OK?
Can We Remove Risk?

Science-based
Dose/Response
Objective
Rational

Community-based
Community Standards
Subjective
Irrational

Figure 4.5   A representation of risk defined by hazard and outrage.

and group perceptions.* In addition, we will be viewing this emotional risk assessment through a particular lens that we will refer to as *public outrage*, borrowing a term from Sandman (1993). As will be discussed in more detail below, public outrage identifies the public perception of harm associated with a potential or known risk. Unlike objective risk (termed *hazard* by Sandman), public outrage is based largely on more subjective values, including, but not limited to, public perceptions, social norms, and biases.

One take-home message is the power of outrage in risk assessment generally, and environmental decisions particularly. In some cases, public outrage can even trump the value of objective scientific information, leading decision-makers to opt for policies that pander to public opinion, rather than follow the hard evidence that is presented. By the conclusion of this section, you should have a new appreciation of the power of perception in environmental decisions. You may ask yourself whether subjective values should play a significant role in such decisions, or whether objective evidence should be the sole means by which environmental decisions are made. To begin, we focus on the relationship identified by Sandman between objective information (hazard) and subjective information (outrage) in shaping environmental decisions.

Sandman develops an argument about how we perceive risk. According to Sandman: risk = hazard + outrage. A visual representation is shown in Figure 4.5.

Based on Sandman's definition, risk is not solely dependent on the actual likelihood of harm (hazard), but also on how the public perceives the harm. This is important because it highlights the role subjective considerations of risk play in decision-making. It is also important when we consider how risk is quantified

---

* There has been a good amount of research done on how group dynamics impact individual decision-making. Said another way, individuals sometimes act in ways they normally would not in the presence of a group. Peer pressure is probably one of the more commonly known terms that refers to this behavioral characteristic.

through outrage. Recall our discussion of the dose-response method of establishing an objective risk (termed hazard by Sandman). We ultimately know the quantification of risk in relation to the dose-response relationship. For instance, a small dose might make someone sick, while a larger dose (beyond a particular threshold) might kill the person. Under such cause-effect relationships it is pretty clear a risk exists, at least from a human health standpoint.*

It is less clear when we think of subjective forms of risk, particularly how to quantify outrage as a way of identifying and weighting risk. Relevant questions we might consider in this context of outrage include the following: How is outrage formulated? When does outrage culminate in sufficient public sentiment to equate to a high level of risk? Can public outrage ever outweigh objective forms of risk, meaning can an objective finding of little to no risk be overcome by a strong subjective finding of outrage? Can public outrage change direction over time, say from being relatively high at an earlier point, to diminishing toward nonexistence at a later point? If public outrage can change direction over time (unlike most objective forms of risk assessment), how does this impact decisions that are made based on outrage? These questions are important considerations in understanding the dynamics of risk. We will now try to answer some of these questions in the context of summary case examples. The goal is to see the interactions between objective and subjective factors in risk assessment, and when subjective factors might outinfluence more objective factors.

Public outrage can be formulated and communicated in a variety of ways, chief among them being a strong public sentiment that is reinforced through media and other means of communication. Essential in understanding how subjective outrage can formulate perceptions of risk is understanding the underlying components of risk communication (Sandman 1993). There are a variety of ways risk communication has been described, including the following questions to highlight the manner in which risk is being communicated (Sandman 1993, 11):

- Is the risk familiar or exotic?
- Is the risk voluntary or coerced?
- Is the risk controlled by the person identifying the risk or by others?
- Is the risk knowable or not knowable?

One example occurs when risk perception is influenced through heuristics, what may be referred to as a habit of mind. These heuristics can often overcome

---

* In Chapter 3, we discussed overall risk assessment methods, such as benefit–cost analysis. These methods employ a further level of cognitive framework to the question of risk, placing the output (dose-response) in relation to a set of standards (what is a benefit and what is a cost). We have already discussed some costs in relation to our priorities in objective risk assessment, human health being the primary cost associated with a dose-response methodology to understanding risk.

objective information, especially where the objective information is based on difficult underlying methodologies and statistical analyses (Margolis 1996). It is also
important to understand that this process of risk perception can occur at both
the individual and group levels. A specific heuristic can be connected to personal
knowledge or comfort; in our list above it would be the question of whether the risk
is familiar or exotic to the person perceiving the risk. The more familiar the activity,
the less risk will generally be perceived; the more exotic the activity, the greater the
perceived risk.

An individual might continually discount the objective risks of smoking
cigarettes simply because his or her personal experience tells him or her that he
or she has smoked for decades with no ill effects. In this case his or her habit of
mind, or heuristic knowledge, is driving his or her valuation, even though objective
information exists to support a high risk of cancer with continued and prolonged
cigarette smoking. Now, place this same individual within a group context, say
have him or her interact with a large group of individuals who all have cancer as a
result of cigarette smoking. The group knowledge dynamics change, and a collective habit of mind might create the kind of peer pressure or group-think that alters
the individual smoker's perception. Even if the individual perception is not altered,
social pressures might influence the individual to conform to the group line of
thinking. The point is, individual versus group dynamics matters, something we
will discuss in more detail later in this chapter. Also, we learn from this example
that heuristics, or habits of mind, can sometimes overcome objective information
about the same topic. Thus, subjective information can effectively trump objective
information about a risk, and perceptions have sufficient influence under the right
circumstances to overpower scientific information.

Some additional points about the risk communication are worth mentioning
in summary here. Whether the activity is perceived as voluntary or coerced alters
the perception of risk to the individual, regardless of the actual objective risk. For
example, skiing is an inherently dangerous activity. The risks of speeding down a
hillside smattered with a combination of snow, ice, rocks, trees, and other debris
should be obvious. However, consider how risky you would perceive skiing if you
voluntarily chose to go skiing versus being forced into skiing? Regardless of the
objective risk, your perception of the overall riskiness of the activity will depend on
your level of comfort. Your level of comfort, in turn, will be based in large part on
choice: voluntary versus compulsory (Sandman 1993, 14).

Choice matters when we think about risk perception. There is some connection
between risk perception and risk communication. For example, who controls the
risk matters. I have a friend who feels very comfortable around poisonous snakes
so long as he is handling them personally. As long as he controls the risk of being
bitten by the snake, he feels the risks are limited. However, if he is not personally
controlling the snake, I would bet his comfort level is diminished, and he would

perceive a higher degree of risk being in the room with the poisonous snake but not handling the snake himself.*

Finally, knowability of the risk is important and can be defined through three inquiries. A risk is knowable if it is certain, detectable, and there is expert consensus on the matter. If this risk in uncertain, lacks easy detectability, and there is expert disagreement on the risk, then the risk is perceived as unknowable. When a risk is perceived as unknowable, it is considered much greater regardless of whether this is objectively true (Sandman 1993, 34). Some of these perceptions are highlighted in greater detail by the following example on climate change.

Climate change is an interesting environmental problem. The reasons why are varied, but in simplifying the case, we can establish a few facts regarding our understanding of risk associated with climate change. First, we know there is evidence to support a changing climate (Intergovernmental Panel on Climate Change 2007). In fact, biogeochemical evidence suggests the climate has varied widely throughout most of the earth's history, and only very recently (say the last 10,000 years or so) has there been a general level of consistency in climate trends (Ruddiman 2001, 352–82). Although we know the climate is changing, we do not know what is the primary cause of that change. There is strong—and growing—objective evidence to support human-caused climate change, but the objective evidence is not absolute, meaning it cannot offer a 100% prediction with complete certainty.†

Another problem with climate change is time. Most scientific predictions indicate the impacts of climate change don't take place overnight. Rather, they tend to take place over several decades to hundreds of years (Intergovernmental Panel on Climate Change 2007). If we think about it, this time component impacts the way in which we view risk. For example, consider our highest priority of risk assessment—human health. If we think about the worst-case scenarios associated with climate change (massive flooding, sea level rise, drought, extreme temperature ranges, more intense and greater number of heat waves, etc.), we can certainly connect them to human health concerns.‡ However, because these events cannot be stated with certainly as happening now, but rather over some indefinite time period spanning decades to centuries, we perceive the actual risk of climate change as being lower than we might from a more immediate threat, like nuclear fallout. Thus, even though the hazard of climate change is potentially quite high, our associated outrage about these potential impacts is somewhat lessened because there is a

---

* Paramount to understanding the difference in perception of risk here is knowing that the inherent objective risks of the poisonous snakes are the same no matter who is handling the snakes.

† It should be noted the scientific method does not approve anything to a 100% absolute. The scientific method is really about finding out what does not work, thereby limiting our uncertainty (ignorance) incrementally over time. The point is that we tend to ask science to do something it is not really meant to do when we ask for absolute proof of climate change caused solely by human actions.

‡ Consider the argument that climate change will bring about stronger hurricanes, increasing the likelihood of Katrina-like events in greater abundance as one clear example.

perceived lack of immediacy of threat.* This perceived lack of threat may be termed a lack of outrage, and it is worth exploring in a bit more detail to understand the relationship between immediacy of threat and outrage.

The public's perception of harm is generally reduced when the harm is not immediate. Thus, it will be hard to create a sense of public outrage, or risk when a threat is not proverbially "knocking on the front door." An economic term that relates to this behavioral phenomenon is called *discounting*.[†] A risk that is not imminent is discounted, while a risk—perceived or actual—that is imminent is not discounted. Consider cigarette smoking as one example. We all know the medical risks associated with smoking (there is ample scientific evidence to support them), but those who smoke do so knowing these risks. Most do so because they discount the risk knowing the cigarette they smoke today will not kill them today. However, imagine if smoking a cigarette today actually did kill you today! The immediacy of this risk might influence many a potential smoker to never take up the habit. Probably one reason we don't hear of more people becoming closely acquainted with radioactive waste is they "know" it will kill them.[‡] So time considerations matter when we think about subjective forms of risk. How fast will the risk present itself to me? If the risk is immediate, then I will perceive the risk as significant. If the risk will present itself over a longer period of time, then I will be more likely to discount the risk, at least as it relates to my desire to have something done about the risk in the near term.

Let us compare subjective perceptions of risk to the more objective forms of risk in a bit more detail, specifically looking at the relationship between objective

---

* I say "perceived lack of immediacy of threat" because the impacts cannot be readily seen, but this is not to say the impacts of climate change are not aggregating over time. The issue of aggregation gets into systems thinking, which is discussed in Chapter 2. Recall that natural systems are dynamic by nature, meaning they operate in a nonlinear fashion; their actions cannot be predicted easily as is the case with linear relationships. Consider the riddle of the lily pad as outlined by Firestone and Reed in *Environmental Law for Non-Lawyers*. A lily pad doubles in size each day. In 30 days the pad will completely cover the pond (which is a bad result). On what day will the pad cover half of the pond? The 29th day. Because the pad *doubles* in size each day, it represents exponential growth (like nature). Thus, we might not be aware of the problem until the pad covers half the pond. However, this will only give us one day to respond to the problem, which is probably not enough time to respond effectively. Many cite the exponential aspect of nature when warning about climate change; like the lily pad, we might not be aware of the problem until the symptoms are staring us directly in the face. If this is the 29th day, then we may have too little time to deal with the problem. (For explanatory purposes, if the lily pad showed linear growth, it would cover half the pond on the 15th day, so there would still be 15 days to deal with the problem, rather than the 1 day under exponential growth).

† Discussed in greater detail in Chapter 3.

‡ Actually, I doubt very many people actually understand the chemistry behind the danger of radioactive waste. However, they "know" it will kill them because this idea has been accepted as "fact" within the community at large; there is a high degree of community outrage connected to nuclear radiation—consider Three Mile Island, Chernobyl, and most recently the Fukushima Nuclear Plant in the 2011 Japan tsunami.

information and its impact on subjective perceptions of risk. Let us consider our almost complete subservience to government regulation of pharmaceutical drugs.

When the Federal Drug Administration (FDA) in the United States decides to pull a drug from the open market because evidence has surfaced of the potential ill effects of the drug, we rarely hear of the public becoming outraged over the pulling of the drug. This includes the proportion of the population that regularly used the drug. (Imagine how outraged cigarette smokers would be if the government pulled cigarettes from the market for health concerns.) Why is this so? What special power does the government have when it comes to the enforcement of drug safety? One possible explanation is it seems we have generally accepted the idea that pharmaceutical drugs are dangerous. It seems we have also accepted the notion that our government has good objective information about the dangers of the drug (dose-response types of risk assessment), and probably the government would not intervene in powerful drug manufacturing interests unless there was a good reason.

Other possible reasons include the idea that many of these drugs are meant to combat symptoms of illness, meaning the persons who take these drugs are acutely aware of the immediate health impacts because they are usually treating a health condition with the drugs. This is a bit different from healthy persons who make the voluntary choice to smoke cigarettes. They are not making a direct connection between the use of the product (cigarettes) and the potential effects the product can have on their otherwise healthy condition—likely because the impacts take years to become symptomatic. Of course, like climate change, when the symptoms do present themselves (say lung cancer), it may be too late to do anything meaningful to stop the worst impacts from occurring.

Objective information can help channel our understanding of risk, but only to a point. When the information reinforces aspects of human perception ("I am already well aware of my human frailty, and I believe the government regulates drugs using objective information to ensure my best possible health"), then we tend to allow the objective information to guide our perceptions. However, when there is a disconnect between the objective information and its *direct* relationship to human choice ("The government tells me cigarettes are bad for me and its opinion is backed by objective studies, but I am making a personal choice and I do not show any symptoms of ill health today"), then we tend to discount the objective information and favor our personal choices. These personal choices are influenced by our worldviews on an individual level and common experience on a more group level. Without getting into too much detail on the difference between individual and groups choices (discussed in depth below under "Scaling Value Decisions"), we will now explore some of these other kinds of values and how worldviews influence our perceptions of risk, and thus our values in relation to the environment.

NIMBY and Other Perceived Values

Most values come from views of the world that individuals and groups create and share through common experience. Judith A. Layzer offers an interesting assessment of the values of those who participate in environmental debates based on differing beliefs about the relationship between humans and the natural world (Layzer 2011). She divides belief systems regarding environmental values into two groups, environmentalists and cornucopians. Environmentalists believe in limited environment, while cornucopians believe in an unlimited environment. She indicates the following regarding competition in defining environmental issues between these groups:

> The competition between environmentalists and cornucopians to define an environmental problem thus revolves around three attributes: the scientific understanding of the problem, the economic costs and benefits of the proposed solutions, and the risks associated with action or inaction. (Layzer 2011, 6)

We already understand the first attribute, scientific understanding. This attribute relates to our objective valuation discussion above. What Layzer suggests here is that, depending on one's general viewpoint (a limited world versus an unlimited world), that viewpoint will influence how that individual perceives certain aspects of information. So, for example, one who holds a viewpoint of limits (the environmentalist according to Layzer's categorization) might conclude scientific evidence supporting climate change is a warning that we are approaching a limit in the earth's capacity to deal with human-caused carbon manipulation. However, the cornucopian who does not believe in limits might see the evidence as an indication that we humans are moving to a point where alternatives or substitutes might be appropriate, but that does not mean much in terms of altering human activities in a fundamental sense.

The way these two ideological groups view scientific information is informed by the second attribute, the economic costs and benefits of the proposed solutions. As indicated above, a cornucopian might perceive the scientific information as making a case for substitutes or technological solutions to a problem, while the environmentalist will seek dramatic shifts in human behavior patterns because he or she perceives the earth as being more fragile than resilient; cornucopians believe the exact opposite is true.

Finally, the third attribute, the risks associated with action or inaction, is a way of identifying the relative weights each group gives to certain information regarding the environment. Information, objective or otherwise, that tends to support a theory of limits will be weighted higher by environmentalists than cornucopians, while information supporting a theory of no limits will be weighted higher by cornucopians and discounted by environmentalists. At the heart of this debate is a question of philosophy; what foundational views are driving a particular person or group to adopt an environmentalist worldview, and alternatively, what views are driving a similar person to adopt a cornucopian worldview? We need to explore the foundations of these values in a bit more depth to begin answering these important questions.

We may consider the broadest range of value perception coming from the philosophical background of ethics and morals. Where do we get our ethics and morals from precisely? Certainly, most people are taught basic forms of personal ethics and morality from parents (right versus wrong, kindness, politeness, the golden rule, etc.). Later, our personal sense of morality is expanded in school with social settings, and then further expanded with courses in civics and the role of citizenship and the body politic. We may also learn, or have reinforced, important values from religion. Social norms also help to influence both our private and public value systems. All of these influences help us identify and differentiate questions of right and wrong. Over time, our sense of right and wrong tends to become settled, even rigid, making it difficult to alter our long-standing belief systems (Siegler, Deloache, and Eisenberg 2006, 530–69). It is this system of beliefs, or worldview, that ultimately becomes the foundation for decision-making. Take, for example, the question of sustainability. One who favors sustainability as a general principle might have the following chain of logic to support his or her position:

> What we are doing now as people is **not** sustainable. Therefore, who we are now is bad (a subpresumption is that not being sustainable is a bad thing). Thus, we must come up with new ways of being in order to become sustainable.

Some might argue the statement above emanates from a number of *normative* presumptions about *what should be*. Others suggest the above premise is simply a natural consequence of our scientific understanding (and therefore based on *descriptive* presumptions) of the world. They might point to current scientific literature on climate change, suggesting current human interactions with the earth system are causing substantial disruptions (including global warming), which appear unsustainable if continued. Therefore, the statement is more *objective*, being based on an observed phenomenon, and a reasonable interpretation between that phenomenon and its effect on human well-being.

So, who is right in your mind? Is the statement defined by normative presumptions? Or, is the statement more of a natural consequence of our understanding of how the world works? Do your personal beliefs of right and wrong influence how you perceive the statement? What about proposed solutions to fix the problem (as stated above)? What are the new ways of being we would have to implement, and what are the effects on civilization? Would you be morally agreeable to changes if those changes made life more expensive? Is your moral basis for agreeing or disagreeing with the statement above fixed, or will it change depending on how much its affects your personal life? These are the very difficult but necessary questions we need to individually answer before we formalize our personal beliefs about how we relate to our environment. Once we have created our moral and ethical foundation, we can then proceed to see how decision-making (actually putting our beliefs into action) occurs. A further exploration into some of the foundational environmental values that influence perceptions follows.

NIMBY is an acronym for not in my back yard.* The statement is a pejorative description of undesirable land uses. The uses are undesirable in the sense the proposed land uses are disfavored by local landowners. For example, a group of residential landowners might oppose the nearby development of a landfill because of the potential impacts it might have on the residential properties (lower land values, smell, etc.). There generally is little concern for the objective risks associated with the landfill development (human health), focusing rather on the idea that it will be built near these particular people.† In this example, we might say the community outrage toward the proposed land use is inversely proportional to the distance of the project relative to the community members; outrage grows the closer the proposed project is to the community members.

We might conclude NIMBY represents a perception of risk that is generated through a disassociation with reality, even at the level of basic self-acknowledgment of needs. The landowners are aware of the need for landfills, as they regularly produce waste they do not wish to store in their houses, and they do not wish to be responsible for personally. So what might this tell us about environmental values of NIMBY individuals? Well, we can assume some of these "nimbies" likely consider themselves environmentally conscious individuals. They believe in basic tenets of sustainability, that is, leaving the earth in about as good of shape as it is now for future generations (this is especially true if they have children, grandchildren, etc.). However, they tend to differentiate between these general concepts of environmentalism and their application to their immediate circumstances. Why might this be so?

Let us consider the impact or perception that having a landfill sited in our local community might have on us individually. First, if we purchased a home in the community, this revelation might, for some, call into question our good judgment (landfills are probably not the type of amenity the average homeowner seeks out when looking to purchase a home). So, we might say the proposed siting of the landfill (not the landfill itself) challenges our intelligence in some measure, and this can influence our perception about the benefit of the landfill (it might cloud our judgment). As such, we might seek to distinguish our decision to live in the area (the good idea) from the decision to site the landfill in the same area (the bad idea).

---

* See *Green Issues and Debates*, edited by Howard Schiffman and Paul Robbins (Thousand Oaks, CA: Sage, 2011), 358–360.

† These community members likely agree with the need for a landfill in general; they no doubt generate trash and believe the trash should be removed from their immediate proximity. So, their outrage is not a source of philosophical objection to trash in general. Rather, the outrage is based on their perception of risk rising because the proposed landfill site will be situated within their personal zones of influence.

Our normative ideals of good and bad can be made conditional to our personal situation, and this is certainly true in the landfill example. While we might agree with the idea of landfills (a designated place to hold waste), we do not agree with the idea within the context of the landfill being located near our particular home.* Another way of saying this is that our perceptions often cloud our judgment, and this can lead to a shift in how we make value judgments. So while we think an issue is valuable conceptually (a healthy environment), we diminish the value when it is in our personal interest to do so. In this way, NIMBY attitudes offer an example of how subjective values can impact our attitude toward environmental issues, further complicating what decisions we might make in relation to the environment.

A more categorical value system associated with the environment is that of deep ecology, a philosophy based on a deep appreciation of our environment. Arne Naess coined the term *deep ecology* in the 1970s.† The essential tenet of deep ecology is to identify the importance of nature beyond utility; all living things have intrinsic value, even if that value cannot be reduced to an economic utility. It sees humans and the earth are intricately linked, forming at best a symbiotic relationship. We might say some of the indirect and nonuse values identified in our total value approach (see Chapter 3) can be related to this idea of intrinsic value. We mention deep ecology here as another way of viewing environmental decisions because it helps us to expand what might be considered value by some individuals. If value can go beyond human utility, then how might we begin to judge environmental decisions?

Consider a group of people who identify with the main tenet of deep ecology (all things, living and nonliving,‡ have intrinsic value). We would expect these individuals to favor environmental protection over human actions that impact the environment. Because of how highly they value the environment, they would tend to discount human well-being at the expense of environmental protection. They are, for our purposes, the opposite of the NIMBY individuals identified above. They do not make their environmental values conditional to circumstances (such as proximity of a landfill to where they live), but rather hold fast to a principle of environmental protection for the good of the environment itself. These two types of value systems can represent two ends of a spectrum: one end representing a preservationist mentality, and the other end representing a pure development mentality.§

---

* It would be interesting to see if the issue is about siting the landfill near "our" home in particular, or near any residential area? My guess would be that our bias about siting a landfill near residential neighborhoods would lessen so long as the landfill was not near *our* neighborhood.
† See *The Deep Ecology Movement: An Introductory Anthology*, edited by Alan Drengson and Tuichi Inoue (Berkeley, CA: North Atlantic Books, 1995).
‡ In the scientific vernacular, all things biotic and abiotic.
§ The label "development" refers to a belief system that places humans at the forefront of considerations. In our economic analysis, we can relate a direct value analysis as the main methodology employed in determining the relative costs and benefits of a proposed activity for those categories in our development category here.

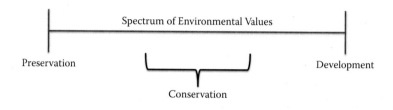

Figure 4.6　Spectrum of environmental values.

Somewhere between the two ends of this spectrum, we can find conservation as yet another set of values. A representation of this spectrum is shown in Figure 4.6.

This spectrum helps us place the question of perceived values into a framework for understanding how subjective values can lead to certain environmental decision outcomes. For example, as already highlighted above, those who are categorized closer to the development side of the spectrum most likely align with the NIMBY-type principles discussed above; they would tend to place human well-being ahead of environmental considerations, and this includes thinking of humans as a priority over other environmental consideration, much like our objective dose-response priority list that places human health at the forefront of importance. However, unlike the objective dose-response evaluation, these people will make decisions based on a more subjective implementation of human well-being. While many who lean toward a development end of the spectrum identify with environmental ideals, they are more likely to discount those ideals when they directly impact the individuals themselves ("I'm ok with the idea of landfills as a concept, but not ok with a landfill being sited near my residence").

Those who identify more along the preservation side of the spectrum—including our deep ecology adherents—are more likely to value environmental considerations as a standard, and not make these considerations conditional on circumstances. In fact, they may go so far as to suggest environmental protection should be a priority even where it harms human well-being. The reason is that they tend to place environmental values at least on par with human values. Said another way, those along the preservation side of the spectrum would reorganize our objective priority list under dose-response analysis, and likely place environmental considerations as high as, and maybe higher than, human considerations.

Those who fall in the middle of the spectrum identify with varying degrees of prioritizing the environment and human welfare. *Conservation* is a term that often reflects a general preference for balancing the interests of human welfare against environmental welfare (Hunter and Gibbs 2007, 346). The key in conservation is to strike a balance. For those who lean toward the environmental side of the spectrum, they might weigh environmental values equal to or greater than human welfare. For those who lean toward the development side of the spectrum, they might weigh human welfare concerns against environmental concerns.

One point to be highlighted here is the idea that the values defined above (development, conservation, preservation) create a kind of spectrum. A spectrum implies a continuum, where there are, essentially, an infinite variety of combinations of values to be considered, with the exceptions being the absolute extreme points of the spectrum (in our example, either an extreme preservationist or an extreme developmentalist). So, for instance, I may lean more toward preservation when the question is one about transitioning open-space land used for recreational purposes into development. I understand that development might increase human welfare to some degree, but I might see the impact of nondevelopment as negligible, and the impact to open space significant (especially if I am living in a well-developed area with limited remaining open space).

What goes into my calculation? Certainly my worldview is an important consideration because it helps to share my relative weighting of the interests at stake (I am not a developer, but if I were, I might place greater weight on the ability to develop open space because I would connect this to a personal preference and sense of well-being; the more land that is developable, the more financial security I see in my future). Also important is the way that I perceive the interests. I may actually be prioritizing human well-being, but I may be giving greater weight to the maintenance of open space over development as an indicator of human well-being. Even if I don't relate the open space to immediate human well-being, I might identify with the ecological values associated with open space (habitat for species of plants and animals important to the region, biodiversity considerations, etc.). No matter my particular values, I might likely lean toward preservation here simply because I perceive no immediate threat to human health (or welfare) by not allowing the development of the open space.* If I did perceive an immediate threat to human health, I might lean toward development (or some other human-centered) factor.

The point is that when we are dealing with subjective forms of valuation, and specifically perceptions associated with valuation, our relative weighting of variables in particular settings might place us further on one end of a spectrum of subjective values than another. There are numerous consequences associated with this revelation in relation to environmental decision-making. One obvious one is that we cannot count on subjective forms of valuation to offer us replicable outcomes; we simply cannot know how an individual or group might perceive values in a particular environmental context. Because we cannot know precisely what may drive public sentiment, we must pay close attention to the factors that are driving public sentiment in order to understand what may influence an environmental decision in one direction or another.

Before we move on to our final consideration of values, the question of scaling value decisions, let us take a moment to discuss an important aspect of subjective

---

* Those involved in advocating affordable housing in certain areas of the world might argue the threat to human health and welfare is greater than one might think, especially under particular circumstances.

valuation, and that is how our perceptions influence the way we approach problems. We will use some of the ideas developed by those who focus on dispute resolution as a way to summarize how value judgments impact decision-making.

By means of a quick primer on the subject, society has always sought ways to resolve disputes between members of the society (Rousseau 1893). In a social system like the United States, the rule of law is the formal means by which disputes are resolved (Cass 2001). The very fact that laws exist, but there are still disputes about the *application* of the law to a particular setting, supports the notion that people can come to differing conclusions about how a situation should be resolved.

Perceptions are a main factor in driving legal disputes, and the law takes notice of this fact in the adage "reasonable minds can differ." In addition to formal means of dispute resolution (say filing a civil lawsuit by the aggrieved party against the allegedly responsible party), there are more informal methods of dispute resolution. Examples include negotiation, mediation, and arbitration. Informal methods of dispute resolution exist to help parties with different opinions about right and wrong in a particular setting resolve their complaints without seeking formal means of resolution (Mackie 1991).

Those who work in the area of dispute resolution must often find creative ways to deal with individual perceptions because most of these types of resolution procedures are voluntary, meaning a party to the procedure does not have to come to a resolution necessarily, or otherwise accept the recommendation of the neutral party, often referred to as the mediator or arbitrator.* Our focus here is on identifying some of the lessons learned by seasoned mediators and arbitrators in getting parties with a particular viewpoint to (1) alter their viewpoint, (2) expand their viewpoint, or (3) move to a resolution regardless of their viewpoint.

There are numerous experts in the area of alternative dispute resolution, all with valuable insights on working with people who have particular worldviews. For our short discussion here, we will focus on the work of Robert Fisher, William Ury, and Bruce Patton (2011). Specifically, we will focus on what Fisher, Ury, and Patton have coined *principled bargaining* as a means of achieving negotiated agreements between parties. I believe we can find significant value understanding what principled bargaining is, how it differentiates from traditional *positional bargaining*, and how this difference aids in our understanding the dynamics of subjective valuation in environmental decision-making.

To summarize the major points expressed by Fisher, Ury, and Patton, there is a natural human tendency to engage in positional bargaining. Position bargaining occurs where individuals take up a position and then defend that position. The interesting aspect of this phenomenon is that defending the position itself becomes

---

* Informal dispute resolution procedures can be both binding and nonbinding. So, in certain cases the parties to the proceeding can agree ahead of time that the final decision of the neutral party will be binding on the parties. This is usually done in binding arbitration proceedings, and the parties usually agree in writing to this binding effect of the proceeding.

the goal, rather than working toward the actual goal (the reason everyone was so upset in the first place). For our purposes, we might see a NIMBY individual in our example defending the position of "no landfill near my home" regardless of what information comes to light. This is true even if the position were taken to defend a specific goal, like ensuring that the value of the home and quality of life in the neighborhood are not affected by a nearby landfill development.

Fisher, Ury, and Patton (2011, 4–8) argue that the focus on a position entrenches the individual to defend the position, even when this has little to do with their true concerns. For example, what if new information was to be offered to show that land values would not decrease, and quality of life would be maintained after the installation of the landfill? Shouldn't this information have an impact on the perceptions of the NIMBY homeowner? What is informative here is the insight that sometimes the perception is not a difference of opinion about values, but rather a misplaced defense of values, in this case, defending a position rather than the underlying value perception at stake.

While the authors argue positional bargaining has its uses, they ultimately determine that a focus on positional bargaining fails to meet their basic criteria for a good resolution to a dispute: a wise agreement, achieved efficiently, producing amicability between the parties to the extent practicable (Fisher, Ury, and Patton 2011, 4). The better direction, according to the authors, is to move to a negotiation that is based on *principle* rather than one that is based on *positions* (Fisher, Ury, and Patton 2011, 10–15). In essence, the goal should be to keep the person focused on the underlying interests that are influencing his or her perceptions about the world.

In our NIMBY example, the underlying interest is the impact the landfill will have on things the homeowner values in the vicinity of the proposed landfill (the home, family, quality of life in the neighborhood). By focusing on interests rather than positions, there is a greater likelihood of seeing what motivates sentiment. Knowing this can lead to deeper insights into how the subjective value is being defined. Once we know how the subjective value is being defined, we are better equipped to consider what kind of impact these views might have on environmental decisions.

For example, if community members opposed an offshore wind farm, we might want to analyze whether there are objective (science-based) reasons supporting the opposition. If there are not, then we turn to subjective values as a way of understanding the problem. Say there is outrage at the project. According to what we have just read, we might do well to distinguish between outrage based on a position ("no building wind farms in my backyard") versus outrage based on a specific interest ("I'm concerned the farms will reduce tourism in my community and my livelihood is based on tourism"). Knowing what is actually driving a person or group to take a position (going beyond the position itself) can make a difference in how we approach the problem, and ultimately come to a solution. This needs to be remembered as we consider values and their impact in environmental decision-making.

The preceding discussion helps us understand the relationship between objective and subjective risk assessment, specifically when perception of risk might match objective risk assessment, and when perceptions might trump, or go against, objective risk assessment. Combining this understanding with knowledge about how public perception culminates in a strong sense of risk (regardless of what objective information is available) gives us a better understanding of the role subjective risk assessment plays in overall risk valuation.

What is left for us to consider in this section now is the role of scaling value decisions. The term *scaling* here is meant to refer to how risk assessment is actually done. We will look at two primary forms of scaling: the individual decision-making process and the multiparty decision-making process. The reason we separate the two is because there are different dynamics that occur at the individual and multiparty scale. Consider the example we have used above of the cigarette smoker. Left to individual devices, a person chooses to smoke cigarettes for generally very personal reasons. However, place that same individual within a group context, and we might see very different choices being made about smoking (whether to smoke, when to smoke, smoking alone or within a group, etc.).

The point is that our *process* of making decisions changes between an individual and group setting. In some ways, we can say what we value changes between individual and group decisions. Just ask any responsible person what happens to his or her value systems when he or she becomes a parent, responsible for a new life! We will now explore some of these scaling issues within the context of environmental decision-making, seeing how scale impacts the choices we make regarding the environment.

Scaling Value Decisions

In the preceding sections we have examined values from both the objective and subjective viewpoints. The goal has been to understand the dynamics that impact how environmental decisions are made from a value-based approach. Most environmental decisions are value driven and because of this, questions about what we value are important when thinking about environmental decision-making. Also, questions that focus on the process of decision-making, including how our value judgments (both objective and subjective) influence our decisions, are important considerations in understanding the ways in which we formulate opinion and how that opinion drives our decisions.

In this section, we move beyond the detailed examination of where values come from to a more generalized review of how value decisions are made at different scales of society. For simplicity purposes, we divide our examination into two broad categories: individual decision-making and multiparty decision-making. The goal is to see how scale impacts decisions. This issue of scale was touched upon earlier in this chapter, seeing how group dynamics can influence a decision-making process. To place this final part of the chapter in perspective, we begin by relating scale back to foundational questions of the various factors that combine to make sound decisions.

A key to making sound (and repeatable) decisions is to ensure that you are valuing the same information in the same way at the same time. This tenet is a foundation of science, in which experiments must be replicable in order to be validated. When we talk about decision-making, we are talking about a *process* of deliberation. Key to this process is an agreement on the *variables* considered in the decision-making process. This is where morality plays a foundational role, as mentioned earlier in this chapter.

In our discussion on economic principles, we reference *benefit–cost analysis* (BCA). We can think of BCA as one way of making a decision. One considers and weighs multiple variables, identifies the benefits and costs of a proposed action, and then, based on this weighing, comes to a decision. As was stated earlier, and reinforced now, the key to a good BCA is to fully realize *all* relevant benefits and costs within a proposed action. If you think about it, understanding *earth systems*, *box modeling*, and methods of *valuation* are all ways of establishing an *objective truth*.* This objective truth is related to the *variables* that need to be considered when making environmental decisions. The goal is to make the decision as objective as humanly possible (realizing our method of valuation is somewhat flawed because of the *weight* we may give to certain variables—based on our personal preferences and internal value systems).

One way to move toward objectivity is to identify the *presumptions* we are making at the outset of our decision-making process. Ethical and moral underpinnings are the sources of our presumptions, and as such, they really color our process of making decisions (Bales 2001, 88–90). To the degree we can objectify our analysis, we should. It makes our arguments clearer and more acceptable to social adoption. We should endeavor to create a strong understanding of what influences decisions. We have previously discussed how different categories of value influence environmental decisions, focusing our attention on objective and subjective forms of valuation. It is easy to understand what influences objective forms of valuation, especially in the context of risk assessment. It is more difficult to see how subjective information influences decisions. A focus on one variable over another can trigger the same information to be perceived in opposite directions; this is where heuristics, or worldviews, play a role and beg our attention.

What we have not discussed is the impact of looking at values from different scales. Below we will view how scale influences value-based decisions. This section will begin with a focus on individual-level value-based decision-making, looking at the main drivers at this most specific scale. The section will then move on to an

---

* The term *objective truth* used here is judged by the criteria of replicability, meaning the process of coming to the decision can be replicated. In order for this to occur, both the means of producing the result and the variables used in producing the result must be rigorously defined and applied.

evaluation of legal and policy analysis, and how these steps aid in further refining the environmental decision-making process. A primer for understanding legal analysis will be given based on a modeling of the U.S. system of government and hierarchy of laws. This will then be supplemented by analyzing a problem-solving process and alternatives analysis.

Values and Individual Decision-Making

Most of us are familiar with making decisions from the individual standpoint—we do it every day! But do we consider the actual *process* we undergo when making an individual decision? Many decisions might be termed simple, almost instinctual, where there is a connection between stimulus and response—"I am hungry, so I need to get something to eat"—or something similar. If we look more closely, however, we might find additional questions being asked (based on different personal *values*). For instance, your initial stimulus ("I need something to eat") may be simple enough, but the response may be conditional. You may not want to eat everything available, because you may limit your consumption to healthy foods. Moreover, you may have personal values that limit certain kinds of food (say no meat because you are a vegetarian). There can be many other questions and considerations that alter the answer to your first question, or otherwise make the analysis a bit more complicated than at first glance.

So, what is it about these considerations that make decisions hard? For one thing, they become the *criteria* by which individual decisions are judged. If they are rigid (exceptions are not likely), they can become powerful limitations on the types of decisions one can make. For example, eating meat to satisfy hunger is unacceptable if you are a vegetarian. The condition (no meat) creates the criteria (meatless food) by which the act of eating is judged. Now, we can argue the merit of the underlying reasons for choosing the condition (i.e., the reasons for choosing to be a vegetarian). What we cannot argue with is once this value is established (once we accept it as a premise even if we do not like the premise), it becomes the criteria by which the action of eating is judged. Thus, the decision to eat or not to eat will be made based on the conditions present (is there food available to eat), and the criteria by which the decision is judged (even if food is present, I cannot eat meat if that is the only food present).

This admittedly basic example is meant to highlight the *process* of decision-making in general. Can you see the importance of individual values as they drive the decision-making process? Consider this application in the environmental field of sustainability. In order for us to make valid decisions about sustainability, we need to first understand what our major assumptions are regarding what is and is not sustainable. If we can identify major categories of action that define sustainability, our task is somewhat simplified. However, if the majority of our sustainable thinking is *context specific* (meaning what is or is not sustainable depends on the context of the situation), then our job is more difficult.

Consider the question of using coal to power our electric energy demand. Is coal unsustainable because there is only a finite (limited) amount, and since we will run out at some point, it is unsustainable to continue using coal? Or, is coal unsustainable because it is made of carbon, and continuing to burn coal will release carbon dioxide into the atmosphere, helping to warm the planet? Or, is coal unsustainable because once burned, it causes a sooty smoke sometimes filled with sulfur, and this poses health risks to humans and the surrounding environment? Or, is coal unsustainable for *all* of these reasons? The answer to these questions inevitably must be, it depends. Why? Because any of these reasons could justify referring to coal as unsustainable depending on how one defines the term *sustainability*. Thus, what matters is how we define the term *unsustainable*, which will also depend on our values creating the conditions and criteria by which the term *unsustainable* will be judged in relation to the use of coal.

Besides the criteria used to judge a decision, there are other factors that influence individual decision-making. One such factor is *cost*. Carrying forward the vegetarian example, one might argue the cost of being a vegetarian may influence individual decisions. If one is adamant about his or her vegetarian beliefs, then maybe cost is not an issue (he or she will eat a vegetarian diet within his or her means). However, if one is less adamant in his or her beliefs (he or she thinks it is a good idea so long as it does not substantially interfere with his or her personal well-being), then cost may be a deciding factor in his or her decision-making. If eating meat is substantially cheaper, the individual might feel the personal benefits from eating meat (cheaper nutrition) outweigh the costs (failure to advance a vegetarian ideology).

Decision-making becomes much more complex when we begin to consider what is driving the decision. The fact that these drivers can vary from person to person only adds to the complexity in understanding the process of decision-making. Does a person have strongly held personal beliefs that are a significant driver in his or her decision-making? Or, are more generalized drivers, such as cost, influencing the individual's choice? Knowing what is influencing individual choice helps us see how those choices are being made and how they might be further influenced. One way in which individual incentives can be discerned is by looking at various ways of understanding *self-interest*. The following section takes up the topic in some detail.

Self-Interest

So what does this all mean in relation to our understanding of the scale of individual decision-making? One way of answering this question is to suggest that individual preferences are the main driver of decisions when they are being made solely by that individual. Preference, in turn, is influenced by worldviews and life experience, as described earlier in this chapter, and is highly subjective in most circumstances. Thus, individual decisions that are heavily influenced by subjective factors of value can sometimes trump objective factors of value. In fact, this can happen often.

So how can we better understand how individual incentives drive decision-making? We may do so by exploring the theory of *self-interest* and its impact on individual decision-making. We begin by exploring the concept of self-interest, identify it through a strategic game exercise known as the *prisoner's dilemma*, and finally set the stage for understanding individual choices and their collective impact on larger multiparty decision-making through reviewing *agent-based modeling*.

The concept of self-interest and its impact on the *process* of decision-making may best be highlighted by Mancur Olson's seminal work entitled *The Logic of Collective Action* (Olson 1971). Olson describes how self-interest on the individual scale can be very different from collective group action, challenging accepted beliefs about the interrelation between individual and group action. Accepted beliefs of self-interest prior to Olson suggested that *if* every individual in a group setting has interests in common, then each individual collectively acts to achieve those common interests. Olson found this premise to be incomplete, especially when considering collective group action in relation to *public goods*, or goods that have characteristics of nonexcludability and nonrivalry.* His main point was that individual interests diverge from group interests in a variety of circumstances, but especially where the benefits are distributed equally among all members of a group, even when certain members have contributed little or nothing to obtaining the benefit. This generally occurred with public goods because public goods contain the unique characteristics that allow for benefits to be distributed to all members of a group (nonexcludability being an important consideration) regardless of individual merit or participation. Thus, according to Olson, certain individuals within the group will, through self-interest, free ride on the efforts of others when the group is working to provide public goods. Free riding is less likely to occur when the benefits of group action are meted out based on some criteria, such as merit or active participation. Let us give an example of free riding to help make the point more transparent.

Consider you are among four people who are sharing the rent in a house. None of the four own the house or have any interest in ownership; you each simply pay rent to use the house for living purposes over a set period of time. Assume the house contains four bedrooms with an adjoining bathroom to each bedroom. You each maintain a bedroom as your private area along with the bathroom that is attached

---

* Gravity is probably the best example of a public good because one cannot be excluded from the resource (no matter how hard I try, I cannot prevent another from accessing gravity); thus it is nonexcludable. Also, it is nonrival (no matter how much of gravity I try and use, there is just as much available to others to use). A more practical example, although not an ideal example of a public good, would be something like air or water. However, even if access is regularly granted to air or water (they are nonexcludable); the units of air and water (at least clean air and clean water) are divisible, so these are not ideal examples of public goods, but rather something defined by Elinor Ostrom as common pool resources, which are resources that contain the characteristics of low excludability but high divisibility (Ostrom substituted the term *divisibility* for *rivalry*). The more difficult environmental issues today generally contain the characteristics of common pool resources.

to the respective bedroom. Outside of the four bedrooms, there is also a living room and kitchen, both considered common areas. They are common areas because each roommate has equal access to these areas for use and enjoyment. The living room contains the one common television and couch and an area for general entertainment. The kitchen contains all things for cooking and eating, equally accessible by the four roommates. An issue arises that requires the attention of all the roommates in the house. The kitchen area and living room have both becomes victims of common access. The kitchen is generally dirty with unwashed dishes being piled up in the sink area. The refrigerator is full of outdated food; inside the milk has turned bad and the leftover pizza is growing mold. The living room has not been cleaned in months. Dirty dishes and empty pizza boxes are strewn across the coffee table, and empty beer and soda cans are everywhere. A distinct smell has taken over these two rooms, and it is beginning to impact the relatively clean private bedrooms of each of the roommates. Now is the time for action!

You and the rest of the roommates get together to discuss how to handle this situation. You all agree on a common goal, keeping the kitchen and living room clean so the living conditions can be healthy and prosperous to the benefit of all four roommates. You all decide that everyone will make a commitment for the common good of the household and simply work together to ensure the goal (a clean house) is constantly met. The next day, you decide to take the initiative on meeting the community goal of a clean kitchen and living room.* The result is a clean kitchen and living room by your individual labor. The benefits of your action accrue not only to you, but also equally to the other roommates in the house.

Something interesting happens over the next few weeks. Each day you notice the kitchen and living room are getting a little dirtier. You yourself are taking steps to clean up after yourself, washing your own dishes as they are used and making sure to put your empty cans and garbage immediately in the trash. However, some (or all) of your roommates are not following suit; the kitchen and living room are slowly moving back to the condition of disarray and dirtiness. After a few more days, you decide no one else will immediately begin to clean the area, so you take it upon yourself again to do the cleaning, thinking your second initiative will spur others to understand the importance of everyone pitching in to keep the common areas of the house clean. However, after your additional labors and a span of about a week, you notice the same trend; no one else is taking up the mantle of cleaner, and some or all of the others are still practicing dirty habits. What is going on here? Why are you the only one who is taking this goal seriously? You all agreed the goal

---

* You might take this initiative for a variety of reasons. For example, you might believe in the goal itself for the betterment of everyone. Or, you might think that if you take the initiative, you will have built up equity for yourself in the eyes of the roommates leading to social prestige. Or, you may simply believe that you will have done your share of the cleaning for a while, and thus you can enjoy a relatively long period of time where the other roommates will be responsible for cleaning without you needing to take additional action.

of a clean kitchen and living room was important. So why are you the only one who seems willing to take action to achieve the goal? The answer lies in what Mancur Olson describes as free riding and the dynamics between individual self-interest and group goals.

Without interviewing each roommate to determine his or her specific motivations as to why he or she has not engaged in the community goal of a clean kitchen and living room, we can use some of Olson's insights to discern likely reasons for his or her inaction. Specifically, Olson would conclude the individuals were free riding off of the work provided by you. Consider the fact that from the roommate's perspective, the goal of a clean kitchen and living room has been achieved with no effort on his or her part. This means every other roommate (besides yourself, of course) can enjoy all of the *benefits* of your work without engaging in any individual *costs* to achieve those benefits.*

Olson would suggest the roommate's actions are simply a rational response to the circumstances laid out before the roommates. Why would they voluntarily engage in individual labor (costs) when their goals can be achieved by doing nothing? So long as there is someone willing to do the work, and so long as the benefits of the work accrue to everyone, then the circumstances motivate the many (the three roommates) to free ride on the work of the few (the single roommate—you). Now we need to look a bit deeper at the underlying reasons why the roommates are capable of free riding in this situation. Specifically, what unique characteristics exist here that allow free riding, and what might be changed to prevent it from continuing in the future?

Let us begin by focusing on the *property right* characteristics that present themselves here. The kitchen and living room were identified as common areas, meaning they were accessible to all roommates (also friends of roommates, family of roommates, etc.). Note this is a different kind of property right characteristic than the private bedrooms. In the private bedroom, each roommate has the capacity to *exclude* other roommates from entering the room. Thus, there is a greater level of control, or dominion, held by each roommate when it comes to the private bedroom. This is not the case with the kitchen and living room. Because these rooms are common, there is not an equivalent right to exclude among the roommates; each roommate has equal access to these areas of the house. So, one main difference between the private bedroom and common kitchen/living rooms is the characteristic of *excludability*. The bedroom has the property right characteristic of *high excludability*, while the kitchen and living room have the property right characteristic of *low excludability*.

There is another property right characteristic at play here besides excludability. To understand it, we have to identify the *interest* that is the focus of this example;

---

* Note that we are using the terms *benefit* and *cost* to outline individual incentives, and how this differs from a benefit–cost analysis as outlined in Chapter 3.

the interest at stake here is the value of *cleanliness* of the kitchen and living room.* Cleanliness is the common goal between the roommates. In looking at cleanliness as a goal, we can make a few observations about it in relation to characteristics of the kitchen and living room. First, we must agree that the kitchen and living room are of fixed, finite proportions; the dimensions of these rooms are set and do not change. The second point is related to the first: because the dimensions of the rooms are fixed, the relative amount of cleanliness of the rooms will change in proportion to the amount of actions taken to dirty the rooms.

For example, let us assume the kitchen begins in a totally clean state. Every incremental action taken to dirty the kitchen (leaving a dish unclean, dropping food on the floor, etc.) lowers the amount (or ratio) of clean kitchen left. This conclusion is directly related to the fact that the kitchen is a finite space; it does not increase in size to accommodate the dirtying of the kitchen. Because of this characteristic, we can say the kitchen and living room are *divisible* in the sense that every action that dirties these areas lowers the amount of clean areas remaining. Left unattended, continual dirtying of the kitchen will ultimately lead to all of the clean areas of the kitchen being gone. Divisibility, then, is an important characteristic that helps define the problem at issue here. The kitchen and living room are *highly divisible*, meaning the spaces will increasingly become dirty, resulting in less clean space left for the enjoyment of those who have access to the resource.†

We see here that the common areas of the house share two property right characteristics: they are both *highly divisible* in terms of the condition cleanliness, and they share a *low excludability* characteristic, meaning the roommates cannot prevent one another from accessing the kitchen or living room; they are common areas by definition. These two characteristics create the conditions for free riding because they allow access to the resource for free (low excludability), but the resource itself is the kind that can be degraded by the actions of those who access the resource (high divisibility).

---

* The term *cleanliness* is more subjective than objective unless we provide some criteria by which to judge the term. For example, if we define *cleanliness* as a condition of the room where no area of the room has more than 10 *E. coli* bacteria per square meter, then we have a pretty objective standard by which to judge the term. Without such a definition, however, we are left to define the term from a more subjective standpoint. In such case, we would need to look toward community standards or generally agreed principles to help us understand the meaning of the term. However, even without explicit definition, we can likely conclude that the roommates in our example had a general sense of what the term meant when they met to discuss setting the goal of cleanliness in solving the problem at hand. Many times, this general community understanding is what establishes the standard (at least initially) that helps to formulate an action plan to do something about an environmental issue.

† Contrast this notion of *high divisibility* with the public resource of gravity. Gravity has *low divisibility* because, no matter how much I use of it, I cannot divide the amount of gravity into units; there is just as much gravity available for someone else to use. Moreover, I cannot dirty gravity the way I can a kitchen or living room, meaning the overall integrity or quality of gravity remains no matter how I treat it. This is very different from what happens to the kitchen and living room in our example.

Garret Hardin explained this unique type of property setting—the term he used was *commons*—when explaining resource depletion and overexploitation (Hardin 1968). Elinor Ostrom later gave more definition to this concept, identifying resources that have property rights characteristics of low excludability and high divisibility as "common pool resources" (Ostrom 1990). Both Hardin and Ostrom were able to identify these property characteristics as being unique to major environmental problems. For example, based on their observations of property right characteristics, we can see that the forcing of carbon into the atmosphere creates a commons or common pool resource issue in relation to the atmosphere and the amount of carbon in it. The carbon is the equivalent, metaphorically, of trash in our roommate example, dirtying the atmosphere as it relates to climate change. The more carbon in the atmosphere, the greater the greenhouse effect, thereby reinforcing climate changes.

The atmosphere shares the characteristic of low excludability because everyone has access to it, especially for the purposes of sending carbon into it.* The atmosphere also shares the characteristic of high divisibility; every unit of carbon placed into the atmosphere increases the overall concentration of carbon in the atmosphere.† In this way, the unique property characteristics of large-scale environmental issues like climate change help to reinforce the problem identified by Mancur Olson; while everyone collectively might agree with the goal of preventing climate change, most of the individuals will free ride off the efforts of a few, complicating a solution to the problem. Businesses have little incentive to unilaterally care about the carbon they are forcing into the atmosphere because they are allowed to pump the carbon into the atmosphere without consequence; they have access to it but do not have to pay for damaging it.

So how might we go about solving this problem? What tools exist to limit the self-interested free riding that has been explained by Olson and placed into context by Hardin and Ostrom? In order to best answer this question, we must begin by setting out the variety of property rights that can be achieved by combining the different options of property right characteristics explained above, divisibility and excludability. A representation of the different property rights that result from several combinations is outlined in Figure 4.7.

Based on the figure, we can see there are four different types of property rights that can be characterized by divisibility and excludability, depending on the

---

* Industrial facilities, like a coal burning power plant, can emit carbon as a by-product of burning coal into the atmosphere just as easily as an individual can burn leaves in his or her backyard during the fall, or burn wood in his or her fireplace during the winter. In each case, carbon is being sent from the coal, leaves, and wood into the atmosphere. Everyone can access it, but no one has to pay for the consequences of dirtying the air with carbon.

† While carbon does cycle through the atmosphere, ultimately being taken up and stored in the earth's crust for long periods of geologic time, the time it takes the additional carbon to move through the atmosphere and return to a major sink is on a timescale long enough (thousands of years by current research) for human purposes for the carbon to be considered a permanent addition to the atmosphere.

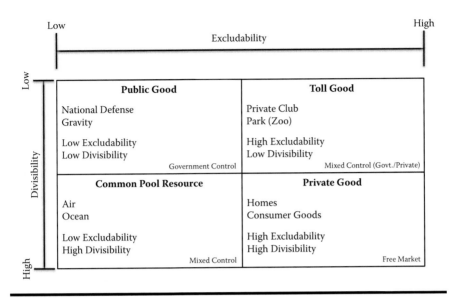

Figure 4.7 Representation of property rights based on the characteristics of excludability and divisibility.

combination of the two characteristics involved: *private property, public property, common pool resources,* and *toll goods.* We can discern how one type of resource can be changed into a different type of resource by altering the characteristics that define that particular resource. For example, a common pool resource can be changed into a private resource by taking the low-excludability characteristic of the common pool resource and changing it to a high-excludability designation; the result is a property right with the combination of high excludability and high divisibility, or private property. The same can be said for the other property rights identified in the figure.* Let us see the impact this might have, changing a common resource into a private resource, on our roommate situation described earlier in this section.

Recall the roommates in our example above were "defecting" from cleaning the common areas of the home, the kitchen and living room. The reason for the defection was that, although they agreed with the goal of clean common areas, they were free riding on the cleaning you, the other roommate, were providing; the goal of clean common spaces was being achieved without any effort from the other roommates. Most importantly, because these rooms were common in nature, you could not exclude the others from the benefits of your work; they could access the common areas as easily as you, and the benefits of your cleaning were imbued onto them as much as they were onto you.

---

* A private property right can be changed into a public property right by changing excludability and divisibility from high to low, and vice versa. A common pool resource can be changed into a toll good by making the common resource highly excludable with low divisibility; a toll good can be made into a common pool resource by doing the opposite.

Could the observed free riding be solved by changing the underlying property right characteristics of the kitchen and living room? One could not change the divisibility characteristic of the rooms in relation to dirtiness; the rooms are of finite space and are therefore divisible by nature. However, one could change the excludability characteristic of these rooms, making the rooms highly excludable. If this were done, then the rooms would be considered private because they exhibited the characteristics of high excludability and high divisibility. If the rooms were private—say you were now the sole owner of the kitchen and bathroom—then you could simply exclude the other roommates from the rooms. Once they were excluded, you could then control the condition of the rooms, ensuring they were kept at a level of cleanliness you determined appropriate. Since the other roommates were excluded, they would no longer be able to free ride on your cleaning work; the benefit of your cleaning would no longer be available to them for doing so.

Of course, the solution here seems impractical because to make the situation livable among the roommates, everyone needs access to the kitchen (and probably the living room for social considerations). So maybe it would be better to allow access to the resource (the kitchen and living room), but only under certain terms. The terms can outline who can access these areas, under what conditions access might be granted, and when access might be denied or taken away. The terms and conditions can focus on access as a privilege based on the individual treating the area with consideration; in this case consideration means keeping the area clean and tidy.

Translating to our environmental example of climate change, we might suggest privatizing the air as it relates to human-induced carbon. One clear way to do this is to charge carbon emitters for each unit of carbon they emit into the atmosphere (Cole 2002, 94–95). The charge should reflect the value of the harm caused by the additional carbon in the atmosphere. This way, the emitters cannot free ride on the causes and impacts of climate change; rather, they must internalize these costs as part of doing business.*

Consider what we have done here so far in this section. We have identified an important consideration of scale when it comes to values of individual decision-makers. As outlined by Mancur Olson, self-interest can cause an individual to act in a way that does not support the attainment of group goals. This is especially true in cases of common resources, or resources that exhibit characteristics of low excludability and high divisibility. Self-interest can be tamed to some degree by removing the characteristics of the resource as described above, say from a common resource to a private resource. This does not change individual self-interest, but rather the conditions by which self-interest can lead to free riding, or defecting from the group interest.

---

* You may be able to connect this strategy of charging for carbon emissions with some of the discussions in Chapters 2 and 3. Here you can see how underlying theories of valuation help to support the development of policies aimed at internalizing the costs of environmental harm with the goal of preventing free riding by those who create the harm.

Before we move on to the next section dealing with multiparty decision-making, we need to take a closer look at how individual values, through an analysis of behavior patterns—specifically learning—evolve and influence both individual and group dynamics. The reason why is because an understanding of how decisions evolve is required to fully integrate what impacts decision-making at multiple levels of scale: individual, group, state, country, global community. We will attempt to summarize some of the major theories that deal with behavioral theory of choice below, which will then set the stage for a more detailed examination of larger-scale value systems and decision-making.

Learning Dynamics

We learned in the previous section that self-interest alters the goals between an individual and a group. This is especially true when the goal is to protect a resource that has common property characteristics. Since most environmental issues deal with common property characteristics in some way, we tend to focus on the impact of individual decisions, especially self-interest and the phenomenon of free riding described above. Now we will take a step back and think about individual learning dynamics in general. The link I am proposing between learning dynamics and values goes something like this: preferences are the manifestation of values; preferences are exhibited as behavior; behaviors presented over time (patterns of behavior) are the basis of learning. Thus, learning dynamics can be stated to be the field that encompasses an understanding of individual value expression (Vriend 2004, 130–33).

To set up this section, we will begin by addressing two major forms of learning as a way of understanding how individual decisions progress. We will then focus on a type of noncooperative game called *prisoner's dilemma*, which is often used to understand how individual preferences and learning evolve with one other person over time. We will then shift to a cooperative form of game known as the *stag hunt* to see the major differences between a cooperative and noncooperative interaction among individuals, and how this difference impacts decision-making. Finally, we will discuss a game known as *standing ovation* to see how individual behaviors begin to impact, and be impacted by, the larger group setting. This will bring us to our next section, where we look at the scaling of values in multiparty decision-making.*

---

* It is important to note what we will not be discussing in this section. For those who might read this section and who have a background in learning dynamics (to include cooperative games, noncooperative games, agent-based modeling, etc.), understand that certain subjects were purposefully left out of this section due to length considerations and the general audience for which the text is meant. As a primer in environmental decision-making, there is a need to gain a sense of how learning dynamics theory is evolving, and how certain parts of the theory might be applied to modeling behavior and understanding the relationship between actions and responses. I consider the concepts chosen to highlight learning dynamics sufficient for the purposes of gaining a basic insight into the subject matter. Those who seek greater depth of knowledge in this area are encouraged to look to additional resources for greater insights. This goes with all parts of this text.

We will break down learning as a way of understanding value development and behavioral actions into two major divisions or types: *belief learning* and *reinforcement learning*. For our discussion here, we will say belief learning occurs when one forms a belief or internal representation of the world and uses those representations to make decisions. Under this definition, belief learning is similar to the term *worldview* identified earlier in this chapter under our subjective value discussion (Layzer 2011). The key characteristic of belief learning is the emphasis on the belief, which can range from passive (low) to unshakeable (high) under different circumstances. An example might be a person who has a strongly held religious view. No matter what evidence might be presented to dispute or discredit the view, the religious observant stands by his or her belief. This is an extreme example of belief learning because the learning itself is limited.

A more moderate example is where the internal belief—representation of the world—forms the basis of decision-making, meaning all decisions flow from that belief, but the belief does not prevent learning from occurring. One might argue Americans in general had a strong belief in the security of the United States prior to September 11, 2001. Events such as the bombing of the World Trade Center in the 1990s and the Oklahoma City bombing did not substantially change this belief. Rather, many people found ways of explaining or accommodating those events around their belief of safety. It took a substantial event like September 11 to shake this concept of security, requiring an individual and government response that perceived the belief in a new way. (Incidentally, this often happens in science, where a law—a long-standing theory that fits most explanations of phenomena—is finally proven to be invalid. The process of accepting the new theory takes a lot of time because many scientists hold on strongly to their belief in the old law.)

Reinforcement learning is different from belief learning. Reinforcement learning describes a form of learning that is based primarily on experience and not closely held beliefs or worldviews. In reinforcement learning, a person increases the probability of acts that have been rewarded and decreases the probability of those that have not been rewarded (Staddon 2007, 161–65). This kind of learning is based more on actual experiences than it is on belief systems. In this type of learning, the person identifies the likelihood of an action based on pure experience. For example, a person who has experienced "good luck" finding work by going to a particular agency on a particular day at a particular time will tend to continue this strategy to find work because of the accumulated rewards from the past experiences.

To make the distinction clear, a person using belief learning might have a strong belief that there will be a messiah visiting the earth in the near future because of religious doctrine. This belief will influence that person's decisions. A person relying on reinforcement learning alone will have no good reason to believe a messiah will be forthcoming because he or she has never experienced this phenomenon before, and therefore there is a very low probability of this occurring in his or her mind. Can you see how the different forms of learning identified here value different aspects of knowing? Beliefs are very important in one context, while experience is key in the other context.

These different ways of viewing the world as an almost precondition to learning are important because they set the stage for value-based decisions. A believer will place a lot of weight on his or her worldviews, while a reinforcer will place the most weight on past experiences, for better or worse. Why is this important to consider in the environmental context? Consider the impact the baseline values of an individual have on setting policies. Say you are a government official in charge of developing policies for setting quotas on the total amount of fish that can be caught in 1 year. You develop a rule that limits the amount of fish available in a given year such that it significantly impacts the economic well-being of the fishermen subject to the rule. Now, say that you find out the rule was based on bad information, and more fish can be caught.

How will this new information be received by the fishermen? If the fishermen are reinforcers, the change in policy direction might not impact their view of your office too negatively because they rely on previous experiences to inform their value system. However, if the fishermen are believers, then the actions you take will have less impact overall because the fishermen have a belief system that colors their view of you and government. If the belief is negative ("government is out to harm us"), then changing your policy direction might have limited impact on relations. This is just one example of why it is important to understand how your actors perceive the world and the ways in which they engage in making value-laden decisions.

Let us now look at how learning evolves in a variety of settings. We begin by looking at noncooperative games, specifically the prisoner's dilemma. We then move on to a cooperative form of learning, the stag hunt. Finally, we conclude with linking individual decisions to the larger group context by introducing the standing ovation problem.

Prisoner's dilemma is a strategic model used in game theory. It has been used to understand how individual choices impact cooperation (Axelrod 1984). Since prisoner's dilemma is a game, the focus of attention in understanding behavior is on strategy. For example, given what is known about a particular situation, what is the likelihood that a person will do action A versus action B?

The strategic part of game theory is based on the premise that two parties are in an adversarial setting toward one another; they are being competitive toward one another. In such a setting, and based on limited information availability, what is the likely outcome? In limiting the information, and then changing it over time, one can review how individual choices are made and whether those choices consistently change between players. Common themes are sought out to see if basic principles arise. If they do, those principles then inform interested parties about how individual choice dynamics work under certain conditions. The prisoner's dilemma is a certain type of game that offers insights on cooperative strategy based on limited information availability. The way in which the game helps understand the

Suspect 1

	Confess	Remain Silent
Confess	5, 5	0, 7
Remain Silent	7, 0	3, 3

Suspect 2

Figure 4.8 A representation of prisoner's dilemma outcomes.

individual decision-making process (referred to as strategies) in a limited situation is best explained by an overview of the game itself.

Two people are arrested for the same crime. Both of the people know one another, and they both partook in the criminal act—they are both guilty. The two people are separated into different rooms and told the same thing by the arresting officers; they have enough incriminating evidence to put both of them in jail for a short sentence, say 3 years. However, if one confesses on the other person, that person will go free *so long as the other person does not confess*. If the one person confesses and the other person does not, then the person who does not confess will receive a large sentence based on the evidence provided by the confessor, say 7 years. If both confess, they will each receive a longer sentence than not confessing, but less than if only one person confesses, say 5 years. Based on these rules, we have the matrix of possible outcomes shown in Figure 4.8.

In looking at the potential outcomes listed in the figure, we can try and determine what we believe to be the best strategy overall. For example, confess/confess has a payout* of 5 and 5, meaning each person gets 5 years in prison if both confess. Alternatively, silent/silent has a payout of 3 and 3, meaning each person gets 3 years in prison as long as both remain silent. Finally, there are two instances in the matrix where confess/silent are options (one person confesses and the other party remains silent). The payout here is 7 and 0, meaning the silent party will receive a 7-year sentence, while the person who confesses will serve no time—he or she will go free.

Now that we know the various outcomes, we next need to decide what is the best strategy? If you were one of the accomplices, which strategy would you choose? At first glance, confessing seems a good option because it gives you the potential to serve no time in prison. Of course, this is only true if you are sure that the other person will

---

* The term *payout* is often used to express the outcomes in game theory. Much of the vernacular used in this field resembles the terms that would be used if we were actually playing a game, like a board game.

remain silent; remember, if he or she confesses you will each serve 5 years in prison. The next best option seems to be to remain silent because if both of you do so, you will only serve 3 years each in prison. Again, this makes sense only if you are certain the other person will remain silent; if he or she confesses and you remain silent, you will be serving 7 years in prison—the longest sentence possible. Difficult, isn't it?

What makes this dilemma especially difficult is the fact the two prisoners cannot share information; each person has been separated into different interrogation rooms and there is no opportunity to discuss strategy. So, you have to rely on your best guess, or instincts, in trying to determine what the other person might do because his or her choice significantly impacts your choice. As suggested above, there are a variety of choices one might make, depending on how he or she views the likelihood the other person will choose one strategy over another. Some believe there is an optimal strategy in a basic first iteration of the prisoner's dilemma, referred to as a *Nash equilibrium* after the author of the theory, John Nash (Nash 1950, 48–49).

The superior strategy, or Nash equilibrium, is confess/confess, meaning each person would be subject to 5 years of prison. Note this is not the best outcome for each person (neither 0 or 3 years apiece if each person remained silent), but it is superior because it limits the amount of risk. Also note I qualified this superior strategy by limiting it to a first-iteration game. In multiple games, where people play prisoner's dilemma again and again, keeping track of the individual strategies, learning occurs. The learning is in the form of knowing which strategy your opponent had chosen in the previous game. While not a complete sharing of information as in a situation where the two prisoners communicate before they make a decision, the previous strategy chosen by the other player helps to inform you about his or her likelihood of choosing a similar or different strategy in the future. When prisoner's dilemma games are played out over multiple iterations, certain trends become common. See if you can pick out the trend in Figure 4.9.

Can you follow the learning that is happening during these multiple games? Player 1 begins by confessing (denoted as a D for defect). Player 2 begins trusting

			Number of Games Played			
	1	2	3	4	5	6
Player 1	D	D	C	C	C	C
Player 2	C	D	D	C	C	C

D = Defect
C = Cooperate

Figure 4.9 A representation of multiple game outcomes in a prisoner's dilemma game.

player 1 and remains silent (denoted as a C for cooperate). In the second game, player 2 punishes player 1 for defecting, choosing to defect himself or herself, leaving us at a Nash equilibrium strategy. However, in the third game, player 1 attempts to coerce player 2 back to cooperation (maybe because he or she sees the lesser sentence as a potential based on player 2's initial willingness to cooperate). Player 2 does notice this willingness after the game (remember, the players choose their strategies simultaneously), and thus by game 4, they both learn to engage in the strategy that will collectively yield them the least amount of time in jail.

It should be noted that this initial punishment and then trust sequence tends to be a regular occurrence when this game is played through multiple iterations. This sequence represents a form of cooperative evolution referred to as tit for tat (Axelrod 1984). It is a telling insight about the dynamics of individual behaviors and choices, and how individual behaviors evolve over time based on interactions with others. From a scaling standpoint, this reinforces the notion that individuals can use one set of criteria when making choices without information about others, but then can alter those choices when they have more information about how others might act. Add in other factors, including resource designation and the potential of free riding, and we can begin to paint a picture of individual decision-making dynamics and how such dynamics impact environmental decisions.

We have just seen how understanding individual decisions in relation to strategies can occur in a noncooperative environment. Let us now turn to learning in a cooperative environment to see how a different form of interaction between individuals can yield more positive results. As we do, consider the impact that cooperation versus noncooperation might have on the evolution of environmental decisions.

The *stag hunt* is an example of a cooperative game.* The main distinguishing characteristic we can highlight for our purposes is the following: cooperative games include collaboration between players, while noncooperative games have no collaboration between players (Axelrod 1984). The lack of collaboration in noncooperative games is highlighted in the prisoner's dilemma by the fact that the two players are separated from one another and cannot share information or strategy prior to either confessing or remaining silent. The stag hunt differs in that players can coordinate their strategies prior to actually making a decision; this is why the stag hunt is known as a coordination-type game (Binmore 2007, 57–70). Both the stag hunt and prisoner's dilemma are pure strategy games, where an optimal strategy is sought. This can be further contrasted with elements of group decision-making (as opposed to individual decisions—our current focus), such as *consensus decision-making* and *majoritarian voting*.

---

* Although we are distinguishing between cooperative and noncooperative types of games here, there is some strong evidence that all games can be defined as noncooperative, depending on where the focus is placed in analyzing interactions between players. John Nash was a proponent of suggesting all games are noncompetitive, and he has had some substantial support since in the game theory literature.

Hunter 1

		Stag	Hare
Hunter 2	Stag	10, 10	0, 7
	Hare	7, 0	7, 7

Figure 4.10   A representation of stag hunt payoffs.

The stag hunt is interesting because it operates on a question of trust; either go it alone and be assured of some small measure of success, or trust another and have greater success. Here is how the game works. Two players are going hunting. There are two options of animal for the hunt, either a stag (deer) or a hare (rabbit). One person alone cannot successfully hunt a stag; they are too big and too fast. It requires two people working together to successfully hunt a stag. One person can successfully hunt a hare alone, but the payout (benefit) is smaller; the amount of food available from hunting a hare is much smaller individually than the ration of food available to each person from a stag. So, it is better to hunt a stag—more bang for the buck. However, in order to do so, one needs to cooperate because it takes two people to successfully hunt a stag. The payoff matrix for the stag hunt based on what has been described is shown in Figure 4.10.

We can see the superior strategy here is for both players to agree to hunt stag, resulting in each player receiving 10 units of value (10/10). We can also see the risk of hunting stag without the cooperation of the other player. In such a situation, the stag hunter receives a 0 because it takes two people to successfully hunt stag. In this situation, it is clear the Nash equilibrium strategy is stag/stag, meaning both players agree, or coordinate, to hunt stag. Contrast this with the Nash equilibrium strategy in the prisoner's dilemma, confess/confess. Confessing is against the interests of the other player, and thus represents noncooperation as the superior strategy. So, why the difference in strategy between the two games presented? Why is cooperation sought in one instance while noncooperation is the best bet in the other instance? The answer lies in the capacity to share information.

Information sharing is a key element to earning trust and creating socially acceptable interactions among human beings. Behaviors reinforce values, but behaviors are also a result of plans between species with the ability to communicate and strategize. In the prisoner's dilemma, there was no opportunity to communicate beforehand; the prisoners were separated before they could strategize collectively. Thus, the superior strategy was one that did not result in the best payoff (both remaining silent), but one that was the safest bet not knowing what the other player would do (both confessing). The stag hunt is different in that both players have the ability to communicate and plan ahead of time. As such, the best payout can occur when there is agreement among the players, cooperation toward a similar goal. This should be a hint about how individual humans build alliances and trust among other members of a community.

We might also consider strategies in the larger context of learning (belief and reinforcement) described above. Imagine a player who has a strongly held belief that he or she cannot trust other people, no matter what a person does or says.* If this is true, then we can assume this person would confess in the prisoner's dilemma, and also choose to hunt hare in the stag hunt regardless of what the other player does or says. If there were multiple games being played, even the history of cooperation from the other player would likely not convince a strong believer to change his or her strategy.

Contrast this with a player who uses experience (reinforcement) to define his or her strategy. We can assume this player will move toward cooperation in both games so long as the other player shows a willingness to cooperate through his or her chosen strategy. After a few iterations we would likely find the parties cooperating nicely. This brings us to our final part of this section, the *standing ovation*. Here, we see how individual decisions begin to influence the actions of others, a precursor to understanding how values impact multiparty decision-making.

The standing ovation problem is a study of group dynamics introduced by John Miller and Scott Page to help explain how individual decision-making occurs within the larger context of group interactions (Miller and Page 2007). The problem is different from both the prisoner's dilemma and stag hunt discussed above. Both the prisoner's dilemma and stag hunt dealt with one-on-one interactions, where the strategy of the individual player was limited to considering the interaction of the other player. The standing ovation problem, like the prisoner's dilemma and stag hunt, considers the strategy chosen by the one player, but differs by having the strategy chosen dependent on the choices/actions made by many other players (or actors) in the particular setting. In this way, the choice of the individual player is based on *multiple strategies* being played out by the other actors, not simply the actions of one other actor. A quick summary of the problem will help to place this difference into context.

The basic facts of the standing ovation problem are as follows, using you, the reader, as the agent at the center of the problem. You are attending a brilliant musical performance in a theatre with hundreds of other audience members seated around you. The performance ends and the audience begins to applaud. The applause builds and somewhere along the way it becomes obvious that some of the

---

* Maybe this lack of belief is due to past life experiences, say being abandoned as a child, for instance.

audience members are contemplating standing. So, does a standing ovation ensue, or does the enthusiasm fade?

This is the question raised by Miller and Page, and they have done work modeling different types of interactions from the point of view of one individual, or agent, using a process generally known as *agent-based modeling*. While the results and manipulations of the modeling exercise are interesting explorations in themselves, we remain focused on understanding what kinds of value questions are raised here, specifically in reference to how the individual behaviors of our agent (you the reader in our example) are influenced by the actions and inactions of others. So, let us consider what might occur and go through a kind of thought experiment to work out possible actions, stopping along the way to consider the impacts of these actions on our decisions.

To our original question: Does a standing ovation ensue from the applause? Well, let's begin by defining a proper standing ovation as one that must include *all* members of the audience. So, in order to have a standing ovation, every member of the audience must participate by standing and applauding. Let us now assume that a few members of the audience decide to stand while applauding. Does this alone create enough incentive for you to also stand and applaud? What factors do you think are relevant in making your decision? For example, what if you never intended on standing to applaud in the first place?

Let us consider the factor of *proximity*, looking at how close to you are the people who decide to stand. Do you think proximity makes a difference? Say you are sitting in an area where the person immediately in front of you and the two people on either immediate side of you stand. Do you think this creates a compulsion to stand? You are definitely the odd person out in this small section of seats, even if everyone else in the theatre is not standing. It is probably likely that proximity has an impact here. Based on this reasoning, we might suggest the following assumption: the closer you are to those who stand, all other things being equal, the more likely it is that you will also stand.

Other factors beyond proximity include the total number of people who stand in the theatre. Say you are sitting in the back of the theatre and notice people begin to stand starting from the front of the theatre. The "wave" of those standing begins to move toward you from front to back. At what point does the number of those standing accumulate to a level that makes you want to stand as well? In exercises where this problem is modeled, there is often a critical mass reached beyond which everyone (or almost everyone) stands in the theatre because a certain percentage of the audience has chosen to stand.

What we are interested in here are the factors that can lead an individual to make a decision that goes against his or her personal beliefs, desires, or intents. Recall the previous discussion about free riding and the peer pressure of the group. One tends to free ride in situations where he or she can benefit from others without receiving consequences for his or her inaction. Group pressure is a way of limiting this practice even when it is the desire of individual self-interest. But *how* is this pressure being exerted in our standing ovation problem?

Consider that each audience member is providing a *signal* through standing or sitting, and signaling is tantamount to showing an individual preference. Even though these signals tend to show preference, there is really no way of knowing the intensity of the individual preference. For example, does a person standing next to me suggest he or she has a strong preference for standing to show appreciation? If the preference is strong, he or she might indeed want me to stand as well. However, if the preference is weak, he or she might be fine with my not standing. In fact, he or she might not personally want to stand either, but is only doing so because others are standing; he or she felt compelled by group pressure and is reacting to the compulsion.

The inability to express intensity of preference in a group setting can lead to a herding effect, which is often referred to as an *information cascade*. An information cascade occurs when people in a group setting ignore their personal feelings by choosing to follow the actions of others (Miller and Page 2007). In our standing ovation problem, conditions in the theatre may lead to a point where those who begin to stand for the ovation cause others to stand, and at some level of aggregation the compulsion to stand becomes a cascade, meaning others still sitting will be compelled to stand not because they desire to stand necessarily, but because they are reacting to the actions of others and assuming the others are showing a preference for standing and that preference is strong. Since those still seated cannot ask each person standing about the intensity of his or her preference, a form of pressure to stand builds to the point that everyone might stand, simply following the early leaders who are the most likely to actually want to stand.

The implications of the standing ovation problem are interesting when we link these actions back to basic questions of value. Most directly, we see in the problem an example of how individual values can be put aside because of group dynamics; an individual can feel compelled to stand and applaud based on group pressure. So, the group hegemony can prevent individual expressions or defections from the group. This is even the case when the relative intensity of the overall group for preferring a particular idea is not known. We might now link this to larger-scale societal norms and systems, such as rules of law. People may conform to rules not because they necessarily agree with the rule as an individual, but because they are coerced by the actions of the majority. This leads us now into the final section of this chapter, understanding how the larger dynamics of group interactions impact questions of value at the scale of multiparty decision-making.

Values and Multiparty Decision-Making

As you may have identified in the previous materials of this section, the formulation of value systems is dynamic. How we define *value* is very much dependent on our framework for evaluating the term. We have seen how objective values are defined through a rigorous process and methodology that can be replicated to identify a level of risk based on probability and direct causal relationships; the dose-response analysis as a form of risk assessment is a prime example. Of course our values are not simply based on objective observations; values are also influenced by subjective drivers. We saw how individual and group perceptions can identify a risk through outrage, as outlined by Sandman. This outrage is highly influenced by a community component. Indeed, we can see how some of the group pressure discussed in that section is related to our scaling discussion through the example of the standing ovation. Individuals can be influenced in their personal thoughts and actions by what others around them are doing, even if there is no clear understanding of intent or veracity toward the particular ideal. Thus, we can see how a standing ovation-type scenario can lead to community outrage as a perception based highly on subjective factors (at best), and how such a community perception can completely disregard more objective forms of information.* Add to this the additional complications of self-interest under appropriate circumstances, and we have a dynamic setting in which to discern how values play a role in environmental decision-making.

The purpose of this final section is to step back from some of the details that we have been working through for the majority of this chapter. Here, we will review more institutional issues associated with values at an aggregate level, focusing mostly on how social systems engage in value decision-making. If we as individuals are somewhat confused about whether we should care about certain environmental issues, and more importantly, what we might be willing to give up to protect the environment, then why do governments often take a lead in establishing and implementing environmental protections?

In this section, we will explore the basic role of government and how environmental decisions are made at this level. We are going to keep this section primarily conceptual, meaning we are going to think in a bit more abstract sense, rather than looking at institutional actors and current systems of governance. Specifically, we are going to scale up our analysis of game theory to a macro-level and look at how the difference between cooperative and noncooperative games helps us understand different large-scale strategies at environmental decision-making.

Consensus Building and Majority Voting

Recall games can be divided into two categories, cooperative and noncooperative. Cooperative games have the hallmark of collaboration among the players; the example we discussed was the stag hunt. Noncooperative games are defined by a lack of collaboration between the players; the prisoner's dilemma was the example we

---

* If many of the individuals are simply cascading or following along with a few in the group, then it is entirely possible the group as a whole does not have a clear idea of the basis upon which they are outraged about an issue. This is certainly true in the environmental arena, where many of the issues are purposefully made complicated and vague, pushing public sentiment toward a bias that is not based on objective evidence.

highlighted. If we scale up these types of games to a societal level, we can find two types of government decision-making processes, one representing elements of cooperation, referred to as *consensus building*, and the other representing a lack of cooperation, referred to as *majority voting*. Before we get into the details of each type, let us quickly review the connection between government decision-making and values.

The purpose of a government, at least in a free society, is to represent the interests of the people. In most democratic institutions, where people have the right to vote representatives into office, the way in which the interests of the people are fundamentally carried out is through the passage of laws (Rousseau 1893). Lawmaking is generally done through a legislative body, such as the Congress in the United States. To pass a law, there has to be some process for validating a proposal into formal legal existence. For our purposes, we can separate that process into two options; the lawmaking body of government requires either a majority vote, or it otherwise requires a consensus of all voting members. From a game theoretic standpoint, there is a substantial difference in choosing one system over the other because of the effect the particular system has on strategies employed. Let us begin by differentiating the two forms of lawmaking by the level of cooperation required to secure the passage of a law. As we do, consider what elements of human behavior derive from the different theories outlined.

The first theory we will look at is majority voting. In majority voting, a law is passed by getting more individuals of a lawmaking body to vote for the proposal than those who vote against it (Forman 1911, 9–10). For example, say there are 100 members of a lawmaking body. If 51 of the 100 vote for a proposal, then there is a slight majority. Under a basic majority system of government, this is enough to pass the proposal.* Contrast this with a consensus decision-making system, where the lawmaking body is required to achieve complete consensus from the members of the group (Roseland 2005, 191–92). For example, if there are 100 members of the lawmaking body under a consensus form of government, then the proposal will only be passed if all 100 members are in agreement.

A majority form of government is placed into the noncooperative category of games because not all members are required to coordinate with the ultimate decision. In essence, majority voting reduces the commitment of each individual decision-maker to the decision; the minority losers may have a reduced sense of responsibility for the ultimate decision because they did not favor the successful proposal. In this sense, the majority does not have to cooperate with the minority. Also, because the minority proposal does not win the day, the losers may have a

---

* The assumption here is that everyone eligible to vote on the matter actually does vote. Also, there are a variety of majority forms of voting. For example, there can be a simple majority (51% or more required) or some form of supermajority (say 66% or more required) in order to pass certain pieces of legislation. The higher the percentage of participants required to agree in a majority system of voting, the more like a consensus style decision-making dynamic arises, including the attendant issues.

greater incentive to defect from the majority rule; a lack of ownership over the decision may lead to free riding incentives, as we saw in the property right discussion above under individual decision-making and self-interest.

Consensus decision-making contains a different commitment to defining cooperation among participants. Rather than focusing on building a majority vote and thereby dismissing minority objections, consensus building seeks the agreement of all (or mostly all) participants. It also seeks to resolve or mitigate the objections of the minority to achieve the most agreeable decision. In this way, consensus is defined as meaning both general agreement (a focus on outcome) and the process of getting to such an agreement; the focus on process and mitigating minority objections differentiates consensus building from majority voting.

One of the key differences between majority voting and consensus building is the treatment of group preferences in a way that minimizes the opportunities for defection from the norm. Remember, we are trying to understand the dynamics of values scaled up to a group setting. All values are observed as preferences, and preferences begin as individual choices based on a variety of stimuli, both external and internal. We have seen how stimuli can alter value choices of the individual; for example, sharing information between participants can change a noncooperative prisoner's dilemma-type situation into a cooperative venture like the stag hunt. Sharing information between participants and coming to an understanding on interests is a strong way of establishing commitments between individuals and minimizing conflicts such as free riding and defections that result in nonoptimal outcomes.

The same principles apply at large-scale levels. Groups take on the role of individuals by establishing a set of principles of agreement between the members. Some of the members may have a strong personal connection to the group principles, while others may simply be following the party line and going along with what others in the group are advocating—a phenomenon outlined in the standing ovation problem described earlier in this chapter. In our group setting here, consensus building sends a message that all interests are relevant; all divergent views have value worth considering, and the final outcome should represent consideration of these views (even if some of the views are not incorporated into the final outcome). In this way, consensus building seeks to minimize the feelings of marginalization between competing factions; in doing so, there is greater acceptance of the final decision, meaning there will be less likelihood of defection and the attendant costs associated with policing against defections.* Majority voting may contain a process

---

* Placing this theory into practice, consider the development of an environmental law that is made through consensus building. The final law will have a greater likelihood of acceptance by everyone (or close to everyone), meaning enforcement costs will be minimized. If we are wearing a cost-effective lens when thinking about superior forms of developing environmental policies, enforcement costs are a substantial consideration. This is especially true where valuation is being determined using something *less* than a total valuation approach, as discussed in Chapter 3.

that involves negotiation with minority interests,* but there is generally much less emphasis placed on minimizing conflict among the various interests. The end result is usually a compromise that leaves some interests dissatisfied, opening the potential for defections among the minority interests.

Dissatisfaction among members of a group is one way to see how large-scale values impact environmental decision-making. We see this play itself out all the time in the political debates surrounding environmental issues. In the United States, environmental laws that have been established are often the focus of attention by dissatisfied groups looking to change the law; the Endangered Species Act, passed in the 1970s, is often the target of such groups (Firestone and Reed 2008, 4–30). For some, the entire law itself should be repealed. For others, the law is inappropriately applied by listing certain species; the listing of certain species impacts the interests of these groups.

Environmental decisions can be problematic no matter the method employed in establishing the decision. This is because of a variety of factors, such as the application of the law changing, as was just described under the Endangered Species Act. In other cases, current social conditions can create dissatisfaction with an environmental policy. For example, when economic conditions change for the worse, the public may become wary of environmental policies that place additional economic burdens on the public. So, beyond the methods employed by a society to limit defection of an environmental policy, the organic nature of changing conditions can also impact the overall acceptance of a particular environmental decision. Having an awareness of these factors is important in understanding the system in which environmental decisions are enacted. Let us now turn to a few examples of larger-scale decision-making, and some of the issues that arise at these larger scales.

Other Collective Value System Considerations

National and international decision-making takes on many of the same components of values identified earlier, including self-interest, learning dynamics, and various forms of strategy in cooperative and noncooperative forms of interactions. What we can provide here now is some additional context to gain insights on how these dynamics interact at aggregated levels. First consider national forms of decision-making.

Nations are bodies of politics, and therefore they are traditionally developed to provide a measure of security for the common person. One person who highlighted

---

* There are various forms of consensus building and negotiation that occur in any majority voting system. Early ideas for policy development are vetted by seeing what groups might be interested or recalcitrant to the idea. Negotiations then begin to take hold to see if a majority can ultimately be established to pass the proposal into law. While it is necessary for us to make distinctions in order to best understand the concepts being expressed, real life is much more dynamic, representing a continuum of variation between a majority vote and consensus building distinction. This is to say we are focused on the hard distinctions in our conceptual understanding rather than the more subtle distinctions that exist in reality.

the nature of this benefit of a formalized government was Jean Jacques Rousseau (Rousseau 1893). Rousseau identified a *social contract* between people as the center-piece of a government, particularly a democratic system of government. The basic idea is that people are willing to give up certain natural rights through the adoption of social laws because the benefits gained in adopting the social laws outweigh the benefits lost by giving up those natural rights.* Thus, a nation is a collection of social laws that provide for the benefit of the members at large. Each member of the nation has particular incentives that drive him or her (well discussed above), but this occurs within limits set by the national body itself—the laws created and enforced by that body.

Nations can act like individuals when it comes to value-based decisions. For example, nations often engage in self-interested decisions. We see this play out in the role of international discourse, or arguments between nations. Even though nations can act like individuals in terms of self-interest and preferences, they are very different in the goals outlined for the entity as a whole. Looking through an environmental lens, we can see that nations must consider a timescale that is much longer than that for most individuals. Nations are meant to survive from one generation to the next. As such, you and I might not consider climate change to be a top priority, especially if the effects are not realized for 100 years, but a government must think differently about the issue. Also, nations have priorities that extend beyond such things as bottom lines. Nations are meant to be concerned with the social welfare of their citizenry (Rousseau 1893). So issues such as clean air and water may take precedence over economic prosperity, at least where that prosperity puts a basic level of quality of life directly at risk. Let us look a bit closer at the difference between individual and social values of a society.

A fundamental difference based on the ideas expressed by Rousseau in his *social contract* may be summarized as the difference between *individualism* and *collectivism*. As indicated above, there is an inherent conflict between these two

---

* Consider under natural law one has a kind of a Darwinian survival of the fittest perspective. Humans must rely on their individual strengths (cunning, power, etc.) in order to gain advantage for themselves. One is only as good as his or her personal traits, and can be overcome by some other person who is faster, stronger, smarter, or some combination of these traits. There is essentially no safety net for the individual under natural law conditions. Government provides social law, or a set of rules that help to govern a civilized society. Included in these rules are prohibitions against certain acts, say stealing and murdering. Although these prohibitions prevent certain actions, they also ensure a certain level of safety for members of the society. For example, under social law a stronger human cannot use his or her strength as a means to gain advantage over you, assuming doing so breaks a social law. The power of the state (collective agreement of the majority of the population) exerts influence to prevent the stronger individual from harming the weaker. This goes for all of the stronger people who might want to harm one weaker person. Thus, in this example, the one weaker person is prevented from exerting influence over others through strength, but he or she is also protected by the same law from all who are stronger than him or her from doing the same thing; the social law provides more benefits to the individual than it takes away.

systems of value. For example, a value system based on individual considerations highlights the importance of individual freedoms. Collective value systems must take into account the well-being of others, and thus must place limits on individual freedom (to the extent those limits ensure the collective well-being of all members of the society).

The extent of limits placed on individuals from society is the inherent conflict that occurs at this level of aggregation. One way of knowing how far a society can go in limiting personal freedoms (or should go) is to determine the overall balance of benefits received versus benefits given up in the trade-off. The transaction will generally seem fair so long as the benefits accrued to the individual from society outweigh the benefits lost to that individual. The interactions between individual and collective value systems may be summarized as follows:

- Individuals may act freely so long as their actions do not harm others' individual freedoms or societal needs.
- Societal needs cannot harm individual freedoms unless it can be shown the harm is based on a proscription (law) determined by the majority of members of that society, and the application of that law is to benefit the well-being of each member of the society.
- The restriction of individual rights by a society is generally acceptable if it meets the following conditions:
  - It was passed by at least a majority of members of the society.
  - It is meant to prevent a violation of rights assigned to the members of the society at large.
- It leaves the individual with more benefits than the individual has given up.

An idealized situation is when two value systems, say an individual and societal value system, are consistent. Consistency here suggests the two systems bear no contradictions or exceptions between them (Bales 2001, 183–224). When we look at environmental decisions through the lens of societal values, we often find instances where societal values contradict with individual value systems. As mentioned earlier, individual values are subject to change contextually, meaning the individual might place one value ahead of another because of changing preferences. Preferences for environmental values, for instance, tend to be inferior to more immediate concerns, like human health, safety, and welfare considerations. When individuals have a sense of security about personal security, then they tend to emphasize a preference for environmental considerations (Peterson del Mar 2006, 61–81). However, if that sense of security wanes for any reason, then environmental considerations tend to take a back seat to the more immediate and pressing considerations. Governments may show a capacity to change priorities based on changing conditions, but this is generally less so than individual behavior patterns. For example, a government might establish laws to protect the environment, and then fund a federal agency to carry out the implementation and enforcement of those laws. Once created, these government institutions tend to be long-standing, as the laws were created to be implemented by the institutions (Weimer and Vining 2011, 178–181). As such, the value preference for environmental protection is more long-standing and less capable of being completely removed because of changes in external factors (economic, etc.). In this way, it may be that social values and individual values become inconsistent at different periods of time; individuals may not care about the environment as deeply as before, but government has created a system of laws, regulations, and bureaucracy that is less capable for changing preferences, which may be a very good thing! Individuals do not always engage in long-term considerations that many environmental issues require. Thus, we must trust in our government to make the difficult decisions that might include protecting the environment for future generations even when doing so causes "pain" for the current generation of citizens. It is important to acknowledge this type of value inconsistency that can develop between individual and societal scales.

We can also mention the difference between national governments (two or more countries) when it comes to value systems; like individuals and societal values, the issue of consistency arises. From a societal-to-societal value comparison, many countries may share similar value systems; these countries might be said to have value consistency between countries. However, some countries may have vastly different value systems, leading to inconsistency between the countries. We often see this external inconsistency play itself out on the world stage. Whether it is issues between two countries, or it is a set of countries unified as a bloc against another bloc in an international forum, the differences that drive the issue are generally based on differences of value.

The implications of inconsistent value applications between countries for global environmental issues like climate change are substantial. If countries cannot come to common ground on an issue of global importance like climate change, then our collective capacity to make meaningful decisions on the subject is limited. Consider the following example; country A and country B are both involved in activity that generates greenhouse gas emissions. Country A is a developed rich nation that wants to limit its emissions through technological innovations, most of which it can further innovate because of the wealth it has developed over the years through early industrialization and emissions. Country B is a developing nation that is growing in wealth but is still considered relatively poor in comparison to more developed nations. Country B is currently going through industrialization, and it does not feel capable of altering its reliance on greenhouse gases as a means to its development. While country A might be placing a high value on reducing emissions, country B is more focused on the immediate well-being of its citizenry. Indeed, both countries might be sharing the same value system (protection and well-being of their respective citizens), but they are at different viewpoints in relation of how to best achieve the goal of protection.

We may pause here and recall some of the previous information about negotiation, particularly the portions that discussed focusing on *issues* rather than *positions* as a means of creating common ground (Fisher and Ury 2011). Consider the example above between country A and country B. What do you think is the major sticking point here? What would the issue be here? How might you go about getting both parties to focus on the issue? If we find the value systems of the two parties *as related to the issue under consideration (climate change)* are consistent on the issue, but there are differences of perception, then a focus must likely be placed on working to change the perceptions of the parties to show where the common interests exist. This is a large part of environmental decision-making, knowing how to identify the true issues of the participants and how those issues are related to the larger goal. Connecting the issues to the goals is a big part of unifying values no matter the scale presented.

Conclusion

In this chapter we have reviewed the concept of value from three different but related viewpoints: objective value through the basis of scientific quantification of risk, subjective value through the notion of perceptions, and the scaling of value from an individual to a group perspective, including national and international bodies. The first summative point to make is hopefully somewhat obvious as we are at the conclusion of this section: value systems are complex. The objective nature of determining value is a complex enough process, but it is made more complex through the addition of subjective considerations. From an environmental decision-making standpoint, there are a few key lessons to take away from this chapter.

Objective values help to create a means of grounding environmental decisions in fact. The capacity to replicate objective valuations is a key component to grounding environmental decisions. This is probably the most important starting point for any environmental discussion; it helps to establish what parties are capable of agreeing on and can also help to identify potential sticking points between parties. If someone or some group is unwilling to accept objective information, then you can be relatively sure their position will be recalcitrant toward the conclusions of that objective information.

One who is engaged in environmental decision-making should begin by finding all forms of objective evidence relating to the question at hand. This objective evidence should be analyzed to see correlations where appropriate, and should also be offered to various stakeholders in the decision-making process to get their insights and opinions on the information. Much can be learned from starting here. One must remember to review the methodology employed in the objective analysis to make sure the results are telling and legitimate. The ability for the results to be replicated and the likelihood of a cause-effect relationship are important criteria for ensuring that the information is relevant.

We must remember that the reliance on objective forms of information is dynamic, meaning the level of scientific certainly about a subject changes over time.

This means one must be willing to refine his or her position about environmental questions as the objective evidence is refined through the scientific method. Connected to this point is how to treat objective information when the availability of information is lacking. Environmental issues such as climate change rely on a lot of correlations and feedback through a dynamic system; in this way it is hard to judge cause and effect with absolute certainty. In such dynamic environments where objective information might not provide absolute directions, an environmental decision-maker must be willing to act without perfect objective information. This might include relying on precaution, or some other value-based decision guide; the natural inclination to help here is to turn to subjective forms of valuation.

Subjective values help to further shape and refine the difficulties involved with a particular environmental decision. Our subjective value systems run the gamut of basic morality to community and group pressures. We discussed the importance of looking at the impact of community sentiment—termed public outrage—on value decisions. We saw how even well-defined, objective risk assessments can be set aside when community perceptions dominate a particular issue. The obvious point here is that community perceptions matter in environmental decisions; how much they matter depends on a number of factors that are hard to determine outside the specific context of the situation being reviewed. However, we can make some generalized statements about the veracity or intensity of the community outrage.

For example, we can try and determine the extent to which the risk is being defined from a positional rather than issue-based standpoint. Many times the community is taking a positional stance on an environmental issue, and that stance is not based on an objective sense of hazard or risk, but more on a fear or interest that is outside the environmental context of the debate. We used the example of community members recalcitrant toward the development of a landfill within the community. The outrage is not necessarily based on a consideration of actual environmental harm, but more on the idea that their choices were less than ideal, choosing to buy a home in an area where a landfill is ultimately located being one example we highlighted. In such cases, one who is looking at or making environmental decisions must be able to refocus attention on the issues rather than the positions. Many times, getting parties to agree on and openly discuss the issues can lead to important breakthroughs for environmental decisions. This is especially true when the fears can be positively dealt with, which then allows the environmental decision to be focused on the objective information that is available, or where lacking, on an honest discussion about subjective values related to the proposal.

In our final section of this chapter, we reviewed the concept of scaling value decisions, specifically, how are value-based decisions impacted at different scales? We broke down the scales into two major groups, individual decisions and multiparty decisions. Multiparty included anything from groups to national governments and international bodies. Important considerations included understanding the difference between incentives at the individual and group levels. This included an overview of self-interest at the individual level, highlighting the difference between cooperative and noncooperative forms of strategy. In noncooperative settings, individuals determine a best strategy through complete self-interest; this included examples of individual defection from group goals like "free riding" off the work of others. Property rights were discussed in this context to help understand how they impact the potential for free riding. Cooperative strategies were also discussed, including those where the benefits of cooperation are made clear.

We finally saw how group dynamics can impact individual decision-making, specifically in the context of the standing ovation problem. In this scenario, we were introduced to the idea that sometimes individuals will be influenced by a group to express a preference that is not held by that individual; the point here is that group influence matters. Aggregating the group value system to public institutions like government, we saw how different mechanisms for determining preference—majority versus consensus voting—can impact the expression of preferences of a society. Moreover, we also observed how government value expressions sometimes contain legacy issues, which can lead to inconsistencies between the societal value and the individual value.

Understanding the dynamics of values is critical to understanding the development, implementation, and evaluation of environmental decisions. As you should see, it is difficult to determine precisely how value judgments will influence environmental decision-making. Rather than being clear, the process is messy and convoluted. Still, by understanding the basic principles discussed in this chapter you are well armed with information from which to better judge the purpose of values in a particular environmental context. You must take what you have learned in this final section and add all of the considerations discussed under the science and economics sections in this text. For example, some of the scientific principles discussed help us understand how to support objective forms of valuation. They also can help us connect an environmental issue to more personal or subjective preferences, helping to place the issue into the correct perspective; doing so can aid in both making and analyzing environmental decisions in context. The substantive portions of this text are now completed. The information learned here must now be applied to case study examples, of which there are three that follow.

References

Axelrod, Robert M. 1984. *The Evolution of Cooperation*. Cambridge, MA: Perseus Books.

Bales, Robert Freed. 2001. *Social Interaction Systems: Theory and Measurement*. New Brunswick, NJ: Transaction Publishers.

Barrow, Christopher J. 2006. *Environmental Management for Sustainable Development*, 2nd ed. New York: Rutledge.

Binmore, Ken. 2007. *Game Theory: A Very Short Introduction*. New York: Oxford University Press.

Caldwell, Lynton Keith. 1998. *The National Environmental Policy Act: An Agenda for the Future*. Bloomington: Indiana University Press.

Cass, Ronald A. 2001. *The Rule of Law in America*. Baltimore: Johns Hopkins University Press.

Cole, Daniel H. 2002. *Pollution and Property: Comparing Ownership Institutions for Environmental Protection*. Cambridge: Cambridge University Press.

Cooper, John R., Keith Randle, and Ranjeet S. Sokhi. 2003. *Radioactive Releases in the Environment: Impact and Assessment*. West Sussex, England: John Wiley & Sons.

Crawford-Brown, Douglas. 1999. *Risk-Based Environmental Decisions: Culture and Methods*. Norwell, MA: Kluwer Academic Publishers.

Fazil, Aamir M. 2005. *A Primer on Risk Assessment Modelling: Focus on Seafood Products*. Rome: FAO.

Firestone, David B., and Frank Clooney Reed. 2008. *Environmental Law for Non-Lawyers*, 4th ed. South Royalton, VT: SoRo Press.

Fisher, Roger, William Ury, and Bruce Patton. 2011. *Getting to Yes: Negotiating Agreement without Giving In*. New York: Penguin Books.

Forman, Samuel Eagle. 1911. *Advanced Civics: The Spirit, the Form, and the Functions of the American Government*. New York: The Century Co.

Hammit, James. 2007. Risk Assessment and Economic Evaluation. In *Environmental and Occupational Medicine*, 4th ed., edited by William N. Rom. Philadelphia: Lippincott Williams & Williams.

Hardin, Garrett. 1968. The Tragedy of the Commons. *Science* 162:1243–1248.

Hunter, Malcolm L., and James Gibbs. 2007. *Fundamentals of Conservation Biology*, 3rd ed. Malden, MA: Blackwell Publishing.

Intergovernmental Panel on Climate Change. 2007. IPCC Fourth Assessment Report: Climate Change 2007 (AR4). http://www.ipcc.ch/publications_and_data/publications_and_data_reports.shtml (accessed September 23, 2011).

Johnson, Barry Less. 2007. *Environmental Policy and Public Health*. Boca Raton, FL: CRC Press.

Layzer, Judith A. 2011. *The Environmental Case: Translating Values into Policy*. Washington, DC: CQ Press.

Lazarus, Richard J. 2004. *The Making of Environmental Law*. Chicago: University of Chicago Press.

Mackie, Karl J. 1991. Dispute Resolution: The New Wave. In *A Handbook of Dispute Resolution*, edited by Karl J. Mackie. New York: Routledge.

Margolis, Howard. 1996. *Dealing with Risk: Why the Public and the Experts Disagree on Environmental Risk*. Chicago: University of Chicago Press.

Miller, John H., and Scott E. Page. 2004. The Standing Ovation Problem. *Complexity* 9(5): 8–16.

Miller, Tyler G., and Scott E. Spoolman. 2010. *Environmental Science*. Belmont, CA: Cengage Learning.

Nash, John. 1950. Equilibrium Points in n-person Games. *Proceedings of the National Academy of Science* 36(1): 48–49.

Olson, Mancur. 1971. *The Logic of Collective Action: Public Goods and the Theory of Groups*. Cambridge, MA: Harvard University Press.

Ostrom, Elinor. 1990. *Governing the Commons: The Evolution of Institutions for Collective Action*. Cambridge: Cambridge University Press.

Perrin, Ron. 1994. Rehabilitating Democratic Theory: The Prospects and the Need. In *Critical Perspectives on Democracy*, edited by Lyman H. Legters, John P. Burke, and Artur DiQuattro. Lanham, MD: Rowman & Littlefield.

Peterson del Mar, David. 2006. *Environmentalism*. Lansing, MI: Pearson.

Petts, Judith. 1998. Risk Assessment and Management for Waste Treatment and Disposal. In *Handbook of Environmental Risk Assessment and Management*, edited by Peter Calow. Malden, MA: Blackwell Science.

Ricci, Paolo F. 2006. *Environmental and Health Risk Assessment and Management: Principles and Practices*. Dordrecht: Springer.

Rodricks, Joseph V., and Thomas A. Burke. 1998. Epidemiology and Environmental Risk Assessment. In *Handbook of Environmental Risk Assessment and Management*, edited by Peter Calow. Malden, MA: Blackwell Science.

Roseland, Mark. 2005. *Toward Sustainable Communities: Resources for Citizens and Their Governments*. Vancouver, British Columbia: New Society Publishers.

Rousseau, Jean Jacques. 1893. *The Social Contract*. New York: G.P. Putnam's Sons.

Ruddiman, William R. 2001. *Earth's Climate: Past and Future*. New York: W.H. Freeman and Company.

Sandman, Peter M. 1993. *Responding to Community Outrage: Strategies for Effective Risk Communication*. Fairfax, VA: American Industrial Hygiene Association.

Siegler, Robert, Judy Deloache, and Nancy Eisenberg. 2006. *How Children Develop*, 2nd ed. New York: Worth Publishers.

Smrchek, Jerry C., and Maurice G. Zeeman. 1998. Assessing Risks to Ecological Systems from Chemicals. In *Handbook of Environmental Risk Assessment and Management*, edited by Peter Calow. Malden, MA: Blackwell Science.

Staddon, John E.R. 2007. Is Animal Learning Optimal? In *Constructal Theory of Social Dynamics*, edited by Adrian Bejan and Gilbert W. Merkx. New York: Springer.

Suter II, Glenn W. 1998. Retrospective Assessment, Ecoepidemiology and Ecological Monitoring. In *Handbook of Environmental Risk Assessment and Management*, edited by Peter P Calow. Malden, MA: Blackwell Science.

Suter II, Glenn W. 2007. *Ecological Risk Assessment*, 2nd ed. Boca Raton, FL: CRC Press.

Tong, Wei. 2010. Fundamental of Wind Energy. In *Wind Power Generation and Wind Turbine Design*, edited by Wei Tong. Southampton, UK: WIT Press.

Vriend, Nicolaas J. 2004. On Information-Contagious Behavior. In *Economic Complexity: Non-Linear Dynamics, Multi-Agents Economies, and Learning*, edited by William A Barnett, Christophe Deissenberg, and Gustav Feichtinger. Amsterdam: Elsevier.

Walker, J. Samuel. 2004. *Three Mile Island: A Nuclear Crisis in Historical Perspective*. Berkeley: University of California Press.

Wallis, Allan. 2008. Developing Regional Capacity to Plan Land Use and Infrastructure. In *Urban and Regional Policies for Metropolitan Livability*, edited by David K. Hamilton and Patricia S. Atkins. New York: M.E. Sharp.

Weimer, David L., and Aidan R. Vining. 2011. *Policy Analysis*, 5th ed. New York: Pearson.

Williams, Wendy, and Robert Whitcomb. 2007. *Cape Wind: Money, Celebrity, Class, Politics, and the Battle for Our Energy Future*. New York: Public Affairs.

Zurawicki, Leon. 2010. *Neuromarketing: Exploring the Brain of the Consumer*. New York: Springer.

Case Problems

Introduction to Case Problems

The following case studies are being provided as a means of allowing students to *apply* the major concepts discussed in the sections of this text (science, economics, values) to problems that highlight skills necessary in environmental decision-making. These case studies have been created to allow for individual and group analysis, as well as creating talking points between students and instructor in a shared learning environment. The hope is that these studies will be used as a starting point for applying the major themes of environmental decision-making discussed in this book. Students and instructors are encouraged to expand upon the examples provided here, as well as to develop their own examples of both hypothetical and real-life situations to add context and richness in the application of environmental decision-making principles.

Case Problem 1. Watershed Management: Linking Terrestrial and Aquatic Environmental Problems

Environmental decisions that involve *watershed management* are particularly interesting (some might read the term *interesting* to mean difficult) because they include considerations of both terrestrial and aquatic resources; they span interactions on land and water. This means environmental decisions in watershed areas need to consider both the aquatic and terrestrial resource areas (or natural system components if we are using our systems analysis language) when considering choices impacting one or both resources.

Let us consider the following example as our first case study. There is a major watershed that runs the full length of the United States beginning near Canada and flowing south, ultimately dumping its contents into the Gulf of Mexico. It has been determined that water quality in the Gulf of Mexico is being impacted by activities that occur within the watershed area. This includes nutrient enrichment that ultimately leads to the low oxygen condition hypoxia. The decrease in oxygen impacts the ability of sea life in certain areas of the Gulf to thrive, leading to what is commonly referred to as *dead zones* in the Gulf. These dead zones have been increasing in recent years, impacting the marine ecosystem, including important commercial shellfish industries.

You have been tasked with determining a comprehensive plan to deal with the dead zone phenomenon. The plan has three main deliverables: (1) a report indicating the major causes of the hypoxic conditions of the Gulf; (2) a report identifying how those causes can be mitigated, including alternatives; and (3) a report outlining the economic impacts of the alternatives discussed with a recommendation of the preferred alternative based on explicitly stated criteria.

To aid you in the development of your plan, the following information is made available to you regarding the watershed area.

Relevant Information

- Fertilizers for agricultural and residential uses (specifically nitrogen and phosphorous) make up the majority of the nutrients leaching into the watershed river system, ultimately aggregating into the Gulf of Mexico.
- The dead zone condition in the Gulf was first detected around 30 years ago, but has increased in size and frequency significantly over the past 10 years.
- Agricultural use of fertilizer has been relatively constant for the past 50 years.
- Residential fertilizer use has increased over 1,000% in the last 50 years.
- Application of fertilizer *per unit area* of residential land has increased only moderately over the last 50 years.
- Residential development within the watershed basin has increased at a rate of development four times faster than historical development within the last 10 years. Most of this development has occurred along the banks of major tributaries of the watershed.
- Only a few communities along the watershed require buffer zones. Buffer zones are used to limit the amount of runoff from developed sites that are near waterways. In this way, buffer zones help to prevent nutrients from land entering waterways within the watershed.
- The current use of buffer zones (25% of communities within the watershed) is estimated to limit 10% of runoff from the watershed into the Gulf.
- Studies show approximately 50% of the fertilizer (nitrogen and phosphorous) that enters the watershed is absorbed prior to making its way to the Gulf. Thus, only about half of the fertilizer in the water actually impacts the Gulf's water quality (the remainder is absorbed and decomposed through chemical and biological processes prior to making it to the Gulf).

■ A market alternative to traditional fertilizer is available. This alternative fertilizer breaks down quickly and is more readily absorbed in the target soils. It is estimated that if this fertilizer were used in place of traditional fertilizer, only 5% of the current quantities of fertilizer would make their way to the Gulf. The cost of this alternative fertilizer is approximately three times the cost of traditional fertilizer.

■ A survey of the watershed shows residential fertilizer application occurs 25% of the time by private party (the landowner self-fertilizing) and 75% of the time by contracted services (landscape companies, small businesses, etc.).

These facts should now be used to evaluate the causes, alternatives, and implications of this problem.

Hints for Analysis

You may want to sort out the problem by first creating a box model representation of the watershed, identifying all of the flows into and out of the system, as well as interactions within the system and any feedbacks that are influencing the system. This can help you answer the causes question. You can then decipher the economic considerations, possibly employing a total value approach because it seems some of your alternatives analysis will impact direct market values of local businesses, as well as the bottom line of the homeowner. (Of course, identifying the costs currently being incurred by the commercial fishing industry—not to mention indirect and nonuse costs—is a valid potential offset argument here.) Finally, a consideration of values will be helpful in your analysis. This is the same process you want to engage in through all of the case problems; use the major sections headings of the text as a framework for your analysis on each problem set. Reasonable assumptions can be made in each instance, and you should check your assumptions against the information provided in the relevant section of the text to ensure the assumption is valid (ensure you are not missing something).

Case Problem 2. Fisheries Management: Managing Public Resources through a Mix of Private Incentives

Fish live in the ocean, a public resource. This means that when a private person goes out to fish, whether commercially or recreationally, he or she is accessing a resource that belongs to the public. Historically, this has never been much of a problem because there were always plenty of fish in the ocean. Over the last several decades, however, many target fish populations have declined severely. This has resulted in a need for greater government management of the resource. The question that is difficult to answer is just *how* should the government manage fish as a public resource?

Should it limit the *quantity* of fish that can be taken by any one person? Should government limit *access* to the fish resource, say by limiting the number of days a person can fish in a given year?

In this case problem, you are being asked by the government to review a current policy related to fishery access, and to evaluate a set of alternative ways of regulating access. Your primary responsibility is to assess the current regulatory program, review the proposed alternatives, and then rank order the alternatives based on the criteria of *efficiency*. Rank order means you rate the alternatives, 1 being your first choice, 2 being your second choice, and so on. What is meant by efficiency here is which alternative, in your estimation, will result in the fairest distribution of fishing rights to the greatest number of fishers while also costing the least amount of money for the government in enforcing the chosen regulation. You are free to assume certain facts in your analysis where facts are missing or incomplete, so long as they are a logical extension of the facts as presented. The current government fishery policy and set of alternatives is reproduced below.

Current Government Fishery Policy

- Major areas of the ocean have been overfished, with landings of fish decreasing approximately 50% over the last 20 years even as fishing effort has increased during this time.
- Beginning around 20 years ago, the fishing effort has seemed to outpace the ability of the target fish population to reproduce itself (although this has not been confirmed through scientific studies). The evidence supporting this theory is the smaller landings that are occurring *per fishing effort.*
- The traditional policy has been to provide anyone who pays the fee a commercial license to fish in government waters. In the past there has been little to no issue with depleted fish stocks because there always appeared to be ample supplies of target fish populations to support the total fishing effort.
- The current system of *open access* (anyone who wishes to fish and who pays a license fee can do so) has led to diminished returns for the fishers; they are taking in less fish per unit of effort, meaning it is costing more to capture less value. If this continues, it is forecasted that the commercial fishing industry will collapse entirely.

Alternative Policy 1

- Alternative 1 focuses on creating a *limit* on the total amount of fish available for capture in a given fishing season.
- The policy would operate by having the government first fund scientific studies of the population dynamics of the target fish species. The studies would focus on the life cycle of the target fish species, attempting to understand the age at which the fish reaches sexual maturity and how often the species replicates.

This information would then provide some understanding of how much of the fish (including limits on size and gender) can be taken in a season.

- **Hint:** There are disputes in the scientific community on how much information should be gathered about the species. Some argue a population estimate is sufficient, while others argue ecosystem interactions are critical, such as predator-prey relationships and habitat integrity to ensure where the juvenile fish develop are protected. The extent of the scientific knowledge being used to inform the *catch limit* is important to understand when relying on the total catch limit derived from that scientific process.

■ The scientific studies would result in a *total allowable catch*. The current commercial fishing community would be able to fish until the total catch limit was met. Once the total catch limit was met, all fishing operations must cease for the season.

■ No fisher is entitled to a certain percentage of the total catch limit set for the species, and there are no limits placed on the number of fishers with a commercial license (as in the current policy).

Alternative Policy 2

■ The government sets a total catch limit based on the scientific information provided in alternative 1 above.

■ The total limit set by the government becomes the basis for an allocation of *catch shares* between existing fishers.

■ The allocation of shares is done through an *auction system*, where the total allowable catch each season is divided into shares representing a portion of the total catch. The total shares in the auction are equal to the total allowable catch for that season.

■ Fishers bid for shares at the auction. The winning bids (based on the highest price bid for each share) are then equal to a specific amount of fish that can be taken from the total allowable catch, a catch share.

■ No individual fisher is allowed to own more than 10% of the total allowable catch in a given season. This is to ensure as equitable a distribution of the catch as possible among the fishers with licenses to fish. There is no guarantee that all fishers with commercial licenses will receive a catch share at the auction. Fishers without a catch share cannot fish for the target species in that season.

■ The catch shares are only good for the season. In the next fishing season, a new total allowable catch will be determined and a new auction held for those catch shares.

■ Eighty percent of the funds from the sale of the catch shares are reinvested to fund the government operations associated with the commercial fishing of the target species, including funding the science that yields the total allowable catch limit each season, as well as the auction operations, permitting, and other administrative functions.

- Twenty percent of the funds from the auction go to a program to assist fishers who are economically impacted by the new auction system (for example, those who are unsuccessful at bidding for catch shares, or those who are unable to get enough catch shares in the auction to support their current operations).

Alternative Policy 3

- The government creates a total catch limit established by science in the same manner as described in alternatives 1 and 2.
- The government divides the total allowable catch limit into shares (for example, one-tenth of the total allowable catch would equate to a 10% stake in the total allowable catch).
- The government then determines, roughly, which current fishers in the industry are responsible for what portion of the total catch based on historical data. (For example, fisher A may have, on average, brought in 12% of the annual total catch of the target species over the past 10 years.)
- Based on historical data, the government awards current fishers in the industry a *quota* for a percentage of the total allowable catch to be set each year. This means if a fisher is awarded a 12% quota in the fishery, that fisher is allowed to catch 12% of the total allowable catch limit, whatever that limit is, from year to year.
- Unlike alternative 2, the fisher does not have to bid for the quota at an auction, and the quota is also good from year to year; the quota will not change for the fisher from year to year.
- The goal of this policy is to provide assurance to the fishing community (they know exactly what they are entitled to catch with the exception of not knowing what the science will establish as the total allowable catch from year to year), while at the same time reducing government costs associated with managing the industry. (For example, unlike having to run the auction each year under alternative 2, the government's responsibility is completed after the initial quotas are established and given out.)
- Fishers can sell their quotas, and they are otherwise operated as *individual property rights*.
- Those who wish to gain access to the fishery after quotas are set must either purchase a quota from an existing holder or otherwise establish a right to fish under an existing quota holder (like a subcontractor).

Hints for Analysis

You may want to review the listed alternatives above from a *property rights characteristics* perspective (consider the Ostrom discussion in the value section of the text), analyzing how each alternative creates a slightly different property rights characteristic. This can then lead to questions of efficiency and fairness. You might also want to spend some time discussing the relevant role of the science in establishing the total allowable catch limits. What factor(s) should be important to consider when establishing the total catch limit? Should ecosystem-based criteria be part of the review, or is a simple calculation to total biomass (population estimate) sufficient? Remember, the number established by science in all of these alternative proposals will set the upper limit for any policies established, meaning that number will impact the distribution of the resource to those who wish to access the resource!

Case Problem 3. Sustainability: Setting Priorities between Today and Tomorrow, a Total Valuation Application

Alaskaland is a country awash in natural resources. These include valuable ores and minerals, as well as significant oil deposits. Alaskaland wants to expand its economy to provide its citizens with greater economic opportunities and well-being.

You work for a major planning arm of the Alaskaland government, and you have been charged with coming up with a strategy to expand its natural resource utilization. Alaskaland wants you to review current natural resource utilization, as well as a number of alternative utilization policies. The review process requires you to consider both the current and alternative policies in light of what is best for Alaskaland citizens, both today and in the future. You are allowed to establish your own criteria for judging the current policy and suggested alternatives, but you are required to fully state the criteria you are using, the reasons for choosing these criteria, and any assumptions you are using in the establishment of your criteria.

Below are the basic facts relating to the current use of natural resources and the proposed alternatives.

Current Policy

- Alaskaland currently utilizes its mineral and hydrocarbon resources at a rate that, under current technology, will result in the depletion of available reserves in approximately 100 years. With reasonable assumptions regarding advances in technological capacity, the amount of available resources at current rates of extraction can be pushed to a 150-year horizon. After this time, the mineral and hydrocarbon natural resources of Alaskaland will be fully exhausted.
- The mining and oil extraction industries in Alaskaland, under current rates of extraction, yield approximately 40% of the country's gross domestic product (GDP). These two industries alone provide current citizens of Alaskaland with 30% of total employment. In addition, the revenues generated from the leasing of public lands and the fees and taxes generated provide Alaskaland with 50% of its annual income.

- Currently, 20% of the revenues received from mineral mining and oil production are placed into a *security fund* that is meant for future generations of Alaskaland citizens. The idea here is that these resources are *nonrenewable*, so some of the money received for the extraction of these resources should be kept in trust for future generations of citizens. Even with the 20% set aside for future generations, the remainder of the generated funds provides 80% of the total operational budget of the Alaskaland government. Because of these revenues, current citizens enjoy this "subsidy" in the form of very low tax rates on both income and expenditures.
- It is expected that as the resources become exhausted (in 100 or 150 years), the economy of Alaskaland will have to change. No longer will 30% of employment be covered by these industries. Also, the government revenue stream from these activities will dry up, meaning there will no longer be a subsidy to current citizens in the form of a lower tax base. All that will remain is the aggregate fund from the 20% set aside allocation per year for future generations.

Alternative 1

- Alaskaland chooses to become more conservative with protecting *future generations* from the current use of natural resources. Not wanting to impact the current sources of revenue and jobs provided by the mining and oil production, rates of extraction stay constant. However, Alaskaland increases the amount placed in trust for future generations each year from 20% to 40% of revenues from the leasing, sale, and taxing of the natural resources. This is expected to provide future generations with a sufficient trust fund to cover government expenses (based on rates of inflation, population growth, etc.) for approximately 20 years. Keeping the old rate of 20% would have provided approximately 5 years worth of government expenses.
- Since there is no change in extraction rates under this alternative, *current jobs* are not expected to be impacted. However, personal income tax rates will have to increase from the current flat rate of 10% to 15% per individual in order to make up the difference in lost government revenue from increasing the yearly set aside. This increase in tax rate is likely to have the largest impact on middle-income families in Alaskaland.

Alternative 2

- Alaskaland decides currency is not a sufficient substitute for natural resources (including valuable ores and oil) because these commodities have traditionally appreciated in value significantly more than any conservative investment rates of return placed on the set aside trust fund monies. Thus, Alaskaland decides to decrease current extraction rates to protect the resources availability, ensuring the resource will last, at a minimum, 250 years at current extraction rates (as opposed to the 100 to 150 years under current extraction rates). Twenty percent of current extraction will still be placed into a set aside fund for future generations.

■ The immediate impact here is ore and oil production will now yield 25% of Alaskaland's GDP (down from 40%), provide 15% of total employment (down from 30%), and generate approximately 30% of Alaskaland revenue (down from 50%). This will mean that the new revenues will provide Alaskaland with 50% of its operational budget, down from 80%. Taxes will have to be raised on current citizens to make up for the revenue, as this alternative does not incorporate any new economic activity in other areas to offset the loss of natural resource production.

Alternative 3

■ Alaskaland is currently undergoing an economic recession as part of a larger global recession (luckily the global recession has maintained the value of the ore and oil on global commodity markets). In order to stimulate the economy, extraction rates of minerals and oil are proposed to increase. The increase will bring additional jobs to the current generation, but will lower the expected time horizon for full exhaustion of these resources from 100 years to 50 years. However, the jobs created should be enough to keep the current generation working at historically high employment rates.

■ In addition, Alaskaland can tap the set aside trust fund in order to fill gaps in government budgeting, including increases in social welfare programs such as unemployment and job training. This will further reduce any benefit available to future generations, substantially eroding the value of the natural capital as a mechanism of wealth distribution to future generations of Alaskaland.

Hints for Analysis

In evaluating the alternatives, you have to make decisions (value judgments) about fairness between current and future generations. Value judgments are important here. So too is the manner in which you decide to account for the value of minerals and oil, both today and tomorrow. From a total value standpoint, much of what is being focused on here is *direct value*, but you may see other values at stake and choose to identify those values as part of your analysis in choosing between alternatives.

Case Problem 4. Climate Change: Making Environmental Decisions in the Face of Uncertainty

There is scientific evidence strongly supporting a conclusion that the average temperature of the earth is getting warmer, especially over the past several decades.

While the evidence supporting a *warming trend* is strong (although additional decades of data would be important in confirming a long-term trend), scientific evidence supporting a specific cause of the warming lacks consensus.

There is strong support correlating the increase in average carbon dioxide concentrations in the atmosphere to the observed warming trend. Further, there is strong support indicating that the increase in average carbon dioxide concentrations is related to human-based activities, most directly the mining, refining, and burning of fossil fuels.

While there are strong correlations linking human activities to a warming earth, there is not absolute evidence making this connection. Other factors, including natural phenomenon (geothermal activity, oscillations in ocean current patterns, and the activity of the sun), might have a role to play in the warming trend observed.

You are part of an international organization charged with recommending a plan of action on the issue of climate change. There is unanimous political consensus that something needs to be done about climate change, but almost no consensus on what that something should be. Your group is charged with looking at the evidence, and making a recommendation on what actions governments should take, if any, in response to the observed warming.

Broadly speaking, the proposed actions can range from doing nothing (ignoring the warming trend completely), to a variety of strategies implementing the following kinds of responses: prevention, mitigation, and adaptation. *Prevention* indicates that there are actions humans can take to prevent the warming trend. *Mitigation* indicates there are actions that can prevent the extent of warming, including lessening the impact of warming on humans. *Adaptation* accepts the warming as an inevitable result, and focuses on strategies to limit the extent of harm caused to humans.

Your group is free to make recommendations in any manner you see fit. For example, you can make a specific recommendation and focus your analysis only on that recommendation. Or, you can make a list of alternative recommendations and choose what you believe to be the preferred alternative. Or, you can provide a list of alternatives and rank the alternatives based on a set of criteria (you can also use different criteria to show how the rankings of the alternatives change—if they do—as you change the criteria). The only absolute requirement is that you provide a detailed explanation at each step of the process. If you are choosing only one recommendation, fully explain what went into your choosing that one recommendation. If you are choosing among alternatives, make sure you fully explain the criteria being chosen, including a discussion of why other criteria were excluded from your analysis.

In this case problem, unlike the others, you will not be provided with a detailed set of closed universe facts to drive your analysis. I thought of doing this, but realized the science on climate change is rapidly expanding over time. Rather than limit you to a set of facts that might be obsolete by the time of printing, your analysis should reflect the current state of knowledge on climate change. This way, you are engaging the problem in real time, using the environmental decision-making frameworks of this text to guide your process. Since climate change may well be the most important "riddle" to solve for environmental managers in the future, it cannot hurt for you to go beyond the confines of this book in obtaining your information.

Still, some guidelines should be set for your analysis to get you started. Consider the following questions as you begin your investigation into this problem:

- What impact does the current *state of science* have on your decision-making process? If the science was absolute on the question of humans being the sole cause of the earth's warming, does this fact make your analysis easier?
- What role, if any, does *precaution* play in your analysis? If we cannot be sure of the cause(s) of the warming, can we make certain decisions in light of this imperfect information? Does doing nothing unless there is absolute evidence make good sense?
- Is your analysis altered if you are looking at the question from a prevention, mitigation, or adaptation perspective? Does one perspective allow for easier decision-making than another perspective, say by removing some of the uncertainty as to cause? (It would seem if we are certain the earth's climate is warming, then an adaptation perspective cares little about the cause of the warming, focusing instead on strategies to cope with the warming.)
- What impact, if any, does *intergenerational considerations* have on your analysis? Some policy choices (or alternatives, depending on how you approach the problem) can lead to outcomes that are better for current generations then they are for future generations. Does your analysis/conclusion change if you focus on a policy direction geared toward people today versus future generations?

Hints for Analysis

Allow the aforementioned questions to help guide your analysis. The precise deliverables and extent of your analysis into this problem can be conducted from both an individual and a group perspective. If done by group, it may be helpful to divide the analysis by different strategic responses, for example, by *prevention, mitigation*, and *adaptation*. Also, much of this analysis (beyond the science question) will be driven by *value* questions. The value section of the text (including *scaling* and issues of equity/fairness) will likely influence your analysis and conclusions.

Index

A

Abiotic components, 18–20
Access
    as privilege, 156
Acid rain, 77
Acidification
    in oceans, 55
Adaptability, 20
Adaptation perspective, 188, 189
Adaptive management, 30, 75
Aesthetic values, 98, 105, 123, 128, 129
    as environmental risk assessment priority,
        120–121
    weighting in risk assessment, 123
Agent-based modeling, 150, 157, 165
Aggregate information, 38
Aggregation
    and inability to halt worst impacts, 137
    and systems thinking, 136
Agricultural production
    biodiversity interactions, 25
    as renewable resource, 70
Air
    as asset, 66
Air quality
    impact of burning fossil fuels, 73
Air quality regulation, 22, 28
Alaskaland
    case problem, 185–187
Albedo effect, 14
Alternative dispute resolution, 144
Alternatives, 102
    cost considerations, 79
    in electricity production, 78
Alternatives analysis, 103, 104
Amazon Rainforest, 18, 19, 23
    as biodiversity hotspot, 24

indirect use values, 105
Analytical tools, 7
    ignorance about, 2
Animal feedlots, 33
Anthropogenic forcing, 48
Arbitration
    dispute resolution through, 144
Artificial fertilizer, 25
Asbestos
    faulty risk assessment, 127
Assets
    environmental resources as, 66
Assumed rate of use, 70
Assumptions, 86
    about free markets, 82
    about happiness and economic output, 90
    in environmental decision making, 64
    of incomplete information, 117
    incorrect, about risk, 116
    of knowability of values, 68
    rate of use, 70
    in risk assessment, 124
Atmosphere, 12, 17, 19, 40
    as intermediary for other system
        components, 57
    low excludability and high divisibility
        characteristics, 154
    privatizing, 156
Auction systems, 183
Availability heuristic, 130
Available carbon, 41, 53

B

Belief learning, 158
    versus experience, 159
    and religious doctrine, 158

Belief systems
    regarding environmental values, 138
Benefit–cost analysis, 64, 80, 91, 101–105, 107, 147
    diagram, 102
    and free riding, 152
    shortcomings, 104
Best available science, 119
Best management practices, 64
Biodiversity, 7, 10, 16, 23–24, 59
    considering in environmental decisions, 29
    definitions, 24–25
    honeybee example, 27–28
    importance, 27–29
    interactions and, 25–27
    nutrients and processes in, 27
    and value yield, 28
    weighting, 67
    what species examples, 25–26
Biodiversity hotspots, 24
Biological responses, 26
Biosphere, 12, 17, 19, 40, 42
Biotic components, 18–20
Boundaries, 17. *See also* System boundaries
Box modeling, 39, 40–43, 48, 147
    carbon cycle, 54
    carbon interactions system component, 50
    context, 49–58
    forecasting using, 49
    simple diagram example, 41
    system component interactions, 51
    visualizing interactions using, 40
Brundtland Commission
    definition of sustainability, 123
Buddhism
    roots of GNH in, 86
Buffer zones, 180
Buffering, 104, 105

C

Cancer-causing agents
    costs associated with, 128
    maximum acceptable exposure rate, 127
    precautionary approach, 124
Cap-and-trade programs, 96
Carbon
    available/unavailable, 52
    charges to emitters, 156
    forcing of equilibrium shift by, 55
    increased atmospheric, 42
    inputs and outflows, 51

and mass–energy equivalence, 44
    plant metabolism, 51
    unavailable, 53
Carbon concentrations
    changes over time, 46
Carbon cycle, 45, 51, 52
    box model representation, 54
    feedback mechanisms, 57
    human manipulation of, 80
    role of oceans in, 56–57
    role of soils in, 56
Carbon dioxide, 42
    as food for vegetation, 42
    increase in atmospheric concentrations, 188
    trees' ability to consume, 66
Carbon emissions
    charging for, 156
Carbon forcing, 58
    divisibility/excludability characteristics, 154
Carbon interactions
    system component box model, 50
Carbon management
    between system components, 48
Carbon monoxide, 44
Carbon sequestration, 42, 43, 58
    by plants, 55
    by trees, 72
Carbon sinks, 41, 50
    in hydrosphere, 43
    potential, 55
Case problems, 179
    climate change, 187–189
    fisheries management, 181–185
    sustainability, 185–187
    watershed management, 179–181
Catch quota, 184
Catch shares, 184
    allocating, 183
Cause and effect, 3, 7, 9, 43
Chaos, 46
Chemical processes, 19
Chernobyl
    public outrage over, 136
Choice
    disconnect with objective risk information, 137
    discounting objective information for personal, 137
    inhibiting through uncertainty, 119
    lack of, 118
    role in risk perception, 134

Choices
  values and, 113
Cigarette smoking
  risk perception, 134
Clean Air Act, 32
Clean Water Act, 32, 34
  enforcement issues, 35
  failure of, 34
  information sharing problems, 37
  limitations with non-point sources of
      pollution, 33
Cleanliness
  as subjective concept, 153
Climate change, 16, 80, 173
  aggregated impacts, 136
  carbon dioxide as indicator, 42
  case problem, 187–189
  hints for analysis, 189
  human causes, 135
  incomplete information and stance on, 119
  risk perception and knowability, 135
  scientific understanding of, 9, 188
Climate control regulation, 28
Climate regulation, 22
Closed systems, 10, 48
Coal, 41
  extractive costs, 79
  versus nuclear power, 122
  powering electric energy demand through,
      149
  risks, 118
  as source of electricity production, 118
Coal burning
  discounting example, 77
Coercion
  and conformance to rules, 166
  and risk perception, 133, 134
Collaboration
  in cooperative games, 167
  lack of, in noncooperative games, 167
Collective value systems, 170–174, 172
Collectivism, 171
Commodity markets, 94
Common ground, 173
  and subjectivity of risk factors, 129
Common pool resources, 154, 155
  excludability/divisibility characteristics, 150
  house rental analogy, 150
Commons, 154
Community outrage, 167. *See also* Public outrage
Community values, 1
Community vitality, 86

Complex interactions, 1
  GNH and, 88
Compliance issues, 38
Computer models
  limitations, 119
Consensus building, 167–170, 168, 169
  difficulties with subjective risk factors, 129
  inhibition by subjective values, 130
  and negotiation, 170
Consensus decision-making, 162
Conservation, 86, 143
  as environmental value, 142
Context-specific thinking, 148
Contingent valuation, 92, 100, 101
Control, 152
Control earth, 119
Conucopians
  world views of, 138
Cooperative games, 157, 159, 162, 167
  stag hunt, 162–164
Cost
  as factor in individual decision-making, 149
  and free riding, 152
Cost-benefit perspective, 3
Cost-effectiveness analysis, 91
Cost per unit
  and competitiveness, 97
  of electricity, 78
Cost-reward balance, 38, 39
Criteria
  in decision-making, 148
Crude oil, 52
Cultural services, 18, 20–23, 21, 22, 32, 73,
      74, 91
  valuation by ecological economics, 74
Cultural values, 105
  preservation and promotion of, 86
Cultural vitality, 86
Cumulative impacts
  of non-point pollution sources, 33
Cycling, 53

D

Daisy world model, 13–14
  biodiversity examples, 27
dC/dT = 0, 39, 45–49
Dead zone, 33, 34
  role of cumulative fertilizer runoff, 35
  watershed case problem, 180
Debt servicing, 83

Decision
　as physical manifestation of value choices, 113
Decision-making
　national forms, 170
Deep ecology, 141
　and preservationist mentality, 142
Deer
　provisioning resources for, 21
Defection
　among minority interests, 170
　by losers in majoritarian decision-making,
　　167–168
　minimizing through consensus building, 169
Deficit spending, 83, 85
Deliberation, 147
Depletable resources, 70, 71
Development, 141, 143
　economic decision making regarding, 22–23
　as environmental value, 142
Diffuse pollution sources, 34
Direct uses, 91
　of coal, 77
　natural resource economics focus on, 69
Direct values, 92–95, 103, 187
　differentiation from indirect values, 95
　and provisioning services, 93
Discount rates, 76, 103
Discounting, 65, 66, 69, 76–77, 106
　cigarette smoking risk example, 136
　of environmental ideals, 142
　of objective information in favor of personal
　　choices, 137
Discrete sources
　of pollution, 34
Disease regulation, 22
Dispute resolution, 144
　alternative, 144
　binding and nonbinding procedures, 144
　through positional bargaining, 144
　through principled bargaining, 144
Diversity
　within and between species, 25
Divisibility, 153
　of common pool resources, 150
　and property rights, 155
Dock building proposal, 30–31
Dominion, 152
Dose-response assessment, 123, 130, 133, 167
　actual likely dose, 126
　cancer-causing agent example, 124
　exponential response, 125, 127, 128
　hermetic response, 125, 127

human surrogates, 125
　linear response, 125
　threshold response, 125
Dose-response curves, 126
Drivers
　of decision-making, 145
　in individual decision-making, 149

E

$E = mc^2$, 39, 43–45
Earth fragility, 138
Earth system, 147
　components of, 12
　current stability, 46
　household management, 63, 64
　knowability of value, 68
　well-mixed, 46, 47
Earth temperatures, 14, 15
Ecological economics, 65, 72–75, 106
　comparison with GNH, 87
　contrast with natural resource economics,
　　79
　differentiating from natural resource
　　economics, 68, 72, 75
　equity issues, 74
　relational energy flows, 74
　as subcategory of natural resource
　　economics, 68
　systems thinking in, 74
Ecological impact statement (EIS)
　NEPA requirements, 129
Ecological vitality, 86
Economic activity
　impacts, 88
　positive and negative, 89
Economic perspective, 2, 3, 40
　benefit–cost analysis, 101–105
　discounting and, 76–77
　ecological economics, 72–75
　natural resource economics, 68–72
　relationship to science and values, 3
　relevant categories, 65–81
　substitution and, 77–79
　total valuation technique, 91–101
　trade-offs and, 79–81
　valuation models, 81–90
Economic recession
　effects on extraction rates, 187
Economic valuation, 76
Economics, 115
　of environmental decision-making, 63–65

as functional accounting system, 107
Ecosystem
    valuation of, 129
Ecosystem-based management, 7, 10, 16,
        29–30, 50
    definition and purpose, 30–31
    diagram, 31
    environmental policy management
        examples, 34–39
    role in environmental management, 31–34
Ecosystem degradation
    environmental costs, 97
Ecosystem interactions
    in fisheries management, 183
Ecosystem principles, 10, 16, 17–18, 65
    abiotic components, 18–20
    biotic components, 18–20
Ecosystem science, 7
Ecosystem services, 20–23
Ecosystem size, 18
Ecosystem stability, 28
Ecosystem well-being, 122–123, 128
    as environmental risk assessment priority,
        120–121
Ecosystems, 17
    inherent value, 22
    living components, 19
    nonliving components, 19
Education, 86
Ehrlich, Paul, 80, 81
Electricity
    as human necessity, 78
Emotion
    impact on subjective valuations, 131
    as subjective value, 131–137
Endangered Species Act, 121, 170
Endogenous energy sources, 12, 45
Energy flows, 12, 39, 45, 73, 74
    active regulation of, 13
    modeling with box models, 40
Energy inputs, 45
Energy-matter relationships, 43
Energy sources
    endogenous/exogenous, 12
Enforcement issues, 35
Environment
    linking to human interactions, 81–90
Environment-society-economy relationships, 69
Environmental decision making, 1
    economics categories, 65–68
    economics of, 63–65
    ecosystem-based management in, 31–32

in face of uncertainty, 187–189
    individual *versus* societal values in, 172
    lack of understanding about tools, 2
    natural systems perspective, 9–39
    process in individual and group settings,
        146
    science-economics-values relationships, 3
    science of, 7–9
    systems thinking and, 39–58
    values in, 113–114 (*See also* Values)
    without specialized expertise, 2
Environmental goods
    determining values for, 104
Environmental health
    and human health, 122
Environmental impact, 104
    metrics, 85
Environmental management
    ecosystem-based management role, 31–34
    risk limitation goal, 114
    traditional forms, 32
    using media-specific environmental laws, 32
Environmental policy management
    examples, 34–39
Environmental protection
    preference for, 173
Environmental risk assessment priorities,
        120–121
Environmental services, 66
Environmental values
    spectrum, 142
Environmentalists
    NIMBY syndrome among, 140
    worldivews of, 138
Equilibrium, 10, 47, 59
    dynamic, 15
    movement toward, 55
Equilibrium change, 15
Equilibrium response, 16
Equilibrium state, 11
Equilibrium theory, 39, 43, 45–49, 48, 49
Equity
    in ecological economics, 74
Erosion regulation, 22, 28
Ethics, 139, 140
Excludability, 153
    changing, 156
    of common pool resources, 150
    in property rights, 155
Exogenous energy sources, 12, 17
Experience
    basis of reinforcement learning in, 158

versus belief learning, 159
  strategy design through, 164
Expertise sharing, 36
Exponential response, 125, 127, 128
  maximum acceptable exposure rate, 127
Exposure assessment, 123, 126
  mathematical maximum exposure, 126
  most-at-risk situation, 126
  worst-case scenario assessment, 126
External inconsistency, 173
Externalities. *See* Negative externalities
Extinctions. *See also* Species extinctions
  rate of, 28
Extraction rates, 71
  for depletable resources, 70
  increasing with economic recession, 187
  modifying to protect future generations,
    186–187
  for renewable resources, 71
Extractive costs, 70, 99
Extractive value, 72, 82

F

Fair market value, 93
Fairness question, 80, 187
Familiarity
  and risk perception, 133, 134
Feedback mechanisms, 10, 11, 40, 49–58, 53
  in carbon cycle, 58
  carbon storage and availability, 41
  in daisy world model, 13
  regulating services and, 21
Fertilizer
  application per unit area, 180
  market alternative to, 181
Fertilizer runoff, 34, 35
  watershed management case problem, 180
Filtering functions, 105
Fish population decline, 181
Fisher, Roger, 144, 145
Fisheries management
  alternative policies, 182–184
  case problem, 181
  current government policy, 182
  hints for analysis, 184–185
  limiting total capture, 182
Fishing rights, 36–37
Food and Drug Administration (FDA)
  dose-response assessments, 124–125
  regulation of pharmaceutical drugs, 137
Food sources, 21

Forestry management, 71–72
Forests
  regulating services, 22
Fossil fuel burning
  chemical impacts, 73
  discounting example, 76
  undesirable impacts, 73
Foundational views, 138
Framework, 30, 101, 120
  for environmental decision making, 1
  as regulatory conditions, 38
Free markets, 82, 84
Free riding, 150, 152, 162, 176
  house rental analogy, 150–151, 155
  limiting through group pressure, 165–166
  minimizing through consensus building,
    169
  solving through changes in property right
    characteristics, 156
  tools limiting, 154
Freshwater
  as provisioning service, 21
Fuel economy
  limitations as metric, 86
Full information, 35, 37
  as goal, 23

G

Gaia hypothesis, 13, 14, 18, 23, 26, 59
Game theory, 157, 159, 167
  payout in, 160
  stag hunt payoffs, 163
Genetic diversity, 24
  bottlenecking of, 24
Genetically modified species, 25
Genuine progress indicator (GPI), 88–90, 106
  comparison with GNH, 89
  goals, 88
  links to ecological economics, 107
Geographic isolation, 24
Geothermal power, 77
Goals
  connecting issues to, 174
Gold
  as asset, 66
Good governance, 86
Government
  role in creating prosperity, 82
Government decision-making
  consensus building and majority voting
    processes, 168

Government intervention, 98
  to internalize costs, 97
Government management
  of fish resources, 181
Government spending, 82, 85
  in GDP accounting, 83
Grand Canyon, 105
Greenhouse effect, 73
Gross domestic product (GDP), 82–84, 106
  alternatives to, 84–90
  as blunt instrument, 89
  criticisms, 84
  failure to account for income distribution, 83
  handling of negative externalities, 84
  increasing in socially perverse ways, 83
  as metric of well-being, 83
  and natural resource economics, 107
Gross investment, 82
Gross national happiness (GNH), 85–88, 90, 106
  comparison with ecological economics, 87
  goals, 86
  roots in Buddhism, 86
Group dynamics, 176
  discounting individual values due to, 166
  influence on decision-making, 146
Group hegemony, 166
Group perceptions, 131–132, 166
Group pressure
  limiting free riding through, 165–166
Growth prospects
  impact of deficit spending on, 83

H

Habit of mind, 133
Happiness, 86
  comparing between cultures, 85
  false assumptions about, 90
Harm, 114
  frequency of, 116
  probability *versus* magnitude, 115, 116
  public perception of, 132
Harms
  due to increased GDP, 90
  valuing, 75
Hazard, 132
Hazard identification, 123
Health
  valuation, 129
Healthy environment
  and human prosperity, 88

  as prerequisite for healthy humans, 84, 121, 122
Heat transitions, 12
Herding effect, 166
Hermetic response, 125, 127
Heterotrophs, 27
Heuristics
  in cigarette smoking, 134
  influence on risk perception, 133
  in risk assessment, 130
  trumping of objective science by, 133–134
High divisibility, 153
  of atmosphere, 154
  of common pool resources, 154
High excludability, 152
Home heating system
  as system example, 10=11
Honeybees
  biodiversity implications, 27–28
House rental analogy, 150–152, 155
Household management, 64, 89
  and economics concept, 63
Human actions
  carbon forcing, 58
  and climate change, 119
  effects on environment, 3
  island effects, 25
Human-based interactions, 37
Human-based valuations, 98, 99
Human capital
  substitutability for natural capital, 74
Human-centered governance systems
  establishment of, 86
Human health, 121
  as risk assessment priority, 120, 135
  weighting in risk assessment, 123
Human interactions
  linking environment to, 81
Human system components, 40
Human values, 32
Human welfare, 128
Human well-being, 21, 121
  biodiversity and, 28
  discounting at expense of environmental protection, 141
  as environmental risk assessment priority, 120
  open space as indicator of, 143
  and public welfare, 122
  weighting relative to environmental considerations, 142

Hydrocarbons
    Alaskaland case problem, 185
    electricity production using, 77
Hydropower, 77
Hydrosphere, 12, 17, 19, 40, 42
    carbon sequestration in, 42
    as carbon sink, 43
Hypoxia
    in Gulf dead zone, 33

I

Impacts, 31
Incentives
    for information sharing, 36
    managing public resources through, 181–185
Income distribution, 83
    failure of GDP to consider, 83
Incomplete information, 117
    and clarity of choice, 119
    and climate change stance, 119
Inconsistent value applications, 173
Incorrect assumptions
    about risk, 116
Indirect services, 122
Indirect uses, 91
    ecosystem-based management principles, 98
Indirect values, 67, 74, 92, 95–98, 103
    of buffers, 105
    dollar value of, 96
    externalizing, 97
    and regulating services, 95
Individual decision-making, 175, 176
    in context of group interactions, 164
    group dynamics impact on, 132
    learning dynamics and, 157–166
    process of, 146
    self-interest and, 149–157
    values and, 148–166
Individual freedom, 172
Individual perceptions, 131–132
Individual property rights, 184
Individual values
    discounting due to group dynamics, 166
    influence on individual and group
        dynamics, 157
Individualism, 171
Infant mortality
    as measure of GNH, 86
Inferential rules, 130
Inflows, 40, 49–58, 53
Information cascade, 166

Information sharing, 36, 169
    compelling *versus* volunteered, 38
    game theory results, 161
    impact on individual stakeholders, 37
    incentives for, 36
    policy choices motivating, 38
    between private stakeholders, 36
    role in trust earning, 163
Inherent value, 22
Interactions, 8, 17, 73
    biodiversity and, 25–27
    between biosphere and atmosphere, 51
    between biotic and abiotic components, 19
    of economic activity, 89
    in natural systems, 12
    system with, 11
    visualizing with box modeling, 40
Interests
    focus on, instead of positions, 145
    house rental example, 152–153
Intergenerational change, 80
Intergenerational environmental health, 9, 74, 80
Intergenerational equity, 81, 82, 187, 189
    Alaskaland case problem, 186
Intrinsic value, 99
Irish potato blight, 26
Irreversibility
    of impacts, 48
Island effect, 24
    due to human activities, 25
Issues
    connecting to goals, 174
    focus on, 173

K

Knowability, 9, 75, 133
    about climate change, 188–189
    assumptions in risk assessment, 124
    change over time, 116
    of earth system value, 68
    limitations of, 116
    of risk, 135

L

Lack of choice, 118
Landfill
    risk assessment for, 128
Landscape, 23
Lawmaking, 168

Lawn maintenance
    and non-point pollution sources, 33
Laws
    passage of, 168
Learning
    prevention through strongly held views, 158
Legacy values, 67
Legitimacy
    of science, 8
Limiting factors, 8
    abiotic, 19
Limiting nutrients, 52
Linear response, 125
Lithosphere, 12, 17, 19, 40
    as carbon sink, 41
Local government
    environmental decision making, 2
Local value judgment perspective, 2
Locally undesirable land use (LULU), 129
    NIMBY syndrome and, 140
Long-term planning
    for depletable resources, 70
Lost carbon problem, 49–50
Lovelock, James, 13, 23
Low divisibility, 153
Low excludability, 152, 153
    of atmosphere, 154
    of common pool resources, 154

M

Magnitude of harm, 115, 116, 117
Majoritarian voting, 162, 168
    conflict in, 169–170
    as noncooperative game, 168
Majority voting, 167–170
Management frameworks, 30
Marginal values, 100
Marginalization
    minimizing through consensus building, 169
Market-based valuations
    limitations, 94
Mass–energy equivalence, 43–45
Mass–energy relationships, 43, 44
Maximum acceptable exposure rate, 127
Mean temperature, 11
Media-specific environmental laws, 32
Mediation
    dispute resolution through, 144
Metrics
    for well-being and progress, 81–82
Micro-landscapes, 23

Millennium Ecosystem Assessment, 91
Mitigation perspective, 188, 189
Monoculture planting, 26
Morality, 139, 140
Multiparty decision-making, 146, 166–167, 175
    collective value system considerations,
        170–174
    consensus building in, 167–170
    majority voting in, 167–170
    process of, 146

N

Nash equilibrium, 161
    in prisoner's dilemma game, 163
    in stag hunt game, 163
National Environmental Policy Act (NEPA),
        32, 103, 121
    ecological impact statement requirements, 129
Nations
    similarities to individuals, 171
Natural capital
    indefinite level of substitutes, 81
    as input, 74
    as prerequisite for human survival, 74
    substitutability for human capital, 74
Natural hazard regulation, 22
Natural resource economics, 65, 66, 68–72, 106
    contrast with ecological economics, 79
    differentiating from ecological economics,
        68, 72, 75
    ecological economics as subcategory, 68
    focus on direct uses, 69
    GDP and, 107
Natural system components, 40
    and human economies, 68
Natural systems, 3, 7, 9–17, 59
    biodiversity in, 23–29
    ecosystem-based management in, 29–39
    ecosystem principles, 17–23
    equilibrium response in, 16
    movement toward equilibrium, 55
    provisioning, regulating, and cultural
        services, 20–23
    three recurring themes of, 9–10
Nature
    importance beyond utility, 141
    intrinsic value, 141
    for nature's sake, 99
Negative externalities
    handling in GDP, 84

Negotiation
    dispute resolution through, 144
    in majority voting systems, 170
Net economic output, 88, 90
Net exports, 82
Net government spending, 85
New equilibrium state, 16, 55
NIMBY (Not in my backyard), 138–146, 140–142
Nitrogen
    as limiting nutrient, 52
No-action alternative, 103
Non-point sources
    diffuse nature of, 34
    of pollution, 33
Noncooperative games, 157, 159, 167, 176
    majority government and, 168
Nonextractive values, 98
Nonmarket values, 66, 72, 92, 99
Nonphysical environmental processes, 67
Nonrenewable resources, 69, 70
Nonuse values, 74, 91, 92, 98–101, 103
    determining, 105
    as independent variables, 100
Normative economics, 67
    GNH focus on, 90
    weighting in, 67
Normative metrics, 85
Normative presumptions, 139
Nuclear power, 77
    magnitude and frequency of harm, 116
    well-being values, 122
Nuclear reactors
    risk assessment, 114
Nutrients, 27

O

Objective risks, 128, 174
    disconnect with human choice, 137
    trumping by public outrage, 133
Objective truth
    methods of establishing, 147
Objective values, 115
    quantification methods, 120–129
    risk assessment and science role, 115–119
Objectivity
    of science, 8
Oceans
    consequences of using as carbon sequesters, 57
    photic zones, 52
    role in carbon cycle, 56–57

Oil, 41
Open access fishing, 182
Open systems, 10
Opportunity costs, 80
Option values, 67
Outcomes matrix
    prisoner's dilemma game, 160
    stag hunt game, 163
Outflows, 40, 49–58, 53
Outrage, 132, 175
    based on position *versus* interest, 145
    identifying risk by, 167
    and immediacy of threat, 136
    power in risk assessment, 132
    public, as subjective value, 131–137
    reductions with perceived lack of immediacy, 136
Overcapitalization, 117
Overexploitation, 154
Overfishing, 182
Oxygen
    regulation of, 27
Oxygen abundance, 18

P

Partial market schemes, 96
Partial regulation, 96
Patterns
    in natural systems, 47
Patton, Bruce, 144, 145
Payout
    in game theory, 160
Peer pressure, 132
    limiting free riding through, 165–166
Perceived values, 138–146
Perceptions
    changing, 174
    clouding of judgment by, 141
    influence on decision making, 144
Personal bias
    separating from values, 115
Perturbations, 13
Pest regulation, 22
Pharmaceutical drugs
    government regulation of, 137
Phosphorous
    as limiting nutrient, 52
Physical environmental goods, 67
Physical processes, 19
Phytoplankton
    carbon sequestration, 42

Plants
  carbon storage by, 55
  as provisioning resources for deer, 21
Plate tectonics, 24
Point sources
  of pollution, 32
  stationary nature of, 34
Pollination regulation, 22, 28
Pollution
  non-point sources, 33
  point sources, 32, 33
Positional bargaining, 144, 175
  limitations, 145
Positions
  focus on, 173
Positive economics, 66
  weighting limitations, 67
Positive psychology, 86
Precautionary approach, 117, 118, 189
  in risk assessment, 124, 127
Predation, 183
  preventing through biodiversity, 26
Preferences
  values and, 113
Preservation, 141, 142, 143
Presumptions. *See also* Assumptions
  identifying, 147
Prevention perspective, 188, 189
Principled bargaining, 144
Priorities
  for environmental decision-making, 120
  spectrum of, 121
Priority setting, 120
Prisoner's dilemma game, 150, 157, 159–162, 167
  multiple game outcomes, 161
  Nash equilibrium strategy in, 163
  outcomes matrix, 160
Private consumption, 82
Private goods, 155
Private property, 155
Private stakeholders
  information sharing between, 36
Probability of harm, 115, 116
Processes, 27, 148
  as focus in consensus building, 169
  risk assessment, 125
Progress
  and assumptions of risk, 117
  metrics, 81–82
Property rights, 176
  changing free riding through, 156

excludability and divisibility characteristics,
    152
and excludability/divisibility characteristics,
    135
  individual, 184
  matrix, 154, 155
Property rights characteristics, 184
Proprietary information, 37
Prosperity
  government role in creating, 82
Provisioning services, 18, 21, 32, 91, 122
  and direct values, 92
  direct values and, 93
Proximity, 165
Public goods, 78, 150, 155
Public outrage, 131
  inverse proportion to distance from project,
    140
  over Three Mile Island incident, 136
  pharmaceutical drug examples, 137
  as subjective value, 131–137
  trumping of objective science by, 132, 133
Public property, 155
Public resources, 38
  managing through private incentives, 181–185
Public welfare, 122

Q

Qualitative measures, 87
  of GNH, 86
Quality of life, 121
Quantification methods, 120–129
Quantitative measures, 87

R

Radioactive uranium, 118
Radioactive waste
  poor public understanding of, 136
Rate of use, 82
Recycling
  of nitrogen and phosphorous, 52
Regulating services, 18, 20–23, 21, 32, 73, 91, 96
  in forests, 22
  and indirect values, 95
Reinforcement learning, 158
  basis in experience, 158
Relationships, 15
Relative weighting, 143
Religion
  as source of values, 139

strongly held views, 158
Religious significance, 99
Renewable resources, 69, 70
    agricultural production, 70
    overexploitation, 71
    replacement rates, 70
    trees, 70
Renewable resources management, 71
Replacement rates, 70
    for renewable resources, 70
Replicability, 8
    of objective risk metrics, 130
    and objective values, 128
Reproductive rates
    and species inbreeding, 24
Residence time, 53
Resilience
    and biodiversity, 25, 26
    limits of, 15
Resource conservation and Recovery Act, 32
Resource depletion, 69, 154
    Alaskaland case problem, 186
Resource exhaustion, 186
Resource extraction rates, 71
Resource longevity, 71
Reward systems, 39
Risk, 113, 132
    defined by hazard and outrage, 132
    extent of, 124
    identifying and quantifying, 114
    as indicator of harm, 114
    knowability, 133, 135
    likelihood of, 124
    limiting in strategic games, 161
    limiting through environmental
        management, 114
    objective measures, 130
    objective *versus* subjective perceptions, 114
    perceived lack of immediacy, 136
    voluntary *versus* coerced, 133, 134
Risk assessment, 1, 113
    dose-response assessment tin, 123
    dose-response curves, 126
    exposure assessment in, 123
    hazard identification in, 123
    heuristic methods, 130
    objective *versus* subjective, 146
    and priority setting, 120
    process visualization, 125
    quantification methods, 120–129
    role of science in, 115–119
    spectrum of objective-to-subjective values, 129

three steps in, 123–124
    weighting of values in, 123
Risk assumptions
    updating, 117
Risk characterization, 123
Risk communication, 133
Risk factors
    identifying, 128
    lowest-priority, 129
Risk identification
    through outrage, 167
Risk perception, 114
    choice and, 134
    familiarity and, 133, 134
    heuristics influence on, 133
    at individual and group levels, 114
Rousseau, Jean Jacques, 171
Rule of law, 144
Rules
    conformance to, 166
Runoff, 33
    and soil erosion, 56

S

Sahara Desert, 19, 23
Sanitation laws
    as basis of environmental laws, 121
Scaling
    individual decision-making, 148–166
    value decisions, 143, 146–148, 175
Science
    best available, 119
    change over time, 174
    current state of, 189
    devaluation of, 9
    environmentalists' *versus* cornucopians'
        views of, 138
    equilibrium theory, 45–49
    incremental nature of, 116
    interaction with environmental decision
        making, 2
    mass–energy equivalence, 43–45
    relationship to economics and values, 3
    role in risk assessment, 115–119
    translating into values, 9
    trumping by public outrage, 132
Scientific method, 8, 115
Scientific perspective, 2
    in systems thinking, 43–49
Security fund, 186

Self-interest
    conflict with group goals, 156
    as decision-making value, 149–157
    on national level, 171
    theory of, 150
Self-regulating systems, 18
Services, 72
    assessing, 22
    provided by natural systems, 18
    provisioning, regulating, cultural, 20–23
Signaling, 166
Simon, Julian, 80, 81
Social contract, 171
Social institutions, 40
Social law, 171
Social norms, 139
Social vitality, 86
Soil stabilization
    by trees, 72
Soils
    role in carbon cycle, 56
Solar power, 77
Species extinctions, 25
    background levels, 28
    daisy world example, 27
    increased rate of, 28
Species inbreeding, 24
Spiritual values, 74, 99, 105
Stable climate
    biodiversity and, 28
Stag hunt game, 157, 159, 162–164, 167
    payoffs, 163
Standards
    in priority setting, 120
Standing ovation game, 157, 159, 164, 167
State changes, 44
Status quo, 118
Steady state, 47
Stored carbon, 41
Strategic games, 150, 161
Strategy coordination, 162
Stress levels
    and biodiversity, 26
    equilibrium response to, 16
Strongly held views, 158
    about distrust, 164
Subjective risks, 128
Subjective values, 129–131, 143–144, 175
    emotion and public outrage, 131–137
    spectrum in risk assessment, 129
    trumping of objective factors by, 149
Substitution, 65, 66, 69, 74, 77–79, 106

Subunits, 17
Supermajority, 168
Sustainability, 82, 88, 122, 149
    alternative policies, 186–187
    Brundtland Commission definition, 123
    case problem, 185–187
    current policy, 185–186
    descriptive presumptions of, 139
    as GNH goal, 86
    hints for analysis, 187
    normative presumptions about, 139
System boundaries, 17
System change, 15
System components
    biotic and abiotic, 18–20
System interactions, 11
    based on temperature control, 11
    box model, 51
System stability, 46
System stress
    equilibrium response to, 16
Systems
    closed, 10
    open, 10
Systems thinking, 3, 7, 39–40, 59, 69, 73
    aggregation concept and, 136
    box modeling, 40–43
    in ecological economics, 75
    inflows, outflows, and feedback mechanisms
        in, 49–58
    underlying scientific principles, 43–49

T

Target species
    protecting with biodiversity, 26
Taxes
    self-imposed, 97
Technological advances, 78
Temperature control
    system interactions diagram, 11
Terms and conditions, 156
Thermostat analogy, 13
Threat
    and outrage, 136
    perceived lack of immediacy, 136
Three Mile Island incident, 114
    community outrage over, 136
Threshold, 15
    intergenerational issues, 80
    in rainforests *versus* deserts, 20
Threshold response, 125

Time balance, 86
Timescales
    human, 70
    national *versus* individual, 171
Tit for tat, 162
Toll goods, 155
Total allowable catch, 183, 184
Total valuation technique, 61, 90, 91–92, 103, 122
    direct values in, 92–95
    indirect values in, 95–98
    nonuse values, 98–101
    total value equation, 92
Toxic Substances Control Act, 32
Trade-offs, 69, 79–81, 106
    identifying, 32
Transparency
    in fair/just society, 94
Trees
    ability to consume carbon dioxide, 66
    as atmospheric filter, 72
    carbon sequestration by, 72
    direct uses, 69
    as renewable resources, 70
    soil stabilization by, 72
Trust
    building in stag hunt game, 164
    earning through information sharing, 163
    in stag hunt game, 163
    strongly held views about, 164

U

Unavailable carbon, 53
Uncertainty
    environmental decisions in face of, 187–189
    inhibition of choice through, 119
Underground water sources, 33
Units, 54
Unknowability, 75
Uranium
    lack of choice issue, 118–119
Ury, William, 144, 145
Utility
    intrinsic value beyond, 141

V

Valuation, 147
    of divergent views, 169
    human *versus* environmental welfare, 142
    subjective, 143–144

Valuation models, 81, 106
    alternatives to GDP, 84–90
    genuine progress indicator, 88–90
    gross domestic product (GDP), 82–84
    gross national happiness (GNH), 85–88
    in risk assessment, 129
    well-being metrics, 81–82
Value-based decisions, 159
Value decisions
    scaling, 147–148
Value inconsistency
    between individual and social scales, 173
Value judgments, 127
Value systems, 174
    individual *versus* collective, 172
Value unification, 174
Values, 64
    beyond utility, 141
    as criteria for decision-making, 148
    definitions, 72
    in environmental decision making, 113–114
    and individual decision-making, 148–149
    learning dynamics, 157–166
    misplaced defense of, 145
    and multiparty decision-making, 166–174
    NIMBY, 138–146
    objective, 115–129
    perceived, 138–146
    relationship to science and economics, 3
    self-interest, 149–157
    subjective, 129–146
Variables, 8
    agreement on, 147
Variety
    biodiversity as, 23
Vegetation
    net destruction of, 56
Voluntary coercion, 38

W

Warming trend, 188
Water
    as abiotic component, 19
    as asset, 66
Water diversion
    effects in different ecosystems, 20
Water purification, 22, 28
Water regulation, 22
Watershed management
    case problem, 179–180

hints for analysis, 181
relevant information, 180–181
Wealth maximization, 81
as catalyst for minimum living standard, 86
Weighting, 81
of biodiversity, 67
of environmental risk assessment priorities,
121
limitations in positive economics, 67
in normative economics, 67
relative, 143
worldview effects on, 143
Welfare
valuation of, 129
Well-being. *See also* Happiness; Human well-being
criteria for human, 84
distinguishing from human health, 122
electricity as necessity for human, 78
metrics, 81–82, 106
as quality of life, 121
resource support of human, 70

Well-mixed natural systems, 46, 47
Wetlands
cost of wood fiber from, 97
indirect values, 95, 96
Wheat species
biodiversity examples, 25–26
Willingness to pay, 92, 93, 101
speculation on future, 95
Wind power, 77, 118
aesthetic considerations, 123
Wood fiber
direct valuation, 93
market-based value, 96
from wetlands, 97
Wood products
demands for, 72
Worldviews, 158
effect on value weighting, 143
influence on decisions, 131, 137
and risk assessment, 120
Worst-case scenario assessment, 126